GHT

The full story of cricket's match-fixing scandal

SIMON WILDE

AURUM PRESS

First published in Great Britain
2001 by Aurum Press Ltd
25 Bedford Avenue, London WC1B 3AT

Design by Roger Hammond

A catalogue record for this book is available from the British Library.

ISBN 1 85410 811 5

10 9 8 7 6 5 4 3 2 1
2005   2004   2003   2002   2001

Typeset in 11/15pt Janson by Geoff Green
Printed in Great Britain by MPG Books Ltd, Bodmin, Cornwall

Picture credits
p.1   *top* Popp
p.2   Graham
p.3   Graham
pp.4 & 5 Associat
p.6   Graham
p.7   *top* Allsp
p.8   *top* Asso   lay

To my mother

CONTENTS

AUTHOR'S NOTE

This book is not intended as a complete account of corruption in cricket. Its focus is the modern phenomenon of bookmakers attempting to corrupt active cricketers with a view to achieving betting coups. Some other allegations – such as that made in 1994 by the former Essex player Don Topley that the Essex and Lancashire teams had colluded three years earlier to mutual gain in county championship points – therefore fall outside its compass. Certain other claims of dubious provenance, for example those made about Brian Lara's conduct during a tour of South Africa in 1993, have been ignored.

Throughout, the term 'match-fixing' is taken to mean an arrangement, actual or alleged, either to fix the result of a match, or aspects of a match, for financial gain.

Exchange rates: foreign currencies have been translated into sterling at the following rates: 1.5 US dollars per pound; 10 South African rand per pound; 2.4 Australian dollars per pound; 75 Pakistan rupees per pound; and 62.5 Indian rupees per pound. In India one lakh equals 100,000 rupees, or £1,600; one crore, 100 lakh, or £160,000.

Simon Wilde, Clapham, July 2001

1

THE CONFESSION

Rory Steyn was the first man to see the mask slip from Hansie Cronje's face. He saw it slip at the kind of hour at which it is sometimes hard to disguise the truth. It was around 2.00 on the morning of 11 April 2000.

Rory Steyn was a security officer attached to the South Africa and Australia cricket teams for a series of one-day matches to start the next day at Kingsmead, Durban. A religious, amiable man in his thirties, tall and sinewy, Steyn had been a policeman and a member of former president Nelson Mandela's bodyguard. This was relevant to the position in which he now found himself.

In dragging Steyn out of his sleep and into his own room in the Elangeni hotel at such an ungodly hour, the South Africa captain was calling not on a confidante – Cronje's relationship with Steyn was purely a working one – but a representative of the law. And no one calls up a representative of the law at 2.00 in the morning unless he has something significant to say.

Steyn found Cronje fully dressed and very much awake; in fact, it looked as though he had not been to bed. He saw Cronje's packed bags, as though ready for imminent departure. And then there was his face. A man whose poker-straight features were capable of hiding all trace of emotion, even during the most fraught matches, he now looked wide-eyed and vulnerable, and on the verge of tears.

The first thing Cronje did was thrust a sheaf of paper into Steyn's hand. 'You may have guessed,' he said, 'that I have not been entirely honest and that some of what has been printed in the media is true ... I've decided to write a statement and come clean.'[1]

But Steyn had not guessed. He had heard of the sensational claims by the Delhi police in India four days earlier, of them having recently bugged phone calls between Cronje and a member of an Indian illegal betting syndicate. They had issued charges against Cronje and four other South Africa players of criminal conspiracy relating to rigging matches and betting, and released what purported to be a transcript of one of these conversations. But most South Africans had dismissed the allegations as wild and unfounded. So had Steyn. Cronje's reputation was as near to spotless as reputations got.

Cronje's words left Steyn stunned. But there were more surprises to come. Cronje said something about wanting to turn himself over to the law. 'I got the impression he thought I was still a serving police officer and that he was handing himself over to the police,' Steyn would recall. But Cronje was clearly unaware that after leaving Mandela's protection unit, Steyn had left the police and started working for himself. He was not the representative of the law Cronje was plainly looking for.

It took a while for this fact to dawn. Having steeled himself to take Steyn into his trust, Cronje was stunned to find the process less straightforward than he had hoped. He broke down and crumpled onto a sofa, insisting that he had to go to the police.[2] He told Steyn he had been constantly harassed by the syndicate during South Africa's tour of India. Sometimes they had phoned him twenty times a day. 'He said he couldn't live with the lies, they were eating him up,' Steyn said. 'His family were under immense pressure and it was not fair to them. The players mentioned in the transcript were innocent and he wanted to clear their names.' He implicitly accepted that the conversations with the 'bookie' had taken place; what was not in the transcripts was Cronje telling him 'to get lost and leave him alone'.[3] Cronje's mind seemed to be disturbed. Still intent on surrendering himself, he handed Steyn his wallet with the words: 'Please give this to my wife.'

Steyn fought to get a grip on this surreal nocturnal exchange. He tried to calm Cronje down. 'Wait, Hansie. Wait,' he said. 'Slow down now. There are no formal charges against you, either in India or in this country, for you to confess to. Let's take this thing one step at a time.' Steyn was having difficulty adjusting to the idea that South Africa's captain had no intention of attending his team's practice session later that day or playing Australia the day after that. These games, re-matches of two epic World Cup contests in England the previous year, had aroused enormous interest.

'Who else have you told this to?' Steyn asked.

'Nobody,' said Cronje. 'I don't want to speak to the players. I don't want to speak to Ali Bacher.'

Bacher, the managing director of the United Cricket Board of South Africa (UCBSA), was, along with Cronje, one of the most powerful figures in South African cricket. If Cronje represented the team, Bacher was the board. They had worked closely together for years, and an outsider might have expected Cronje to turn to Bacher in his hour of need.

But Bacher cannot have been an easy man to confide in. A member of Johannesburg's influential Jewish community, he was the last man to captain South Africa before the boycott against apartheid and had dominated South African cricket completely since his controversial masterminding of sanctions-busting tours of the country in the 1980s. Offering large sums of money to top overseas stars at clandestine meetings in hotels and airports, Bacher had been a pariah in the eyes of the game's establishment. Now everything came second to his messianic determination to make his country a major force in the world game. To him, the individual players were subordinate to this task.

Bacher spoke proudly of how well the board looked after its players, but in fact the demands made of them were enormous, their schedule a never ending pursuit of playing and financial success. Later questioned about his relationship with the board, Cronje shrank from answering directly: 'I don't want to get into a situation where I disclose my relationship with the United Cricket Board.'[4]

That Cronje could not now unburden himself of the dark secrets he was holding more or less summed up the extent to which his relationship with Bacher had deteriorated during the six years of Cronje's captaincy. In any case, during the past four days Cronje had several times assured Bacher that there was no truth in the Delhi police's claims. 'They're absolute rubbish,' he had said. Bacher had even called an emergency meeting of the board at which a statement of unequivocal support for the captain had been produced.

Steyn had an idea. 'You can't hand yourself to me,' he had said, 'but maybe we can get hold of Percy Sonn.' Sonn, the acting president of the South African cricket board, was a high-ranking police officer and advocate.

But Cronje was against that idea as well – and was right to be, for Sonn would prove his most intractable enemy. His suggestion of going to a senior government official – in this case, the Deputy Foreign Minister – rather than a colleague or friend may have struck Steyn as odd, but in the light of what had been going on behind the scenes over the past four days, it did make sense. 'I want to go and see Aziz Pahad,' he said.

DID CRONJE'S PAST replay before his eyes during this tortured night? He had had plenty of time to reflect on where it had all gone wrong, because he would later say that he had known from the moment he first heard of the police's allegations that his days as a cricketer were over.

Active sportsmen are often reluctant to dwell on their achievements or calculate their places in history, but it would have been inhuman had Cronje not attempted to assess his position in the cricketing landscape, even if only to measure how far he was about to fall.

Cronje had been one of the most successful cricket captains in history. Under his leadership, South Africa had won half their Tests (27 out of 53) and three-quarters of their one-dayers (99 out of 138). Even if he had never quite done himself justice as a Test player, he was still among his country's most successful batsman, only Gary Kirsten having exceeded his 3,714 Test runs. In 68 Tests he had played some important innings when they were most needed and was prepared to take on danger bowlers like Shane Warne and hit them out of the attack. He had a good cricket brain and a streak that could only be described as bravery. His value to the side could not simply be measured in runs, though.

He was perhaps proudest of his status as a role model within Afrikaner society. Cricket was a relatively new area of interest for Afrikaners; historically, it was the sport of South Africa's English-speakers, and not until the 1970s did that begin to change on the back of the excitement generated by the great South African Test side of the late 1960s, of which Bacher was a member. It was an Afrikaner, Kepler Wessels, who became the first Test captain after the country returned to playing international cricket in 1992, and another Afrikaner, Cronje, the second. Wessels and Cronje had in fact both attended the same school, Grey College in Bloemfontein, one of the oldest and best schools in South Africa, and populated by Afrikaners. Even now, only a third of the pupils are taught in English.

At Grey's, Wessels and Cronje had come under the inspirational spell of Johan Volsteedt, a future principal of the school and one of those gripped by the new passion for cricket. The craze for sport and fitness in Bloemfontein was something of a joke with outsiders, who alleged that there was little else to do in the city. But by the end of the century Grey's could count 90 international sportsmen among its former pupils.

Cronje started playing for the first XI at fifteen and swiftly went on to lead various age-group sides at school, provincial and national level. He was a tall, upright and clean-hitting batsman, but what stood out most about him was his ability to read a game and other players. It was a gift he never lost and one that made his opinion particularly valuable.

Cronje was also academically successful but cricket simply fell into his path. Not only was his father, Ewie, a university sports administrator who had played the game at provincial level, chairman of the Free State Cricket Union, but Volsteedt would spend two years as Free State coach. Cronje first played for the province while still at school and by the time he was in his early twenties was captaining the side. With Volsteedt's help, the team, sometimes containing up to eight old Greys, won their first one-day prize. In the space of six seasons Cronje would lead Free State to seven trophies and establish himself as the leading figure among the new generation of Afrikaner cricketers. Though there was only modest earnings to be made out of the sport, Cronje was making a successful career out of cricket almost before he knew it. Meanwhile, rugby, at which he also excelled, was still rooted in amateurism.

Allan Donald, for years South Africa's leading fast bowler and a childhood friend of Cronje's who also briefly went to Grey's, used to play cricket and rugby at Cronje's house and remembered how talented he was. 'It used to annoy me so much that Hansie could bat too easily against me as I tore in off my long run – and yet he was three years younger than me.' Donald was also struck by the competitiveness of Cronje and his elder brother Frans. 'It's in the South African genes I suppose. When you start playing sport in my country, you soon realise that there's no such thing as a social game, that winning is everything and coming second doesn't interest anyone at all. Even in the winters, we'd go full on at each other with a rugby ball, with Hansie getting a few of the first XV over to his back garden. I'd take out my frustrations on them because I hadn't really made the grade, and we never pulled out of any tackles. I suppose we South Africans know no other way.'[5]

Cronje adjusted swiftly enough to international cricket to show that he had found his natural level. It was not a normal baptism, however, since the whole South Africa side were going through the same learning process as himself as a consequence of their fast-tracked return to international competition within two years of Mandela's release from prison. The sporting barriers that surrounded the apartheid regime were dismantled as fast as they had been erected in 1969 (the year of Cronje's birth), when Peter Hain's Stop the Seventy Tour campaign led to the cancellation of the South African tour of England. Mandela later said that Hain's civil insurrection had done as much as anything to hurt the white community in South Africa, a white community of which Cronje's sports-mad family was very much a part.

Cronje's career as a professional sportsman thus underwent a dramatic change at an early stage and one he could not have foreseen when he first set out. One day, it must have seemed, all there was to aim for was provincial cricket; the next, he and the South Africa team were in Australia competing for the 1992 World Cup. Suddenly cricket was a career offering genuine financial rewards. Match fees, win bonuses and sponsorship deals were all up for grabs. Life changed very fast and Cronje – described by Donald at that time as a 'happy-go-lucky character' who 'enjoyed a few beers and sometimes carried a bit of extra weight' – wanted to cash in like everyone else; indeed, as we shall see, rather more than most.[6]

The new South Africa played their first Test match a few weeks after the 1992 World Cup during a flag-flying mission to the West Indies. Cronje did not cover himself in glory, out for two single-figure scores, the second amidst a miserable collapse when victory was in sight. He lost his place for the next Test match against Mohammad Azharuddin's Indians in Durban several months after but returned two weeks later at the Wanderers for his first home appearance.

That was a game full of drama and irony. The pitch started green and lively, and with the ball moving around, South Africa were soon in all sorts of trouble. Wessels had surprisingly chosen to bat first, and with clever seam and swing bowling Manoj Prabhakar swept away the top order. When Wessels was out, Cronje found himself going out to bat at 26 for four.

Somehow he hung on for nearly an hour and a half. Though again he did not reach double figures, he batted skilfully and laid the foundations for a recovery completed by Jonty Rhodes's century. Cronje fell to a fine return catch by Kapil Dev. In the next Test at Port Elizabeth, Cronje's third, he scored his maiden century, a century that not only won the match but decided the series. After that, there had been little looking back – at least not from an outsider's perspective. A few months later, when Cronje and Wessels played together at Lord's, Volsteedt was in proud attendance, Cronje having kept his promise to pay his teacher's air fare when he first played at the game's headquarters.

Cronje took over the captaincy from Wessels in November 1994. An uneasy ambassador, he was never allowed to forget the diplomatic implications of his role and, indeed, had every reason to be mindful of the threads by which South African society hung. A few months before he took over from Wessels, a seminal event in his life occurred, a tragic accident that shook his comfortable and complacent view of life. He was driving through northern Natal late one night, passing through a village on his way to play in a match for Free State, when his car struck and killed a little black girl.

'Apparently the girl ran out from nowhere, and Hansie couldn't do a thing about it,' Donald recalled. 'He did stop at the scene of the accident while waiting for the ambulance and police to arrive, but it all got very ugly. About forty people emerged from nowhere, threatening Hansie, and the child's grieving mother was screaming frantically. Hansie and our wicketkeeper, Roger Brown, honestly thought they were going to be killed, as they were surrounded by the group, who were brandishing knives. Eventually Hansie and Roger were allowed to leave, and they were very shaken when they caught up with us at the team hotel.

'We later heard that there had been quite a few hit-and-runs in that particular area, and that nobody ever stopped, for fear of being murdered. But Hansie and Roger felt it was the right thing to do, and they got away with it. After that tragedy, Hansie changed his lifestyle and became a committed Christian ... He worked very hard in the gym, became super-fit, and has stayed with this regime ever since. After taking counselling about the incident, Hansie committed himself to God and became a very dignified person ... his new, serious outlook on life gave him even greater stature.'[7]

But not everyone agreed that Cronje should have been elevated to the national captaincy. John Blair, president of the Free State Cricket Union and therefore a colleague of Cronje's father, warned the United Cricket Board of South Africa not to ratify Cronje as Wessels' successor. 'It will all end in tears,' he is reported to have said, believing Cronje had a 'dangerously unstable personality' that was susceptible, under pressure, to irrational behaviour incompatible with leading a national sports team.[8]

Subsequent events would bring into serious question the genuineness of the Christian conversion of a man who wore a wristband bearing the acronym WWJD ('What Would Jesus Do?') but also belonged to an Afrikaner tribe that had effortlessly professed to be Christian throughout 40 years of apartheid. It would transpire that less than a year after the car accident, and only a few weeks after taking on the South African captaincy, Cronje was incapable of resisting the overtures of an illegal bookmaker.

No one could have anticipated the troubles the captaincy would bring Cronje. Or, indeed, what the future held for some of his Indian opponents in that first home Test match, Azharuddin, Prabhakar and Kapil Dev.

Yes, it would be a long fall.

UNBEKNOWN TO Rory Steyn and most other South Africans, the Department for Foreign Affairs had been keeping in close touch with Cronje ever since the Delhi police had gone public with their claims.

Aziz Pahad was the key figure. Within twenty-four hours he had held a meeting with Bacher, who was upset that the integrity of South African cricket was being questioned. The South African cricket board's statement of support for Cronje had stated that it was 'certain that no South African cricket player has ever been involved in match-fixing', and referred to Cronje's 'unquestionable integrity and honesty'.[9]

Bacher, oblivious to the ironies of his role in covertly signing up foreign cricketers to join rebel tours of South Africa during the apartheid years, was also unhappy at the apparent flouting of diplomatic procedure by Indian officials. After his meeting with Pahad, Bacher's rhetoric was more circumspect, but he still claimed, 'The government takes the same view and will be running with the ball now.'[10]

For Pahad, running with the ball meant staying in regular contact with Cronje. Precisely what form this dialogue took is unclear, but Cronje's protestations of innocence failed to convince the minister. The day before Cronje's early morning confession, Pahad's worst fears had been realised at a meeting in Pretoria with Harsh Bhasin, India's High Commissioner.

That meeting had become imperative. Feelings against India were running high in South Africa, threatening to breach the delicate ties between the countries. Indians had played a key role in the activities of the African National Congress during its years of insurrection, and one of the ANC's offices was situated in India when it was banned in South Africa itself; there was, therefore, no shortage of excuses for white antipathy towards India. In short, Bacher was not alone in believing a slur had been cast on the honesty of his country. As one cricket board source said, 'The Indian government felt it was coming in for a battering and needed to defend the integrity of its allegations ... there has been a public frenzy of aggression in South Africa against India over the Cronje controversy.'[11]

Pahad had gone to see Bhasin demanding evidence. He asked for copies of the taped phone conversations between Cronje and the

Indian 'bookmaker', and any other evidence relating to the case that Bhasin could produce. His demands for copies of the tapes were not met but Bhasin satisfied him that the Indian police knew what they were doing. Bhasin gave him the clear impression that the Indians were fully satisfied that the voice on the tapes was Cronje's; convinced him, too, 'of the strength of evidence of Cronje's involvement'.[12] The police were certainly not relying solely on bugged phone calls; as one police source was quoted as saying the next day, 'We have other proof to corroborate the tapes.'[13]

Two things happened after the Pahad–Bhasin meeting. One was that Pahad issued a statement containing a phrase that sounded like a coded warning to South Africa's beleaguered cricket captain: 'We will not protect individuals if there is prima facie evidence of wrongdoing.' The other was that contact was again made with Cronje and, while not overtly recommending a confession, as this would have been 'undiplomatic', Pahad 'conveyed his concerns'.[14] Another source was more emphatic. He said Cronje 'realised the game was up', adding, 'I'm certain that Pahad's meeting with Bhasin turned the tables for Cronje.'[15]

Thus, in now choosing to go to Pahad less than twelve hours after the minister had 'conveyed his concerns' to him, Cronje knew he was turning to someone who already suspected the truth and, more importantly from Cronje's point of view, might know what was the best thing to be done next.

Aziz Pahad was in Cape Town, so Cronje and Steyn waited for the first flight of the day. In the meantime Cronje phoned his pastor, Ray McCauley, and told him he had something to get off his chest. He then faxed him the nine-page hand-written statement he had proffered to Steyn. McCauley had known Cronje a long time. He had been invited to tour with the South Africa team by Wessels, who wanted him to help the players in Bible study; when Cronje became captain he asked McCauley to also be responsible for motivational sessions. These fell by the wayside as the team's backroom staff grew and McCauley's own time was increasingly taken up with his fast-expanding Rhema church, which had attracted 25,000 followers in 20 years. But Cronje and McCauley remained close.[16]

Only then did Cronje attempt to contact Bacher and Sonn. They were staying in a game lodge north of Durban with visiting Australian Cricket Board officials, and it took some time to find a phone number for them.

Neither conversation was long. Bacher recalled, 'The phone rang at 3.00 a.m., waking me up … Hansie came on the line and said: "Doc, I haven't been entirely honest with you." I immediately said: "Have you taken any money from bookmakers?" and he said: "Yes."'[17]

It was now the turn of Bacher and Sonn to abandon their sleep. Within minutes they had met and withdrawn Cronje from the one-day series. At 6.30 a.m. Bacher called Rushdie Magiet, the chairman of the selection panel, and instructed him to find a new captain. Asked later whether Cronje was ever informed of his sacking, Bacher said, 'He did not need telling. He knew.'[18]

Soon, Bacher and Sonn were on the road back to Durban. On the way they decided to ask the South African government to institute an inquiry, a request that was backed by President Thabo Mbeki's Cabinet the next day.

By this time Cronje was en route to Cape Town. As he hoped, Pahad – who may have anticipated Cronje would be in touch – knew what had to be done. He told Cronje to hold a press conference at a public auditorium that afternoon at which he could publicly make his confession.[19]

In one sense it was already too late by then. Through cricket board sources the story had leaked out while Cronje was flying, so that when he reached Cape Town he needed the connivance of air-port officials to elude a scrum of media personnel. But even as the cricket world was in the process of getting the shock of its life, the damage-limitation was already underway.

IN LONDON I read the news pretty much as it hit the wires. I was on the internet when a terse sentence flashed up stating that Cronje had been 'withdrawn' from the matches with Australia. It was obvious this was a euphemism: Cronje had either resigned or been sacked, and was probably therefore guilty of the general thrust of the charges laid by the Delhi police.

I was on to my sports editor within seconds. 'He's gone,' I said. There was no need to explain who 'he' was.

'I told you it was a good story,' he replied.

Unlike Rory Steyn, we had instinctively doubted Cronje's innocence since the Delhi police press conference. The claims were so outlandish, they had to be true. If they were false, it meant someone was working an elaborate hoax; which begged the question, 'Why?' We could find no persuasive answer. Besides, the police story had an unarguable ring of truth about it. There was even authenticity in the disjointed nature of the published conversation between Cronje and his underworld 'fixer'. Cronje's denials had fallen some way short of being convincing. I had written a piece on the Sunday outlining the questions to which he had to provide answers if he was to save himself.

Match-fixing was vaguely known about. People believed in match-fixing the way people believed in the Loch Ness monster: there had been a couple of unconfirmed sightings but, hard though outsiders looked, no one had seen it happen under their noses – at least no one armed with concrete proof and prepared to speak out. There were rumours, some of them persuasive, that match-fixing had gone on. But there was nothing definite.

You could believe or you could disbelieve. Most administrators had neither the stomach nor inclination to believe. India had held one formal inquiry into allegations and Pakistan was on its third, but none had been properly resourced and all had been mired in accusation and counter-accusation, though there was talk that the latest Pakistan inquiry had found some players guilty of match-fixing. Enough smoke had been generated to suggest that somewhere there was a fire, but nothing of real substance had been unearthed.

Until now, perhaps.

Within six hours I was on my way to South Africa. I toyed with the idea of heading for India, the true epicentre of the story, but being on hand to feel the aftershocks of Cronje's fall was compelling.

Thirty hours after Steyn's bizarre encounter with Cronje, I checked into the same Elangeni hotel in Durban. In the lobby, two or three Australian journalists were milling about. Having come to cover three innocuous cricket matches, they found themselves by an unlikely throw of Fate's dice in the right place at the right time.

One of them told me that my *Sunday Times* article had been quoted in the local papers the previous day. I took this as confirmation that its main argument – do not discount Cronje being guilty – had not been one doing the rounds among South African reporters, some of whom treated the national team with kid gloves.

Everyone was hungry for scraps of information, which ensured a good attendance of a press conference held later that morning by Australian Cricket Board (ACB) officials in one of the hotel's banqueting suites. It was a waste of time. They had simply put themselves up to answer any questions the media wanted to ask them. They had nothing to announce themselves, other than their shock and concern at the crisis, but clearly felt that they ought to say something.

Given the poor record of the game's administrators in tackling corruption, their pronouncements were hollow, but entirely appropriate.

2

FOR THE LOVE OF MONEY

Cronje was at rock bottom when he cried for Rory Steyn's help. Tortured by his conscience and deprived of sleep, he could not see how to extricate himself from a tangled web of deceit. Just how emotionally low he sunk no one but himself could know, but he painted a bleak picture when Max Clifford, the English publicist, brokered his first television and newspaper interviews three months later in July 2000. They were estimated to have earned Cronje more than £100,000.

'I honestly struggled to eat and to sleep,' he said then. 'I knew I had lied to my family, to my friends, to my wife and my teammates. I couldn't find a building high enough to jump from. I really felt bad about what I did and I suppose that was the chicken way of getting away with it, to kill yourself.' Again: 'There were dark moments when I wondered if it was worth living. I'd think, "Hansie, you've fallen so far anyway. A few more feet won't matter.""[1]

But these 'confessions' must be treated with caution. The commission of inquiry that Ali Bacher and Percy Sonn requested had now been set up under Judge Edwin King, a former Judge President of the Cape, and King had promised Cronje immunity from prosecution if he withheld nothing from it. Cronje therefore could not disclose any new 'facts' in media interviews. In the circumstances, all that was left was to expand on his inner torment. While his anguish may have been real enough, talk of suicide was possibly a headline-serving exaggeration.

Possibly more accurate was his admission that his sleepless nights started the day he took a call from the cricket board's communications manager, Bronwyn Wilkinson, and was told about the Delhi police's charges (Wilkinson said Cronje's first response was a 'kind of a snort laugh'[2]). Cronje said he instantly knew he was in grave danger. 'I had this horrible sinking feeling in my stomach that my cricket career would be over. Everyone would get dragged into it ... but my first thought was of self-preservation.'[3]

His actions made plain that self-preservation dominated his thoughts, thoughts probably rarely as dark or despairing as they must have been when he summoned Steyn. He went round his house in Bloemfontein in search of incriminating evidence, throwing away mobile phones and hiding money given to him by bookmakers. He telephoned 'bookies', presumably either to alert them or agree on versions of events in case they were ever questioned; he would also, over the coming days and weeks, phone teammates and encourage them to lie to the government's commission of inquiry.

At a press conference Cronje had given upon arriving in Durban two days before his confession, he had denied everything. 'I want to make it 100 per cent clear that I deny ever receiving any sum of money during the one-day international series in India. I want to also make it absolutely clear that I have never spoken to any member of the team about throwing a game.'[4] But he admitted to not reading in the newspapers the transcripts of his alleged phone conversations with his 'spymaster'. He also stopped short of saying he had never met the man; he said he met 40 to 50 people every day demanding autographs, photographs or interviews – he could not be certain whom he had met. He said that one of the ways of clearing his name would be to speak to the players, although quite why they should know whether he had behaved honestly or not he did not explain. 'Sports betting has no place in sport,' he added.

Even after confessing to Steyn, Cronje's instinct for self-preservation quickly resurfaced. Within hours he decided that he was not, after all, going to hand himself over to the police. Indeed, he soon started further covering his tracks. Before Cronje faxed his statement to Pastor McCauley, Steyn saw him skim through it and alter the amount he admitted to receiving from 'Sanjay' to $10,000–15,000. It had originally read $20,000–25,000.[5]

Later that day, when Cronje came to compose the confession that would be read out at his press conference, he implied he had received no money at all. Bizarrely, this confession was drawn up in a room in Cape Town's City Park hospital, where Ngconde Balfour, South Africa's sports minister, was having treatment. Balfour, Cronje and McCauley wrote it hunched over a laptop on the bed.

Balfour's involvement was an important step in the damage-limitation operation and probably down to Cronje's legal advisers. It was decided that Balfour would read out a statement on Cronje's behalf, thus sparing Cronje – sitting alongside him in a white sports shirt, still and stony faced – from being drawn into saying anything to the media.

Cronje owned up to little in the statement. He attempted to pass the whole affair off as a misunderstanding. Essentially, he admitted to having 'played along' with a betting syndicate and 'had some discussions with individuals which could have led to the wrong impressions being created'. He made no mention of Aziz Pahad's role. Far from being shown the writing on the wall, he claimed that what had driven him to confess was his religious conviction; McCauley, his pastor, not Rory Steyn, the policeman, was the first man he had turned to. 'As a Christian, Hansie felt he had to talk to Ray McCauley to tell him he had played along,' Balfour said. 'He's very down right now and is feeling great remorse. He's really hurt about what's happened.' Asked why it had taken Cronje four days to confess, Balfour replied that Cronje had been 'scared'. Ultimately 'his Christian convictions swayed his decision to come forward and talk about it'.[6]

The whole statement was, in fact, extremely misleading, and Bacher was later obliged to correct the suggestion that Cronje had not actually received any money. Bacher had read Cronje's hand-written statement, a copy of which had been passed to the cricket board.[7]

An hour before the Balfour–Cronje press conference, Bacher gave a press conference of his own in Durban. He was unable to shed much light on what had happened, save for announcing Cronje's sacking. His middle-of-the-night conversation with Cronje had been abrupt. All he knew of Cronje's feelings was what had been conveyed to him a few minutes before the conference in a phone conversation with McCauley, who had told him, 'Hansie knows you want to kill him, Doc.'[8] Bacher had met the other South Africa players shortly beforehand, and made Herschelle Gibbs and Nicky Boje, named along with Cronje by the Delhi police, stand up and swear they had not been involved in match-fixing. The players were shown a copy of Cronje's hand-written statement but did not appear to read it in full.

Two days later Cronje read out a statement from Bloemfontein, where he was holed up at his brother's house, and spoke of his regret. He talked of a predicament 'brought about by my own foolishness and naivety', but he still provided few details about his precise deal-ings with his Indian conspirators. 'All I will say,' he remarked, 'is that I was not involved in fixing or manipulating the results of cricket matches. I always play to win.'[9] This claim would come into grave doubt.

Cronje's appropriation of religion to excuse his actions suggests a certain arrogance that was also evident in his original hand-written confession, which was seen by few people before it was made public two months later. 'It has been a tough weekend but also a great weekend for me,' he wrote, 'in that I now have the opportunity to face myself in the mirror again for the first time since the Indian tour.

'I have been a role model for many people in South Africa and this was a lesson for all of you out there: When Satan comes knocking on the door, always keep your eyes on the Lord Jesus Christ and ask him to protect you from any wrong. The moment I took my eyes off Jesus, my whole world turned dark and it felt like someone had stuck a knife through my chest.'[10]

WHEN THE POLICE allegations surfaced, other cricket observers pointed out that Cronje's on-field conduct had not always been above board. Some had even seen him contravening the Laws by tampering with the ball during an international in Australia a few years earlier. He had been seen treading on the ball and 'working' it with his studs.

On an England tour of South Africa in 1995–96, Cronje had successfully coerced umpire David Orchard into changing a decision, also contrary to the Laws. Orchard had turned down South Africa's appeal for run out against Graham Thorpe but, encouraged by sections of the crowd with access to television replays, Cronje lobbied Orchard to reverse his decision. In the end, Orchard relented and called for the third umpire to study the replays, which confirmed that Thorpe was indeed out. The fact that Cronje helped correct an error did not alter the fact that what he did was wrong. He committed a similar breach in a provincial match for Free State. Such actions suggested he had scant regard for propriety and felt he could do much as he pleased.

I had had the chance to study Cronje at close quarters when England toured South Africa in the months before his downfall. Many readily dismissed him as a dull, one-dimensional character: reserved, remote, humourless. Typical Afrikaner traits, they said. But I found him fascinating.

Some of his actions were far from dull. Shortly before England arrived, it emerged that Cronje had been holding secret discussions with Glamorgan to coach them the following English summer, a period that clashed with a South African tour of Sri Lanka. For an active Test captain to try to sign up to something that would prevent him from carrying out his job was a possibly unique step and an odd one for a man leading one of the most successful teams in the world. The South African board vetoed the move and, in an attempt to curb such action in future, appointed him captain only for the first two of the five England Tests.

Although he was soon given charge for the whole series, Cronje struggled with the bat throughout. He wore a distracted air and barely scored 100 runs in the five games. Time and again he got out to ill-judged strokes. It transpired that he had made a half-hearted offer to step down as captain midway through the series, an offer swiftly rejected by the other selectors.

I flew to Harare to speak to him before the series began. He gave away little about his difficulties with the board, though it was obvious they were in disagreement about strategy. But the impression was that here was a man taking on the board and selectors single-handedly – and giving as good as he got. Not many cricketers were this powerful.

When South Africa won the series in Cape Town, Cronje gave a curious performance at the post-match press conference. Usually his features gave nothing away; he met the world with hooded eyes and a slow monotone voice that bordered on being zombie-like. But this was different. He looked crushed and ashamed. Asked why he looked downcast, he replied that he had been disappointed at his own contribution. 'Anyone could have captained this team,' he said.

That was an odd thing to say. Out-of-form captains normally console themselves with the thought that at least they put something in through leadership. It is true that Cronje was not in immediate danger of being replaced; no one, for instance, was in a hurry to hand the captaincy to Shaun Pollock (Cronje's eventual successor) for fear of overburdening a key player. But Cronje was talking himself out of the side. I have often wondered whether there was more to Cronje's aspect that day than the reason he gave.

Throughout England's three-month tour, I was convinced something was seriously amiss with Cronje without knowing what it was. I suspected he was under tremendous pressure to fulfil the role of sporting hero in a country going through an almost impossibly painful cultural assimilation. He was required to meet the whims of politicians while striving to carry out a job that countenanced no compromise.

He was constantly being asked to place his own interests, and those of his players, behind broader concerns, and it was no surprise to me that he might find this an intolerable strain. His bizarre proposal in the final Test against England at Centurion that the sides should stage a finish on the last day after rain had ruined a game on which nothing was riding, looked at first glance like an attempt to demonstrate that he was not the sober-suited character those in authority wanted him to be.

He was suffocating under the impossible weight of the demands being made of him; tired of being righteous. As one observer said, 'The poor man needed desperately to sin in order to stay sane.'[11]

I STILL THINK there was an element of truth in this theory, though undoubtedly other motivations were at work: Cronje's long-running struggle to translate his position into real power, and that real power into money. It was almost as if his status as captain of a national sports team meant nothing if that status could not also be equated to high pecuniary reward.

This was a recognisable Afrikaner trait. When British settlers were in Africa, they were admired as financial wheeler-dealers by the farm-based Afrikaners, whose hardships earned them the tag of 'poor whites'. The Afrikaners aspired to possess these business skills but it was not until the 1920s and 1930s that they began their migration to the towns, and only in the second half of the twentieth century that they moved into the mining, financial and banking sectors. To an extent, their history can be charted by their efforts to match the financial acumen of the white English-speaking people. The ability to cut money deals remained the final rite of passage for many Afrikaners.

One Afrikaner commentator rationalised the part this process played in Cronje's downfall: 'Even when we have made it in the sophisticated world out there, we have a nagging little voice in our subconscious: if only they knew who I really am. The only way to silence that little voice is to prove to yourself that you are as tough and as clever and as wise to the world as the next guy. Which means you sometimes also have to flirt with evil.'[12] Johan Volsteedt's assessment was possibly over-romantic: 'When money talks, even the angels listen.'[13]

It was striking that in the eyes of many Afrikaners – and indeed many whites in general – Cronje's actions were not reprehensible. Days after his fall, a poll conducted by the white newspaper the *Cape Times* showed strong public support for him. Of those questioned, 94 per cent said they wanted to see Cronje back in the national team; the *Daily News* found 80 per cent in favour of him playing again. The day after Cronje confessed, all 1,100 pupils at his old school, Grey College, stood in the main hall and sang: 'Hansie is our hero, we shall not be moved!'[14]

The Afrikaans press was strident in its criticism of the Indian police when they laid their charges against the South Africa cricketers. It was claimed that the allegations represented a plot to sabotage the growing status of Afrikaners within the sport. 'The refusal to countenance the possibility that Cronje erred has much to do with what he has come to mean to South Africa as a nation ... Cronje's actions have done great harm to South African cricket, but the most telling damage may be to white South Africans' sense of themselves.'[15] Others felt his behaviour was part of a wider problem. 'This is Africa, boys and girls,' read one letter to the *Citizen* newspaper, 'Hansie has only done what many are doing.'[16]

Cronje was a man who appeared to have everything – fame,

adulation, an impeccable reputation – but lacked the one thing that would mark him out as a man who had taken his place in the world: the entrepreneurial talent for making money. And in a country whose currency, the Rand, was worth little outside the national borders, wealth was not easily achieved. Acquisitiveness was Cronje's signature emotion but for years he kept it tucked beneath the mask he displayed to the outer world. Once exposed, however, he frankly admitted, 'I had a great passion for the game, my teammates and my country. But the problem is the unfortunate love I have for money. I do like money.'[17]

His teammates knew well of this obsession. When news broke of Cronje's dealings with the bookies, the revelations – shocking though they were – made perfect sense to some of them. Cronje's desire for control and power may have grown steadily during his time as captain, but his interest in money had been sky-high for years. This manifested itself in contradictory ways. While he would save his daily meal allowance by eating take-away food rather than dining in expensive restaurants (unless the restaurateurs were willing to provide a famous guest with a free meal), he was in thrall to the trappings of wealth.

Craig Matthews, one of Cronje's closest friends in the South Africa team, recalled them spending a day on the yacht of one of Matthews's friends off the Cape in January 1996. 'You could see Hansie was just fascinated by this boat. He basically didn't stop asking about what it was worth, what it cost to maintain and so on. And also what somebody had to be worth in order to afford that kind of luxury. That was always quite a big thing with him: what people were worth.'[18]

Cronje claimed he fought a constant battle to overcome his addiction. 'I am not an alcoholic and I have never been addicted to nicotine, but I understand there are times when you give in to the temptation. At various times guilt made me realise what I was doing was wrong. I did not realise ... I was hooked. That only became apparent later.'[19]

In the end he devoted more energy and application to maximising his earnings than to honing his batting technique. By South African standards he became rich. At the end he was estimated to earn £200,000 annually from his contract with the South African board, endorsements, speaking engagements and prize money. During the King Commission hearings, it emerged that he had received a benefit in 1998 worth at least £140,000 (other estimates placed the tax-free amount at £300,000) and that one agent alone had earned him £400,000 in sponsorship deals during the previous five years. His financial affairs were complex. He placed some funds in bank accounts in England, a legacy of a season spent with Leicestershire in 1995, and set up trust funds in his and his wife's names. He owned a £380,000 house on a luxury estate at Fancourt, on the Cape.[20]

The King Commission ordered an audit of his financial affairs from Deloitte & Touche, from which it transpired that about £1 million had been paid into various South African bank accounts held by Cronje during his six years as captain. This included his regular payments from the South African board, and sponsorship and benefit earnings. The audit was abandoned when the King Commission was wound up before Cronje's overseas accounts could be examined (his account in Leicester contained around £7,000). It also showed Cronje had, at various times since 1994, held the deeds to eight properties, though not all concurrently; in February 2001, he owned two properties and part-owned a third. When these details became public, Cronje, clearly angry at the imputations that he had received more money by illicit means than he had confessed to, held a press conference in which he attempted to show he had nothing to hide.[21]

Bob Woolmer, the former England player who coached South Africa for all but the last nine months of Cronje's tenure as captain, recalled, 'He played the stock market, and we regularly had whoops of joy and cries of disaster as the shares bounced around. Cricket was not his only source of income.'[22] Others around the South Africa team were aware he was working on various prospective business deals during the last year of his captaincy, some involving technology partners from India. He had long been in the habit of poring over the financial pages of the newspapers.[23]

Asked whether he was surprised when a professional gambler, Marlon Aronstam, gave him 50,000 rand (about £5,000) as a gift, Cronje replied, 'I am not trying to boast or to try and be big-headed or anything … but I do have a lot of money, I do deal with people with a lot of money and 50,000 rand is a big gift and the first 30,000 rand was a big gift, and I was surprised that he gave me so much, yes, but in my mind it is not uncommon for the practice that I'm in.'[24]

Cronje's case provided many different lessons for cricket, but the starkest was that if the true nature of a person so much in the public eye could escape detection, then so could that of any of the game's other stars. The assumption that cricket's heroes were different from ordinary people, devoted only to the timeless ideals of winning and taking part, unswayed by ordinary emotions such as greed and lust, had been revealed as bunk. 'He was adored. Now we know he was a fake. When we cheered, he mocked us. When we suffered for his loss of form, he counted his money,' one letter to South Africa's *Star* newspaper read. 'Our hero was just another greedy man.'[25]

Tim Noakes, a professor of sports science at the University of Cape Town, whom Woolmer briefly recruited to the backroom staff of the South Africa team, claimed Cronje had actually been a poor captain who inspired little respect. He said it was 'left to the press to build him up'.[26] One newspaper editorial warned that 'his downfall is a moral fable in the dangers of idolatry'.[27] Everyone assumed Cronje had been serving his country; in fact, he had merely been serving himself.

While the South African public wrestled with the shaming of their hero, and Cronje himself retreated to his hideout at the luxury coastal resort of Fancourt, rarely to be seen again, cricket was left to reappraise its heroes, assess them as people and what actually motivated them.

Unfortunately, it would emerge that several other top players harboured 'an unfortunate love of money'.

3

THE WORLD CUP THAT CHANGED EVERYTHING

Cricket was not supposed to be like this. More than any other sport, it retained vestiges of the purity and innocence of its origins. Comparatively speaking, it was unsullied by the commercial imperatives of the modern world. Had there been a corruption scandal in football or boxing, no one would have raised an eyebrow. But cricket was different.

Cricket was synonymous with fair play. While it was true that examples could be produced of eminent figures from the past indulging in sharp practice or financial greed, these were the exceptions that proved the rule. The sport may have had its roots in aristocratic gambling, but convention demanded decency and honesty of its participants and 95 per cent of the time they provided it. What was unique about cricket was that each player, while batting and bowling for himself, was ultimately serving a team cause. Selflessness, not selfishness, was expected of every participant.

Lord Harris's paean to the game perfectly summed up its virtues. 'You will do well to love it,' he wrote in 1931, 'for it is more free from anything sordid, anything dishonourable, than any game in the world. To play it keenly, honourably, generously, self-sacrificingly is a moral lesson in itself.'

Similarly, the sport attracted reporters and broadcasters who were, by and large, escapists and romantics. We were drawn by cricket's gentlemanly code, its ability to allow individual players to express their characters, its essentially tranquil nature. Covering cricket was thought to be one of the most pleasant occupations on earth. Some dreamed of being another Neville Cardus, CLR James or John Arlott. Not so many years ago, some cricket writers had managed to go through their entire careers without ever writing a 'news' story of any description, let alone one about whether a particular player's talents extended beyond executing the leg-glance to money-laundering.

All this was to change. When match-fixing surfaced, we reacted in one of two ways. Some pretended, when they could, that nothing untoward was happening (they were far from alone in this); others got our boots on and started tramping through the scandal's murky undergrowth in search of answers.

Ironically, one of the things we discovered was that it was cricket's peculiar ability to allow the individual to perform within a team environment that made the game so susceptible to abuse.

IT IS HARD to pinpoint when organised match-fixing surfaced in cricket in the modern era. There were claims of isolated malpractice in the 1970s. When in 2000 the International Cricket Council (ICC), the world governing body, finally got to grips with the problem and appointed the former Metropolitan Police Commissioner Sir Paul (later Lord) Condon to head an anti-corruption inquiry, it was suggested that counties fixed matches to mutually secure points and league positions. However, he found the evidence of unlawful betting on such games 'patchy, anecdotal and not compelling'.

International cricket was where money was to be made, and the first event to attract a number of allegations of bookmakers bribing cricketers was Pakistan's tour of India in 1979–80. These two countries, so often at war, had resumed playing matches the previous year and inevitably attracted enormous interest.

The two players who combined to make Pakistan a major force in Test cricket for the first time were its late 1970s fast-bowling partnership of Imran Khan and Sarfraz Nawaz – Imran the glamorous and talismanic figure who would subsequently lead his country to victory in the World Cup, and the burly, moustachioed Sarfraz, whose wayward talent could win or lose a match. Both Imran and Sarfraz, as well as Arif Ali Abbasi, a long-serving Pakistan board official, all said they believed this tour signalled the first sign of trouble. Rumours attached to the Pakistan and former Kent captain Asif Iqbal, whom Sarfraz alleged developed a friendship with Raj Bagri, one of the biggest bookmakers in India. Safraz said Bagri behaved as if he was a member of the Pakistan team. 'It takes a lifetime to build a reputation,' said Asif when I spoke to him in 2001, 'and I do not want to dignify Sarfraz's allegations by commenting on all of them. I met the bookie in question through other players known to him, but no discussions of any such things as match-fixing or betting took place. Sarfraz was a great bowler, but I had been on tour with him before and had told the board that I was not prepared to captain the side if Sarfraz was included.'[1]

Two controversial incidents related to the final Test in Calcutta after India had won the series. One was Asif's decision to declare Pakistan's first innings early on the fourth day when they were still 59 behind; the other was his apparent ceding of the toss to Gundappa Viswanath. According to Arif Abbasi, Asif told Viswanath he had won the toss before the coin even landed. Narottam Puri, a television commentator who interviewed the India captain directly after the toss, said Viswanath had been baffled by what happened. Puri recalled him saying, 'I really don't know who won the toss … I just flipped the coin … Asif turned around and said "Congrats, Vishy!"' Many years later another Indian player, Chetan Chauhan, confirmed Viswanath's confusion, but added, 'We laughed it off as a joke.'[2] Such were the losses suffered by some bookmakers that bets were cancelled. Asif himself told me that there was no confusion: 'Viswanath has denied he was suspicious about the toss, and the claim in the Qayyum investigation that Vishy wrote about the incident in his book is laughable. Vishy never wrote a book!'[3]

Sarfraz had more to say about that tour, alleging that Pakistan threw the Test in Mumbai, but his motives must be questioned. He was bitter because Asif did not select him for the tour, reasonably enough given that he had been Pakistan's best fast bowler behind Imran (Imran said Asif left him out because he feared he could not handle him). He was also by inclination something of a conspiracy theorist – to talk to Sarfraz after he retired about match-fixing was to have a conversation peppered with allegations concerning any number of people in any number of places; the presentation of supporting evidence was always submerged beneath the weight of his own conviction that what he was saying was true.

In his autobiography Imran Khan made no reference to Asif's conduct in Calcutta but did point out that the recriminations over Pakistan losing to India took a terrific toll on Asif, who ended the tour emaciated and on tranquillisers. Asif denied the charges. 'I didn't even know betting existed then,' he said. 'The people who made the allegations about the toss – were they there when I tossed the coin? As far as declaring, we had a chat and felt that losing a series 2–0 is as good as losing 3–0. Unfortunately, we dropped a couple of catches.'

Sarfraz also alleged that Sunil Gavaskar, who captained India in the first five games of the series before handing over to his brother-in-law Viswanath for the sixth, was also involved with Bagri, though he did not specify what the nature of that involvement was.

Gavaskar, who denied any wrong doing, captained India on and off between 1978 and 1986. No one, however, was alleging that Gavaskar, the first man to score 10,000 runs in Test cricket, personally took money to influence events.

None of these allegations were made public until years later, but one Pakistani journalist who covered the tour heard rumours and began making inquiries. Soon after, he received threatening telephone calls, warning him off pursuing the matter further.

From the mid-1970s the game of cricket had been undergoing a transformation. The first one-day World Cup in 1975 had been a huge success, and Kerry Packer's temporary poaching of the world's top players for his own World Series on Australian television had made the administrators and the players themselves reappraise the commercial possibilities. The culmination of this process was the final of the World Cup in England in 1983, which India won against all the odds. In an extraordinary upset they beat West Indies, the defending champions and winners of the two previous World Cups, by successfully defending a small total. Had the mighty West Indies been chasing a bigger target, they might have woken out of their slumber; as it was, they sleepwalked their way to disaster.

I was present at the time and vividly remember how the mood of the game changed the instant Viv Richards, then the undisputed champion batsman of the world, hooked into the hands of Kapil Dev running round on the boundary. There was a big Indian presence at Lord's and after the giant-slaying was complete, the streets outside erupted into a traffic-halting carnival that would have done Calcutta proud. At the post-match reception Clive Lloyd, the West Indies captain, looked utterly shattered.

Even as the evening unfolded there was a distinct feeling that the cricket world had just lurched on its axis towards Asia. It had already been agreed that the 1987 World Cup would not be staged in England again (England had staged all three tournaments to date), and the choice of the subcontinent as venue seemed entirely appropriate given the craze for one-day cricket India's victory inspired. But given the interest the subcontinent's bookmakers were now to take in the sport, there could also have been no place worse.

India's World Cup triumph had a big impact on the Indian cricketers themselves. Lavished with gifts on their return home, they developed a taste for the material things in life and thereby became more open to persuasion. Mohinder Amarnath remembered bookmakers hanging around during the tournament itself, but that they did not then have the courage to approach the players. 'None of the players were directly involved, in the sense that the bookies used to be scared. They were there, but people there never used to bother you.'[4] Such reticence was about to disappear.

There was huge public interest in everything the India team now did. All their games were telecast live, which helped to cement cricket as the subcontinent's broadest religion and elevate the players onto the same plane as Bollywood stars. Indeed, they were perhaps even more popular, given the universality of cricket's language; the popularity of film stars tended to vary from region to region because of language barriers. India started playing far more one-day cricket, home and away. Despite the benefits, this would fuel cynicism among the overworked performers.

With one-day cricket receiving so much exposure, gambling expanded rapidly. Betting was illegal throughout the subcontinent on all but a few select horse race meetings, but laws were so antiquated that they acted as no kind of deterrent. Under India's Public Gambling Act, for example, the maximum sentence for a first offence for anyone owning or keeping a gaming house in Delhi was a prison term of six months and a £16 fine. 'For a bookie or a punter dealing in tens of millions of rupees, the provisions of this Act are no major cause for worry.'[5] A massive industry worth hundreds of millions of pounds, and providing entertainment for millions, was thus allowed to flourish.

India's major betting centres were Mumbai, where a network of several hundred bookmakers largely determined the odds, followed by Delhi, Calcutta, Chennai and Ahmedabad. Dubai, in the Gulf, where there was a large expatriate Asian population and huge concentrated wealth, generated activity second only to Mumbai. Karachi and Lahore, in Pakistan, tended to act as middlemen to the larger gambling centres in Mumbai and Dubai.

It was partly to satisfy the new fanaticism of the Asian population in Dubai that a businessman called Abdurrahman Bukhatir built the sport's first 'offshore' venue, and possibly the most bizarre cricket ground in the world in the desert, at Sharjah, ten miles along the coast. Tournaments were staged there from 1984, usually two per year, and became noted for three things: the absence of urgent competition, the paucity of prize money and, in time, the suspicion that matches were 'fixed'. Similar international venues were set up in the unlikely settings of Toronto and Singapore.

Lord Condon's interim report would highlight the dangers of the relaxed regimes that developed at such venues. 'Corrupt practices took place under the cover of the carnival atmosphere of some of these events ... If national pride was not really at stake then players were more susceptible to corrupt approaches. At some of these tournaments the payment regime to players and others has been vague and the total remuneration for a player could involve cash in an envelope from the organisers, gifts and payments from fans and from bookmakers and gamblers ... which may have led to corruption.'[6]

Bukhatir appointed Asif Iqbal, who had retired from Test cricket after the disgrace of losing in India, as chief organiser. Asif held the post for seventeen years and it involved him in no little controversy. His own name would subsequently be linked to match-fixing, and he himself admitted that there had been matches at Sharjah which he had 'wondered' about, but denied any personal involvement.[7]

Much gambling business was conducted so surreptitiously as to be almost undetectable. The network was spread across the big cities like an invisible web. Shopkeepers and cigarette vendors on street corners joined with industrialists and businessmen in collecting bets from thousands of people who regularly gambled anything from £10 to upwards of £10,000 at a time, passing the wagers onto the bookies and retaining a percentage for themselves. By arranging deals by word of mouth or small indecipherable pieces of paper, and by bypassing normal banking channels, the bookies made it next to impossible for the authorities to assemble evidence against them.

Another major factor was the development of mobile phones and pagers, whose proliferation also eased lines of communication, although these would later bring problems of their own for the bookies.

The system was near impregnable. When the match-fixing scandal was at its height, many areas of gambling remained unaffected. 'We don't see any change in the betting pattern,' said one Karachi bookmaker. 'It has not affected the people. They are still coming to us and placing their bets.' A Mumbai police officer described the difficulties of making charges against bookies stick: 'They change their locations. They change their mobiles. It is impossible to keep tabs on them. Even if we pull off a successful raid, they are bailed and operating again a day later. They ... are virtually untouchable. Even if court is reached, the punishment never fits the crime.'[8]

Gradually, the betting became more organised. 'Initially, betting was restricted to a group of friends, but by the later 1980s it had become more organised, and a number of bookies spawned in major metropolitan cities,' stated India's Central Bureau of Investigation (CBI) report into match-fixing. 'By the middle of the 1990s, with a surfeit of one-day matches being shown live on television ... betting had taken the shape of a massive organised racket.'[9] By the late 1990s estimates put the turnover in India on a one-day international in excess of £16 million.

By the early 1990s the mafia groups that colourfully dominated political and commercial life in the subcontinent's big cities, especially Mumbai, were showing an interest in the gambling trade. Gambling, and eventually match-fixing, were an attraction because they were relatively easy and safe ways of making money, and the mafia's sources of income were shrinking. 'The gangsters got into fixing because their profits on importing gold and white contraband had been cut,'[10] one source said. The mafia's arrival on the scene was a crucial development.

In the 1980s malpractice appeared to be confined to players being paid relatively small amounts of money for manipulating minor aspects of games. The Condon report listed the scope of these side-bets, which would remain a major area of corruption:

* The outcome of the toss at the beginning of a match
* The end from which the fielding captain elected to bowl
* A set number of wides, or no-balls occurring in a designated over
* Players being placed in unfamiliar fielding positions
* Individual batsmen scoring fewer runs than their opposite numbers who batted first
* Batsmen being out at a specific point in their innings
* The total runs at which a batting captain will declare
* The timing of a declaration
* The total runs scored in a particular innings and particularly the total in the first innings of a one-day international

It was not until the bookmakers were more organised and in possession of greater sums of money that match-fixing in its most literal sense – that is, the predetermination of a result – became more common, and that probably could not happen until mafia gangs were involved. 'The proceeds of corruption in cricket are sufficiently large to attract the attention of organised crime,' the Condon report concluded, 'and corruption provides an opportunity for easy profit and simple money-laundering.'

Before 1990, the only games that anyone alleged had fixed results were the India–Pakistan Test in Mumbai in 1979–80 and a World Cup match in 1987. In both cases Sarfraz Nawaz was the accuser. He claimed Bukhatir and Asif Iqbal 'arranged' for Pakistan to lose to Australia in their World Cup semi-final at Lahore, a charge Bukhatir and Asif vigorously denied. Asif asked the Pakistan board to investigate. 'I said that, if what Sarfraz says is true, ban the team and make sure we are punished as well. If not, Sarfraz should be punished. Nothing happened.'[11]

It was generally agreed that a match was hard to fix without several of the best players being involved, another reason why side-bets would remain attractive. Some, such as Azharuddin, would later maintain that for a result to be arranged, 'the entire team has to be in the know',[12] but this was not the general view. Obviously, the more influential a player, the more influence he could wield, which was why captains like Hansie Cronje became such desirable commodities. 'When you've got the main players in your hand you'll have to be really unlucky to lose,' Salim Malik, the Pakistan cricketer, was reported as saying. 'Really there's no chance of losing money … You pay and they will be out. He'll run himself out, whatever, but he will be out … You'll have four or five players in hand and they will be playing just for you. No matter what the rest of the team do, they will do what they've agreed to do.'[13]

Within ten years the subcontinent mafia had become the biggest single threat to cricket's credibility. In its report into match-fixing, published in November 2000, India's Central Bureau of Investigation warned, 'There are clear signals that the underworld mafia has started taking interest in the betting racket and can be expected to take overall control of this activity, if not checked immediately with a firm hand … It does appear that what may have been small-time wagering has now been replaced by an organised syndicate, and this syndicate has started interfering with the purity of the sport. It has been the negligence of the police and the other regulatory authorities, that has allowed wagering to turn into an organised racket.'[14]

Several mafia groups were suspected of involvement, but three names kept cropping up. Two had their roots in Mumbai, though their leaders were exiled abroad – one led by Dawood Ibrahim, the other by his arch-rival Chhota Rajan. They had been allies until Ibrahim, who paved his way to wealth of £320 million through the construction trade, became the chief suspect behind a series of racially motivated bomb blasts in 1993 and took refuge in Pakistan. Ibrahim was known as the 'Muslim don', Rajan as the 'Hindu don'. Rajan set up base in Malaysia.[15] The third group was run by Abu Salem, who governed another splinter of Ibrahim's empire. Salem fled India in 1996 and set up operation in South Africa; one former Test captain later admitted to receiving an approach from him to fix matches.[16]

It was Ibrahim's gang that attracted most publicity. Ibrahim liked cricket but did not bet. He owned a VIP box at Sharjah, and the former allrounder Ravi Shastri remembered him visiting the Indian dressing room there in 1986. He was rumoured to wield great influence, extending even to team selection in the case of one country. His brother Anees liked to mix with the star players, but Ibrahim's top lieutenant, Chohtta Shakeel, denied they sponsored match-fixing. Shakeel claimed the gang's role was simply to act on behalf of punters cheated by dishonest bookies. 'We are punters, not fixers,' he said.[17] But he did not dispute that match-fixing existed. 'Managers, captains, even ICC members are involved,' he commented.[18]

The mafia's arrival on the scene had an obvious effect beyond their superior organisation. The bribes went up in value. Whereas a batsman might have been paid a few hundred pounds to deliberately throw away his wicket in the mid-1980s, a player could earn a small fortune in the regular employ of a syndicate some ten years later. 'In a year you could make three or four million [pounds],' one banned player claimed.[19] But there was a downside – the threat of retribution if co-operation was not forthcoming. Gangsters were not averse to resorting to blackmail or physical violence if people did not comply with their wishes. Many feared the consequences if they were asked to identify the shady characters with whom they dealt, and threats undoubtedly bought the silence of some.

Those who were surprised that players could countenance throwing 'big' matches such as Tests or World Cup games – as opposed to 'dead' games which could not affect the overall outcome of a series or tournament – needed to remember that some players actually had little choice. The blunt message was: 'Co-operate – or we will tell your board you took money, or worse.'

There were stories that several bookmakers who failed to 'arrange' matches paid with their lives. A Mumbai bookmaker who sustained heavy losses after failing to cut deals with players during India's tour of South Africa in 1992–93 – Cronje's first home series – was said to have hung himself. Another was believed to have had more success in recruiting players but was killed in Dubai a few years later.

The precise nature of the relationship between players and bookies would remain one of the great mysteries of the saga, but blackmail featured in many people's thoughts. 'The players do not do it just for money, but because they are in too deep,' said Fareshteh Gati, an experienced Pakistan journalist. 'They are being threatened. That alone explains why they are so desperate to be in charge, because the captain is in the best position from which to manipulate events. Equally, an honest captain is no good. So the corrupt players underperform to get him removed. Junior players too find themselves under threat of being pushed out if they do not cooperate. Many good guys have found themselves losers.

'Precisely which matches are fixed emerges only gradually. The honest players might speak out first. They tell you there had been an argument among the team about the batting or bowling. Then you hear that the bookies cancelled bets, which means they suspected something was going on. Finally, a manager might say that he had advocated one policy and the captain had followed another. Then you would know.'[20]

The captains. Don't take your eyes off the captains.

LORD CONDON described the Indian betting industry as 'the engine-room which has powered and driven cricket corruption'. But he said it would be wrong to lay all the blame for the spread of corruption on the Indian subcontinent.

By the mid-1980s problems had also developed elsewhere. There were suspicious goings-on in Australia and New Zealand, at least according to the former Pakistan batsman Qasim Omar, who toured both countries. In Australia the fascination with betting was ever on the rise; by 1994 Australians were wagering around £200 per person per year, making them possibly the biggest gamblers on earth. Trouble was perhaps inevitable.

Omar's international career ended in 1987 when he sold a story to the newspapers accusing teammates of smoking cannabis. Saying it could find no evidence to support his claims, the Pakistan Cricket Board banned him for seven years. Omar, born in Kenya, was then thirty. He settled in England, married a local girl and spent the next fourteen years playing league cricket and, once match-fixing became topical, selling more stories of corruption from his days on the international circuit. Most of these stories were written with the help of the same journalist, veteran Fleet Street hack Brian Radford.

According to Omar's admittedly lurid accounts, bribery was already rife by the mid-1980s, especially among the Pakistan team. Among his claims were that a world-class batsman was offered £9,000 to throw away his wicket in four Tests of a five-match series; a Test captain was paid for information; and a top Asian bowler underperformed to complete the building of his new home. Omar himself took money to throw away his wicket. He scored two Test double-centuries, both at Faisalabad, and said each innings ended with him getting out deliberately.

He also claimed to have acted as a middleman between bookies and up to fifteen foreign players, 'some of them very big names', from Pakistan, Sri Lanka, India, West Indies and England. Under the heading 'Bowler Bribe', he claimed in the *People* in 1996 that 'an England bowler' took £1,000 to concede a boundary in his first over of a Test. Omar said he knew of the deal because he helped set it up and was paid £500 for doing so.[21]

He declined to publicly name the guilty but stated that among those who turned him down were Aravinda de Silva, of Sri Lanka, and two India players, Ravi Shastri and Sandip Patil. 'I asked de Silva to throw his wicket away in the first Test at Faisalabad in 1985. My bookmaker wanted to bet that de Silva would be out straight after reaching his ton. I put it to de Silva during a meal break – but he said "No" and went on to score 122 before he was caught.'

What was noticeable was that all the bribery activity Omar

referred to related to individuals manipulating side-bets rather than players working together to fix the outcomes of matches.

His most interesting allegations related to what had gone on in Australia. Omar said that an Australian bookmaker had supplied prostitutes to visiting players, among them captains, in return for favours regarding side-bets. He claimed the deals were struck in hotels and restaurants. 'I know plenty of players from a number of countries who had sex with these girls as a reward for doing things for bookies,' he was quoted as saying in an article in the *News of the World*, which appeared five days after the publication of the CBI report. A similar sex scandal was also in operation in New Zealand, he said.

In a subsequent 'exclusive' interview with the *Sydney Morning Herald*, Omar admitted that an unnamed 'prominent Perth business-man' had enticed him to throw away his wicket at various stages of Pakistan's 1983–84 tour of Australia at £200 a time.

Again, Omar volunteered no names except his own, alleging merely that 'prominent players, including national team captains' were offered sex, money and gifts. After selling his stories, he passed on what he knew to Lord Condon's anti-corruption unit. Malcolm Speed, the chief executive of the Australian Cricket Board, said he was relieved to find that 'there are no Australian officials or players involved in these allegations'.

Omar accused the Pakistan Cricket Board of turning a blind eye to bribery and offered to help the Pakistan government clean up the game. But when Justice Malik Qayyum conducted his inquiry into match-fixing, Omar was not called as a witness. Omar may have tainted himself with his eagerness to make money, but his claims were completely ignored.

AMONG THE multitudes captivated by India's 1983 World Cup win was a young, modestly salaried clerk in the Syndicate Bank in Delhi called Mukesh Kumar Gupta. The son of a middle-class government treasury clerk, Gupta lived in a ramshackle house in the old city's

Ballimaran district. He was bright but stuck in a nondescript job, and his imagination had been fired by the slaying of West Indies several thousand miles away.

'One day, he was walking on the street near his residence at Mohalla Dassan and saw some people betting for small amounts on a cricket match and this caught his attention,' read the CBI's match-fixing report. 'He started betting with them on a small scale after banking hours. Since the people involved in this business were not well educated and did not have much knowledge of cricket, he started reading about cricket from books, magazines, newspapers etc. He updated his knowledge by listening to [the] BBC and gathered a lot of information. In this manner, he used to place intelligent bets and made more money than other people involved in betting. Since he was very prompt in his payments, the bookies also started having trust in him and his volume of betting increased...'.[22]

By 1986 Gupta had made a 'good amount' of money and decided to open an account with the biggest bookies in Mumbai. Part of the arrangement was that he should provide them with regular business, so he set up as a bookmaker himself, in partnership with another Delhi bookmaker called Anand Saxena. Saxena knew more about betting than Gupta and educated him in the business. Between them they made a good profit out of the 1987 World Cup.

The following year at a club tournament Gupta met Ajay Sharma, a young batsman who had recently broken into the India team, and gave him £30 in appreciation of a good innings. He gave Sharma his telephone number, he said, and told him to get in touch if he had problems. Gupta did this, 'since he thought Ajay Sharma had talent and it was an investment with the hope that some day he could reap the benefits'.[23] A couple of weeks later Sharma is said to have contacted him and a relationship started that would benefit them both. Sharma's international career failed to take off but his contacts with players helped him become, in the words of the Delhi police, 'arguably the biggest cricketer-bookie we have had in a long while'.[24] In 1989 Gupta resigned from the bank to concentrate on bookmaking.

According to Gupta, Sharma relayed information to him during India's tour of New Zealand in 1990; 'based on that information, he [Gupta] made a good amount of money'.[25] Sharma denied this but admitted introducing Gupta to Manoj Prabhakar, another member of the team, after Sharma was dropped for the tour of England. Several years later, after playing his last match for India in 1993, Sharma introduced Gupta to two other India cricketers, Ajay Jadeja and Azharuddin, then the national captain. Azharuddin in turn introduced him to other players. Sharma has always disputed the allegations against him, however, and told me that he had never been involved with bookmakers, and why would he want to?

Prabhakar came to a similar arrangement with the bookmaker. Prabhakar agreed to introduce Gupta to international players for £800 a time. It was an arrangement that would prove fruitful. 'According to MK, Manoj Prabhakar gave him information about all aspects of the India team and he also underperformed in one of the Test matches which ended in a draw.'[26] This match was likely to have been the high-scoring draw against England at Old Trafford in which Prabhakar took two wickets for 192 runs and scored 4 and 67. Gupta said that in return he gave Prabhakar about £650 and enough money to buy a Maruti Gypsy car 'with wide tyres'. 'MK used to pay him only when his introduction to foreign players resulted in a profitable relationship ... MK used to pay him through one of his servants.'

Prabhakar admitted introducing Gupta to some players but denied fixing, or attempting to fix, matches for him. When the Indian cricket board commissioned an investigation into match-fixing, Prabhakar was cleared of rigging matches. The former CBI director who led the inquiry, K Madhavan, said that there was 'no evidence of any role by him of match-fixing'. Prabhakar himself was more ambiguous in his denials: 'They say I was involved, yes I was involved, to some limit. Then I realised this is too much. They start with information, then they try to grab you and get you involved in fixing. You don't want to but you get fixed.'[27]

Gupta, an affable character typically adorned with fine jewellery, mixed confidently with the star players. He travelled to New Zealand, Sri Lanka, Hong Kong, Sharjah and South Africa in pursuit of contacts and information, building up an extensive network that gave him a vital advantage in his business. He sent someone to England to gather information on his behalf. Gupta was happy to pay well for information but gradually saw that the best way to bring about what he wanted was to bribe players to perform below par. Again, it seemed that he preferred to deal with players on a one-to-one basis, encouraging them to manipulate their personal performances to influence side-bets rather than working collectively in the harder task of fixing results. Even so, many refused. To protect himself, Gupta used a number of aliases, including 'MK' and 'John'. Until he was sure he had a player's confidence, he might purport to be something other than a bookmaker, such as a potential sponsor or journalist.

Gupta claimed to meet eight foreign international players directly or indirectly through Prabhakar between 1991 and 1994, though Prabhakar himself denied there were so many. All eight were prominent cricketers whose help might have been considered valuable to a bookmaker. They were, he claims: Aravinda de Silva and Arjuna Ranatunga, from Sri Lanka; Martin Crowe, of New Zealand; Salim Malik, of Pakistan; Dean Jones and Mark Waugh, of Australia; Alec Stewart, of England; and Brian Lara, of West Indies. Six of the eight either had, or would subsequently, captain their countries.

According to Gupta's testimony to police, Jones refused to get involved in any way; Crowe and Mark Waugh (£13,500 each) and Stewart (£5,000) were all paid for information; de Silva and Ranatunga (£10,000 between them), Salim Malik (£12,800) and Lara (£25,000) received money for either underperforming or fixing results. He alleged de Silva and Ranatunga fixed a Test against India at Lucknow in 1994, Lara played below par in two one-dayers in India the same year, and Salim Malik arranged for his team to lose a match in Delhi between the one-day champions of India and Pakistan in 1991.

That was Gupta's version. All the players themselves vehemently rejected his claims when they appeared in the CBI report, though de Silva, Jones and Crowe did admit to speaking to him. Jones had already publicly admitted several years earlier that he had been offered £30,000 by an unnamed bookie, introduced to him by an unnamed player. He described the player as a retired Indian and said the bookie, who carried the money in a cake tin, claimed to have a 'nark' in every international team in the world.[28] Crowe believed he was being offered money for media articles; Gupta had portrayed himself as a journalist, but once Crowe realised the real nature of his business, he refused to have anything more to do with him.

Those who knew Gupta well said he was ambitious but discreet; he did not seem the kind to show off about his contacts, though that was how many saw his testimony to the CBI. 'MK was always determined to make it big and could go to any extent to reach his goal,' said a long-standing acquaintance.[29] 'The secret of his success,' claimed another, 'was that he never went around town dropping names. He kept everything to himself.'[30] Even Saxena knew little. His role was simply to maintain the books. 'MK was very secretive about his links with cricket players,' he said.[31] The CBI were most concerned about Gupta's confessed dealings with Indian players and were impressed with how often they were proved accurate when they investigated further. 'Whatever he told us turned out to be true. It was corroborated by various aspects of the investigation.'[32]

Around 1994 Gupta even broke off his relationships with Saxena and Prabhakar. He said that two years earlier he had struck a deal with Prabhakar to fix matches but that he had proved expensively unreliable. Some matches turned out as Prabhakar said they would, others did not. Gupta had suffered 'huge' losses during the World Cup in Australia in 1992 and a one-day series against England in India in 1992–93, when Prabhakar forecast only one out of three results correctly (the series was tied 3–3). Although Gupta's charge of attempted match-fixing against Prabhakar was dismissed by Madhavan, clearly something caused the rupture between them.[33] Gupta said he no longer trusted Prabhakar, whose demands for money kept increasing and whom he suspected of dealing with other bookmakers and punters. Saxena, meanwhile, was unwell – Gupta believed he might have had cancer.

Gupta gave up bookmaking and became a punter, operating closely with a bookie in Mumbai called Anil Steel, though the switch had no material affect on the way he operated. Steel introduced him to Asif Iqbal, whom he knew. The CBI report alleged that Asif in turn introduced Gupta to Sanath Jayasuriya, of Sri Lanka, the player of the tournament at the 1996 World Cup, in Dubai. It was understood Jayasuriya was offered £330,000 but turned it down. Gupta noted, meanwhile, that Saxena and Prabhakar had become friends.

Gupta appeared to be working for himself, at least in the early years, a small but successful operator. He claimed his earnings through 'insider information' were modest – up to 1998 only £800,000.[34] The CBI suspected he understated the true amount to keep down his tax bill on this undeclared income, but even they admitted, 'It was only in 1994–95 that he [Gupta] started earning big money.'[35]

UP TO THE EARLY 1990s the fixing of results appeared to be rare and the evidence against those games that did come under suspicion, flimsy. In 1990 Imran Khan had heard talk that four of his Pakistan team were preparing to throw the final of a Sharjah tournament against Australia and persuaded the team to put £14,000, their prize money they had won to date, on themselves to win. The team duly won, but Imran was not convinced that the talk was true. He described the rumours as 'not especially reliable ones'.[36]

The paucity of hard evidence may have had something to do with the onset of what Lord Condon would later describe as the climate of 'silence, apathy, ignorance and fear' prevalent a decade later.

This climate was nowhere more prevalent than in Sri Lanka, where claims that Sri Lanka had thrown a Test against Australia in Colombo in 1992 surfaced several years later when the Cronje affair loosened tongues. This is the earliest Test to come under serious suspicion. The evidence was sketchy but the claim plausible, given that this was a tour on which two Australia players, Dean Jones and Greg Matthews, had said they were approached by bookies.

At the time of the match three Sri Lanka players, Sanath Jayasuriya, Asanka Gurusinha and Roshan Mahanama, went to their board asking for protection after refusing to co-operate with a betting scam. Their concerns were known to several prominent figures in Sri Lankan cricket. Sidath Wettimuny, a former Test captain, said, 'Three of the guys were approached. Roshan was certainly one of them. He spoke to me about it.' Tyrone Fernando, the then president of the Sri Lankan board, admitted the concerns of the three were not treated appropriately: 'It was a different time. Such things were new to us. In hindsight, we should have taken the matter more seriously.'

Sri Lanka, who had won only two of their previous 37 Tests, scored 547 to claim a first-innings lead of 291 and looked set for a famous victory when they reached 127 for two chasing 181 in the final innings. But a spectacular collapse followed and Australia emerged winners by 16 runs, a result that Allan Border, the Australia captain, described as 'the greatest heist since the Great Train Robbery'. Jones believed the result was genuine: 'As far as I am concerned the collapse started from the moment Aravinda de Silva charged Craig McDermott and was caught. He was in such good form he thought he could do anything.' But others alleged that Gurusinha, who saw seven partners come and go during the collapse, was given no support.

Other allegations about Sri Lankan cricket emerged. It transpired that the board had ordered an inquiry into the team's performance following a disastrous tour of India in 1994 (the tour about which Gupta made his allegations concerning de Silva and Ranatunga). The report, the earliest known investigation into cricket corruption, stated: 'There is evidence that a bookmaker of Indian origin has attempted to make his presence felt in the national cricket scene. The subject of "gambling with the toss" had been part of discussions at one of the team meetings on the tour. There is, however, no further evidence available in this field.' The board subsequently imposed a ban on mobile phones in the dressing room but the report was never published.[37]

Another inquiry, into 'a complete batting collapse' that led to defeat in a one-day final in Singapore in 1996, only came to the fore when it was given a passing mention in the Qayyum report on match-fixing in Pakistan.[38] Why had these facts not come to light earlier? While I was in Sri Lanka covering the England tour early in 2001, I met Lal Wickrematunga, who owned one of the island's leading newspapers, the *Sunday Leader*, and was a member of the cricket board when these events took place. We met for a drink on the lawn of the Galle Face hotel, an old colonial pile that was one of the more identifiable of Colombo's landmarks.

Lal explained that Sri Lankan society worked by an antique system of patronage. The system was a direct legacy of the British years of rule because the British had, with typical organisational zeal, parcelled out every aspect of commercial life family by family. These same families still held the strings to many areas of business. Lal himself experienced difficulties setting up his independent newspaper.

Thilanga Sumathipala was part of this elite and made his money as one of the two families who controlled bookmaking. He became president of the cricket board in 1997 and was re-elected two years later not without controversy. Though a rival candidate persuaded the country's president to set up an investigation into the finances of the board, Sumathipala survived until a coup removed him towards the end of the England tour. When bookmaking and cricket became an unacceptable mix after the Cronje affair, Sumathipala resigned from the board of the family firm, though he was kept in close touch with affairs. Among those he employed was Aravinda de Silva's father.

In a society where power was locked in the hands of a chosen few, there was little need for openness or accountability, in cricket or anything else. As in Pakistan, many good guys found themselves losers. 'Things work in strange ways in this part of the world,' Lal said.[39]

4

OUT IN THE OPEN

For years the cricketing public got no whiff of corruption. Rumours may have circulated through dressing rooms, but that was where they stayed. The public, journalists, even many of those working within the game, slumbered on, blissful in their ignorance.

Occasionally, the stench surfaced. In October 1994 India lost a one-dayer to West Indies at Kanpur in circumstances that the match referee, Raman Subba Row, found suspicious. He docked India two points for not playing within the spirit of the game, suspecting them of deliberately losing to increase the likelihood of West Indies, rather than New Zealand, meeting them in the final. India's sixth-wicket pair, Manoj Prabhakar and Nayan Mongia, stonewalled through the closing stages of a run 'chase' and were charged with 'not making an effort to win'. They came together with 63 wanted off 43 balls; they actually scored 16.[1]

Subba Row questioned Azharuddin and Ajit Wadekar, respectively India's captain and manager, and found their explanations unsatisfactory. 'Azhar just said his players were very confused – and I said I was too,' Subba Row stated. Prabhakar and Mongia both felt betrayed by them. Mongia said he was told by Wadekar not to get out because it would damage India's run-rate; Prabhakar, who was already batting, confirmed that this instruction was conveyed to him by Mongia in the middle. Prabhakar wrote, 'The resultant hullabaloo about my going slow should be directed at the team management and not me as I was doing so under their instructions.'[2] Earlier, Prabhakar bowled six overs costing 50. Bizarrely, the Indian board successfully appealed against the points deduction on the grounds that Subba Row had exceeded his authority and disciplined both players by dropping them for the rest of the tournament.

This incident created little fuss outside India. It did not make more than a few lines in *The Times*. It was viewed as a curiosity, a one-off event in a far-away tournament. There were, after all, one-day internationals being played all round the world, all the year round. No one suspected a wider problem.

There were two questions no one asked but perhaps should have done: firstly, was Subba Row right in suspecting India lost to give themselves easier opponents in the final? Secondly, was the result influenced by bookies?

Four months later the right questions were finally being asked. In February 1995 Phil Wilkins, the cricket correspondent of the *Sydney Morning Herald*, ran a story claiming that two Australia cricketers, Shane Warne and Tim May, had been offered 70,000 Australian dollars each (about £29,000) by a 'prominent Pakistani cricket personality' to throw a Test in Karachi the previous September. The approach was alleged to have come on the fourth evening of the game; Warne and May were being asked to bowl badly on the final day. They bluntly refused, though Pakistan, 155 for three overnight chasing 314, won anyway when the final pair scored 57 together. Warne took five for 89.

How Wilkins came by the story was a well-kept secret, but the most enduring theory was that he was tipped off by Bob Simpson, the then Australia coach. If Simpson was the source, it would not have improved his relations with the players, who mistrusted his politicking. But after nearly ten years he was coming to the end of the road. Within a few months he had been forced out.

The claims sent shock waves through the cricket world. Nobody was sleeping now. For the next few weeks every major newspaper office in the cricket-playing world, including mine, was well and truly alive to what Graham Halbish, the chief executive of the Australian Cricket Board, called 'cricket's greatest crisis for 20 years'.[3] My feelings were probably those of every other cricket writer: a sense of having been duped; that if cricket matches could and had been fixed, then we 'experts', paid to explain why one team won and the other lost, had been made to look foolish.

Over the following days a few players even came forward to confirm that match-fixing was reality, not rumour. Allan Border, recently retired as Australia captain, told the *Daily Telegraph-Mirror*, another Sydney newspaper, that he was offered £500,000 to 'throw' a Test match against England at Edgbaston in 1993 when Australia went into the final day on nine for no wicket needing 120 to win. The offer, it was alleged, came from Mushtaq Mohammad, a former Pakistan Test player now living in Birmingham.

Mushtaq was tracked down. He said the conversation had been a hypothetical one: he had asked Border what he would do 'if someone was to offer him a lot of money to lose'. He added, 'Allan said that he never messed around with his cricket and I said neither did I. It was just a hypothetical conversation, nothing was offered by me on anyone's behalf. I meant it as a joke.' But it was a joke Border did not get. He dismissed the offer 'curtly'. One of his players recalled, 'The skipper was taken aback; he was fuming … When the players were told of the offer they were stunned.' Border himself said, 'I got a bit of a shock because something like that had never happened before.'[4]

The *Herald* allegations prompted Intikhab Alam, the Pakistan manager, to admit that his players were asked to swear on the Koran that they were not involved in betting before leaving for their current tour of South Africa and Zimbabwe. Intikhab said the request had come in response to 'ugly rumours'. 'There was so much going on from all corners that, yes, this was done,' he said. 'We just wanted to make sure.' But he also dismissed the ugly rumours out of hand: 'I think that people have gone mad. There is no truth in it.'[5] It would transpire that this was not the first time Pakistan players had been asked to swear on the Koran.

Then, on 15 February 1995, the *Herald* and *The Age*, a Melbourne newspaper, named the 'prominent Pakistani personality' who had approached May and Warne as the Pakistan captain Salim Malik. Sworn statements by the Australian players were apparently on their way by courier to the ICC in London.

When these statements eventually became public, a fuller story emerged. Malik had phoned Warne in his hotel room, which he shared with May, and asked to speak to him. In Malik's room, Warne said, he was offered 200,000 US dollars (about £130,000, thus more than the original newspaper article claimed) for him and May to bowl badly, the money to be shared between them. It also transpired that later on the same tour Malik had allegedly approached another Australian, Mark Waugh, at a reception on the eve of a one-day international in Rawalpindi. Waugh was offered the same amount 'for four or five Australian players not to play well the next day'. Waugh said he rejected the offer. Once again, the Australians lost anyway. Waugh scored an unbeaten 121 out of Australia 250 for six, but Pakistan knocked off the runs for the loss of one wicket, with 11 overs to spare.

These were sensational allegations, not least because of the high-profile nature of the players involved. Warne was unquestionably the greatest spin bowler in the game, very possibly the best in history. His estimated earnings from playing contracts and endorsements exceeded £500,000 – big money in cricket terms. Lloyds of London had offered to insure his right hand for £1 million. Malik, whom the Australian players referred to as 'The Rat', for his facial resemblance to one, and Waugh were arguably among the best half-dozen batsmen then playing. Malik had played Test cricket for thirteen years and been Pakistan captain for one. Blessed with an excellent technique, he had been precocious even by Asian standards. The son of a Punjabi exporter of linen wear to Europe, he began playing in earnest at the age of twelve in Lahore's Iqbal Park. Four years later he scored a century in his second first-class match and at eighteen struck a century in his first Test, the youngest Pakistani to do so on debut.

The day the Australian papers named him, Malik was leading Pakistan in a Test in Harare. He considered pulling out of the match but in the end went ahead and played. He won the toss, elected to bat and contributed a jittery 20 to Pakistan's score of 231. Afterwards, he said, 'I think it's shameful. I don't believe it. This is stupid – 70,000 Australian dollars. I wish I could have that sort of money. I never spoke to anybody like this. I will speak to my lawyer and will take legal action … Do you think after 13 years I can do such a stupid thing? I never spoke to any of them [the Australians] about this. I just say "hello" to them on the ground. I never socialise with any- body. I am a quiet person.' Talking of his innings, he admitted con- centration had been difficult. 'I was just out of my mind. I was under pressure and I was shaking. I got a lot of encouragement from my team. The boys are also quite depressed, but I am glad they didn't believe this.'[6]

Rather inconveniently, though, one of them apparently did. Aamir Sohail was quoted in the next day's *Australian* as saying, 'If I wasn't bound by a code of conduct, I could name so many players in the present national team who have been bribed to lose matches. It's getting so bad that it's getting all the guys who don't do it a bad name.'[7] He later said the remarks were misattributed.

Three days later Sarfraz Nawaz, now an adviser on sport to Pakistan's then prime minister Benazir Bhutto, claimed an anti-cor- ruption committee had launched an investigation the previous year into the activities of 'six or seven' players, tapping phones and trawl- ing bank accounts. Apparently there were suspicions about Pakistan's failure to overhaul Australia's 179 in the Singer World Series in Sri Lanka. Publicly nothing came of this inquiry, though mobile phones were briefly banned from the dressing room.[8]

Sarfraz also asserted that certain Pakistan players had thrown a match against England at Trent Bridge in 1992; Pakistan (led by Salim Malik because Javed Miandad was absent with a stomach upset) had lost by 198 runs after conceding 363 for seven, then a record total for a one-day international. Sarfraz claimed Miandad was willing to testify if provided with government protection.

Pakistan won the Harare Test by 99 runs to clinch the series 2–1, but their dressing room had now descended into near anarchy. A players' revolt was only averted by the intervention of a Pakistan Board official, Arif Abbasi, but the uprising was not long quelled. While the majority of the team was visiting Victoria Falls, Rashid Latif, Malik's vice-captain, and Basit Ali suddenly announced they were retiring forthwith. They faxed their decisions to the Pakistan board and a domestic news agency. They were hardly at retirement age: at 26 and 24 respectively, Latif and Basit were old for swimmers but not cricketers. 'It is very unfortunate,' Intikhab said, 'but they say they are not enjoying international cricket any more.'[9]

Fuller details emerged during a judicial inquiry three years later, but it was apparent even then that they had acted to bring matters to a head. Latif, it was believed, had accused Malik of betting on matches in which he was involved. Imran Khan, who had now retired from cricket and gone into politics, did nothing to stop talk of the Pakistan teams having an unhealthy interest in money by attacking his country for surrendering its identity to Western materialism.

The major point at issue between Malik and Latif centred on the finals of the Mandela Trophy in South Africa the previous month. Latif had got wind of what he believed were his captain's intentions to deliberately lose the first match in Cape Town. He created such a hue and cry in the dressing room that Intikhab asked all the players to repeat their pre-tour oaths and swear on the Koran that they would play honestly. But before Malik could make the pledge, he made his excuses and went out for the toss. When he returned he had already invited South Africa to bat. Given that batting second under floodlights was hard, this decision went against the feelings of Latif and others in the team. Even Cronje, the South Africa captain, publicly expressed surprise at being asked to bat first.

South Africa won the game, Pakistan, chasing 216, collapsing to 178 all out. Their last six wickets fell for 22, three to run-outs. In the second final in Johannesburg, Malik again asked his opponents to bat first; again Pakistan lost. Basit Ali later said that suspicion was rife that the matches were fixed. Rumours of deep divisions within the team had already taken hold by the time of a one-off Test at the Wanderers two weeks later, rumours Malik publicly denied after his team sank to a heavy defeat.

Doubts were also raised about the first Test in Zimbabwe, which the home team won by an innings inside four days. By completely outplaying their opponents, they caused a huge upset: Zimbabwe had won none of their previous ten Tests as a Test nation and they were quoted at pre-match odds of 40–1. Rich pickings indeed for anyone with the foresight to back such hopeless outsiders.

Several Pakistan players would testify that during this tour a man called Hanif Cadbury was a familiar sight around the team. Cadbury, whose real name was Hanif Kodvavi, was an expatriate Pakistani from Karachi, where he operated in the video and restaurant trades but was also one of the city's biggest bookmakers. Cadbury's brother, Idress, claimed Hanif gave up bookmaking when he emigrated to Johannesburg to run an import–export business between there and Dubai, Singapore and Karachi, but it seemed entirely possible that if he was involved in business with those places, his clients were primarily gamblers.

Aaqib Javed, a Pakistan cricketer, saw Cadbury 'freely mixing with the players'.[10] Basit Ali saw Hanif Cadbury – 'the renowned bookie' – 'going into the rooms of certain players'.[11] Miandad said that when he was Pakistan captain (which meant before 1994) he was told by Idress Cadbury that Wasim Akram and Waqar Younis, possibly a more irresistible new-ball partnership for Pakistan than even Imran and Sarfraz, were 'on his brother's books'.[12] And Mukesh Gupta told Indian police that it was his understanding that the Pakistan team had been 'very close to a bookie named Hanif Cadbury ... and most probably they were "doing" matches for him'.[13]

However, when Pakistan's tour of southern Africa ended, things were much less clear-cut. Allegations had been made and denied. There was some circumstantial evidence of wrong-doing and some potent rumours. Even when Salim Malik and Intikhab Alam were respectively dismissed as captain and manager ten days later, not everyone could agree what it meant. I was interviewed by ITN's *News at Ten* and said that it was a day that confirmed our worst suspicions. After all, Pakistan board officials had interviewed both men for eight hours before giving Malik seven days to show why 'disciplinary action should not be taken against him'.

But perhaps I was hasty. Two weeks later Pakistan cricket maintained its reputation for perversity when its board announced an inquiry into the claims of match-fixing. Malik, far from being expected to prove his innocence, was now to be allowed to 'confront his accusers and cross-examine them'. He had been sacked for poor performances, not because of the bribery issue. In the meantime, he was free to play for Pakistan, though he would not be reinstated as captain. To add to the surreal feeling that something-but-nothing had happened, Rashid Latif and Basit Ali both returned to the Test team, having apparently rediscovered their enjoyment of the game.

The inquiry was put in the hands of Fakhruddin G Ebrahim, a former Pakistani supreme court judge. His inquiry was hampered in several ways. The ICC washed its hands of the affair. Bob Simpson said he had told David Richards, an Australian who had served with the Australian Cricket Board before joining ICC as its first full-time chief executive, about the Malik affair several months earlier, directly after the tour. Richards stated that the ICC was not empowered to get involved – a stance with which the Australian Cricket Board took issue. The ICC merely passed on copies of the statements it had received from the three Australian players, declining even to try to persuade them to travel to Pakistan for cross-examination. The Australian board said it was unwilling to send Warne, Waugh and May to Pakistan for fear of them coming to harm.

Had the ICC taken firmer action at this stage, further scandals might have been avoided. But Richards effectively took no action, imploring the chief executive of the Pakistan board, Arif Abbasi, to keep match-fixing allegations hidden from public view. On 13 February 1995 – that is, between the first *Sydney Morning Herald* story and the identification of Salim Malik as the 'prominent Pakistani personality' – Richards sent a fax complaining of Abbasi's comments in the media on the original *Herald* story.

In these comments Abbasi had effectively accused Richards of incompetence, saying he had sat on information about the Malik affair more or less since it had taken place, contrary to the impression Richards and Sir Clyde Walcott, the chairman of ICC, were giving publicly that the ICC had only just learned of the matter. In fact, Richards had been informed of the offer during a meeting with Bob Simpson at the end of the Pakistan tour. 'We asked the chief executive why the ICC had not reported the matter to us,' said Javed Burki, chairman of the Pakistan board. 'He told us he had been informed verbally and he thought it fit not to take any further action.'

Richards complained to Abbasi that his comments had 'caused a heightening of the media coverage'. He added, 'If and when the ACB provides information, it will be extremely difficult to prevent the allegations from becoming public, to the detriment of the image of cricket. I reiterate the need for care in any public remarks, and would hope that you speak to me direct, given the years that we have known each other.' Richards added that he planned to 'discreetly progress the matter with you and your colleagues' when Pakistan toured Australia later that year. He went on: 'The fact that no story had been written after the tour gave credence to this course of action.' He claimed he did not consider Simpson informing him of what had happened as an official complaint, but the fact remained that the Australian board kept Richards informed of developments. A fax from the ACB to the Pakistan board on 22 February 1995 confirmed that the 'ACB had the view then, as it does now, that the allegations were proper matters for the ICC to deal with and not for one board to put to another.'[14]

The ICC seemed to know far more than it was letting on. John Reid, match referee during Australia's tour of Pakistan, revealed that he had been requested by Richards to keep his eyes open. 'I was asked to look into betting, but I certainly did not know about any offers to the Australians.'[15] However, why he had been asked to do this was never explained. *The Australian* newspaper also claimed the ICC had received reports of umpires being offered bribes 'to assist specific outcomes'.

Judge Ebrahim studied the statements of the Australians and cross-examined Malik before concluding in October 1995, only days before Pakistan toured Australia, that, 'The allegations against Salim Malik are not worthy of any credence and must be rejected as unfounded.' He offended the Australians by adding that the allegations 'appear to have been concocted for reasons best known to the accusers'. The Australian board condemned his remarks as 'extraordinary and damaging'.[16]

Pakistan's tour could have been incendiary but passed off without incident. Malik cut a disconsolate figure, spending a lot of time in hotel rooms watching television. 'I hate Australia. It's hell,' he said. On the first day of the series he badly cut his hand and in three innings scored only 81 runs. In Brisbane, Warne dismissed him fourth ball and he declared with grim satisfaction, 'It shows there is justice in the game.'

For all the setbacks, Ebrahim's inquiry could have been more thorough than it was. In rejecting the notion that Malik might have offered the Australia players 'a large sum of money not for any direct personal gain, but for the sake of the nation's pride', he appeared unaware that betting might be involved. Pakistan cricket officials could have appraised him of that; minutes of a board meeting held in March 1995 had made reference to the leading suspects behind match-fixing as being 'Dawood Ibrahim, Mukesh (Delhi), Rahul bhai (Mumbai).'[17]

Unsatisfactory though it was, the inquiry seemed to draw a line under the affair. Without proof, rumours would stay just that: rumours.

CORRUPTION WAS RIFE by 1994. In the mid-1990s the allegations by a number of players from the subcontinent were subsequently revealed. They also maintained that the problem had not gone away.

Two were Pakistanis who featured in the Salim Malik affair, Aamir Sohail and Rashid Latif, and were perhaps frustrated at the failure of their earlier efforts to expose wrongdoing. By 1997, when they went public, Malik was enjoying a career at least as fruitful as theirs. He had played in the 1996 World Cup and later toured England. Latif, meanwhile, had lost his wicketkeeping place to Moin Khan.

Both gave interviews to the Indian press. There were two strands to what they said. The first was to confirm that attempts to fix matches were still being made. Latif described how, during the Lord's Test against England the previous year, he had been telephoned in his hotel room by a bookmaker offering him money to ensure Pakistan, 290 for nine overnight, did not reach 300 the next morning. He rejected the offer and Pakistan totalled 340, Latif scoring 45. He said, too, he had duplicates of cheques made out to teammates by bookies. Sohail reiterated that he suspected teammates of match-fixing.[18]

Sohail's comments led to the Pakistan board suspending him on disciplinary grounds from a tour of Sri Lanka. Latif's plight was even more serious. He was threatened and sought protection. He later said he sent a fax to the ICC at around this time, outlining what he knew about match-fixing, but never got a reply. David Richards denied ever receiving it.[19]

But it was the second strand to their comments that had the

greater impact. Sohail admitted to *Outlook*, an Indian news magazine, that he had been asked by two India players to fix a match during the Singer World Series in Sri Lanka in September 1994, a tournament that had already aroused suspicion. 'I told them they'd come to the wrong guy,' he said. Ajit Wadekar, the India manager, dismissed his remarks but they were subsequently backed up by Latif, who said that he had been phoned at various times by India cricketers asking for information. He claimed a well-known former India player was now acting as bookmaker.

This set Indian journalists on a painstaking search for hard evidence. The Salim Malik affair had taught them to be vigilant, and they were hearing enough rumours about the India team to keep them on the trail. Moreover, the story sometimes came to them because bookmakers saw journalists as potential allies.

One journalist, Pradeep Magazine, was covering India's tour of West Indies in early 1997 for the *Pioneer*, a Delhi newspaper, when an Indian bookmaker approached him asking for help in meeting India players. He offered a dazzling reward: a house in a locality of Magazine's own choice in Delhi. This bookmaker had travelled widely following cricket, having been to South Africa alone six times. Magazine wrote about the incident. His claims were immediately rubbished by the Indian board, Jagmohan Dalmiya, the secretary, demanding that journalists not 'malign the name of Indian cricket for the sake of a juicy story'. It seemed administrators around the world had grown intolerant of the corruption issue.

Magazine's article received a more sympathetic hearing from fellow Indian journalists. Aniruddha Bahal, a reporter with *Outlook* who had covered a recent tour of South Africa, arranged a meeting. 'I believe your story,' Bahal told him. 'I was shocked at what I saw in South Africa. I think bookies have infiltrated the playing arena. I saw journalists openly flaunting their connections with bookies in the press box.'[20]

Outlook ran an article by Bahal in June 1997. Drawing on interviews with players, board officials, bookmakers, gamblers and other journalists, it pointed an accusing finger at Indian players and officials. It built up a persuasive picture of suspicious behaviour. It revealed that while India were playing in a one-day tournament in New Zealand in February 1995, Mumbai police had conducted a surveillance operation on a bookmaker and overheard him talking to two cricketers in Napier shortly before India's opening game. The bookmaker had called to confirm 'arrangements' for the game, which New Zealand won with ease.

It also revealed that after that tournament, Venkat Rao, India's administrative manager on the tour, had privately named to his board four players he suspected of involvement in betting. Rao later claimed to have been misquoted. Subsequently, evidence emerged that a bookmaker thought to be linked to Dawood Ibrahim had paid the Mumbai hotel bill of one of the players in return for introducing him to 'likeminded' colleagues in New Zealand.

Sensational though they were, these allegations were overshadowed by an accompanying article by Manoj Prabhakar, who had recently retired from international cricket.[21] In retirement, Prabhakar had chased publicity and cash in controversial fashion. He had launched a bizarre and ill-fated bid to become a Member of Parliament, losing badly in the Delhi assembly elections. He became known for demanding large fees for giving interviews and attending 'star nites'. Invited to take part in a six-a-side tournament in Hong Kong, he asked for £13,000.

Prabhakar's article added flesh to the skeleton of rumours but his specific claims that those at the heart of match-fixing were the men running the India team shocked his country. 'Unfortunately, in situations where monkey deals are made in the dark and no proof is available, we can only shake our heads in disbelief,' he wrote.

> I noticed that such dealings seemed to be manipulated right from the top and players, who had reached the pinnacle, did not seem to be doing the right thing at crucial times...
>
> Commercialisation of cricket has changed its face – it's no longer just a game; it's a game where money is the main motivator. Sponsors and

bookies have started exerting pressure and games are now being increasingly fixed…

The board is filling its coffers at the expense of the 11 sweating it out on the field … The menace of money power should be checked before it corrupts the minds of cricketers. There must be a concerted effort to filter the bookies out of the system. This needs to be done. Otherwise the Indian public will keep watching the scenes enacted in bafflement and rage.[22]

But his most sensational claim concerned an incident that occurred during the Singer World Series in Sri Lanka in 1994 to which Aamir Sohail had already referred. Without naming the individual in question, Prabhakar said he had been offered £40,000 by a teammate to help sabotage a qualifying match against Pakistan (a match that, in the event, was washed out). The approach came in a hotel room in Colombo, a room in which a door to an adjoining room lay open, meaning that several witnesses overheard part of the conversation, though without all knowing who the interlocutors were. Prabhakar's refusal was voluble and blunt. 'I told him to get out of my room,' he wrote. 'I told him that I would never do what he was telling me to do. Because of this I soon acquired the tag of spoilsport in the group. This did not stop the offers though, which flowed in regularly.'

A journalist happened to be sitting in the next room. 'It became obvious that Manoj was talking with someone in his room. When he shouted, all of us became conscious of what was happening. [Prashant] Vaidya rose and closed the adjoining door so we never heard who Prabhakar was talking with … I overheard Prabhakar shouting, "What do you think you are doing? Can you buy me out in an India–Pakistan match? No amount of lakhs is going to buy me out." He also said, "How can a person in your position do this?"'[23]

Prabhakar reported the incident to Azharuddin and Wadekar, and Wadekar later told Prabhakar that he had referred to it in his tour report. But the Indian board did nothing with the information until Prabhakar's article appeared nearly three years later.

It was a decision he would regret. Prabhakar was persuaded to write the article only at the eleventh hour. 'Things really snowballed after that,' he later admitted, 'and my life spiralled out of control … When the enormity of what I had done sank in, I remember sitting down holding my head in my hands and thinking, "What the hell have I done?"'[24] His life was threatened, which bought his silence, a silence only broken when the Cronje scandal forced Prabhakar into a desperate effort to vindicate the claims he had made in print.

Needless to say, Prabhakar never alluded to his own involvement with Mukesh Gupta. Given this, it was hard to fathom why he should have contemplated switching from poacher to gamekeeper. But Prabhakar was not a straightforward character. Bahal, who would work with him closely, said how difficult Prabhakar was to get to know, describing him as 'brusque and dismissive at first … [but] after the first few minutes he became much more congenial and earthy'.[25] Prabhakar had always had to work hard, especially on his fitness, simply to keep up with more natural athletes, and in his youth he was teased about his fatness and aspirations to be a sportsman. He was bitter at his summary dropping from the India team during the 1996 World Cup, which led directly to his decision to retire. He once admitted, 'I have been a loner throughout.'[26]

Although the *Outlook* article caused him great trouble, Prabhakar nevertheless enjoyed returning to centre-stage. Someone who met him at about this time said, 'Prabhakar's face reflected a mixture of tension, apprehension and yes, a trace of smug satisfaction. It was obvious he was enjoying the limelight he had forced upon himself and yet he was unsure how it would all turn out … By constantly trying to project an image of himself as a "clean" man trapped in "dirty" surroundings, Prabhakar may have earned more enemies than friends.'[27]

Under intense media and political pressure to respond to Prabhakar's allegations, the Indian board set up an inquiry led by Justice YV Chandrachud, one of the longest-serving chief justices in India. Some of the accused did not wait for it to begin. Azharuddin held a press conference at which he rebutted all claims. Relations between himself and Prabhakar never recovered.

The Chandrachud inquiry was a limited affair. The judge interviewed witnesses on a one-on-one basis and no attempt was made to investigate the financial affairs of suspect players. His report amounted to little more than a cursory appraisal of rumours circulating in the press; it cleared everyone associated with the India team of wrongdoing and was not published for more than two years. 'The judge had no interest in how my journalists had got their information,' said *Outlook*'s editor.[28]

Prabhakar refused to give Chandrachud the name of the player who had tried to bribe him, saying he was dissatisfied at the way the inquiry was conducted. 'If I name the player, I might get killed,' he argued. 'I need security. You don't know what kind of mafia controls this betting syndicate. They are dangerous people. Only if I am assured of foolproof security will I name the man.'[29]

But Prabhakar might have been wiser to confide in someone in authority, especially a senior law figure. When K Madhavan reinvestigated the matter on behalf of the Indian board in 2000, he gave Prabhakar short shrift. 'He wanted to disclose everything, but Justice Chandrachud told Prabhakar that he would not record anything which Prabhakar was saying. Prabhakar told [the] CBI that he did not see any point in disclosing facts, as his statement was not being recorded. I do not believe Prabhakar at all in this regard. It is inconceivable that a retired Chief Justice of India would state as Prabkahar now claims.'[30]

But surely neither did Prabhakar deserve the treatment the Indian board meted out once Chandrachud rejected his claims. It filed a suit against him and withheld £12,800 from his benevolent fund.[31]

Prabhakar reacted bitterly. 'The board is making me look like the culprit,' he said.[32] But not all his complaints were justified. He claimed to have been 'thrown out' of the India team and 'shunned by team-mates'. But after the incident in Sri Lanka, he participated in every Test and one-day international India played (except the two from which he was suspended following the Kanpur incident), before his dropping at the World Cup eighteen months later. He maintained he 'still had a few more years of top-class cricket left in me', but it was he who chose to retire.[33]

Once again, efforts to expose the truth had failed to hit their mark, or even cajole administrators into meaningful action.

But Prabhakar's actions did cause alarm among some. He was ostracised by fellow India players, none of whom trusted him. As one former colleague said, 'Perhaps the good is overshadowed by his shady character.'[34] Bookmakers, too, were concerned that he might yet betray them. In 1998 Prabhakar's offices were burgled and police sources said they believed the break-in was the work of bookmakers searching for documents relating to a recent one-day tournament in Sharjah. There, in a 'dead' game, India had surprisingly lost to Zimbabwe.

In the end, the Cronje affair would force Prabhakar to name the teammate he had accused of trying to bribe him, but by then his accusation, sensational though it was, had become overshadowed by disclosures concerning his own murky past.

Everything about his story reinforced the players' mantra: 'Never squeal on your mates.'

5

WARNE AND WAUGH

The moment when the wide world was forced to confront cricket's link with bookmakers was the revelation in December 1998 that two of Australia's top cricketers had themselves accepted money. What made it worse was that it was the same two players who had accused Salim Malik of trying to bribe them. Both, but especially Warne (who was credited with reviving leg-spin bowling), were role models in the sport, idolised by youngsters and courted by sponsors. Neither in the way he played nor in the way he lived was Warne conventional: his blonde hair and earring were more the uniform of a reformed beach-bum than a Test cricketer. Waugh, from the moment of his brilliantly effortless century in his first Test against England, had been an automatic selection for most games.

Warne had been paid about £3,300 and Waugh about £4,000 in return for information – information Warne and Waugh insisted was restricted to weather and pitch conditions. Waugh declined to provide details regarding strategy and selection, having been asked on about ten occasions; Warne, given money as a gift of appreciation and in lieu of recent losses in a casino, took three calls during the 1994–95 Ashes series and responded in general terms about selection and pitches. They were approached during the now-infamous Singer World Series in Colombo in 1994, a tournament that took place immediately prior to Australia's tour of Pakistan on which Warne and Waugh were approached by Malik.

Their actions were, as they later conceded, naive and stupid – and cost them dear. They claimed not to have known what they were doing, but knew enough to know better. Waugh introduced the bookmaker to Warne by describing him as, 'John, who bets on cricket'.[1] And Waugh was warned by a senior player with whom he was rooming that if he carried on providing information, it would one day come back to haunt him. It did.

The explanation for why they should risk so much for so little is that, like so many, they thought they could get away with it. It was, as Cronje would say, 'money for jam'. Warne was subsequently named one of *Wisden*'s five cricketers of the twentieth century; Waugh, too, deserved a place in the pantheon of great Australian sportsmen. But their reputations never fully recovered.

Most damning of all was the part the administrators played in the episode. Had they dealt with the pair with proper severity when they first learned of the affair – in February 1995 – so much might have been avoided. That was around the time Hansie Cronje and Mohammad Azharuddin were being wooed by the bookies. They might – just might – have thought twice had an example been made of the two Australians.

The Warne–Waugh story emerged because the Pakistan government, in co-ordination with the cricket board and its upstanding chief executive Majid Khan, formerly the devastating strokemaker for Glamorgan and his country, had recently suspended Malik, Wasim Akram and Ijaz Ahmed and ordered another investigation, Pakistan's third in five years. Mark Waugh and Mark Taylor, the Australia captain, gave evidence to the inquiry while Australia were playing in Pakistan, Taylor acting as Warne's representative because

Warne was at home recovering from surgery on his shoulder. The board had produced an unsourced letter that suggested Waugh had links with an illegal bookmaker.

The letter was eventually discarded as evidence but a journalist working for *The Australian*, Malcolm Conn, who covered the hearing, pursued the matter. 'Little by little, word filtered from inside and outside the team that all might not be as it appeared,' Conn wrote. 'By [November 1998] it had become clear to me that Waugh had been punished by the Australian Cricket Board for giving information to one or more illegal bookmakers on the Indian subcontinent.' Conn said that more than a dozen calls to players and officials, including Taylor himself and his deputy, Steve Waugh, Mark's twin brother, had proved fruitless until eventually 'some were willing to confirm and expand what I already knew'.[2] Conn was hardly deterred when he quizzed Bob Simpson. 'I don't know what you're talking about,' Simpson had said. 'Why don't you ask Tubby Taylor?'[3]

The night before *The Australian* published the story, David Hookes, a former Australian cricketer, broke the news on a Melbourne radio station.

It came as a devastating blow to the collective integrity of professional cricketers. It now seemed that even the good guys were bad guys too, an impression the exposure of the 'untaintable' Hansie Cronje would reinforce.

Some suspected Warne and Waugh might have had more to do with bookies than they were letting on, but it was their duplicity that stung most followers of the game. They had put themselves forward as the upholders of a decency to which they could not lay claim themselves. There were widespread calls for both to be removed from the Australia team. Three days later Waugh was roundly booed when he appeared in a Test against England in Adelaide. Warne was sacked as columnist by *The Age* and the *Daily Mirror*, although within five months he would be back contributing a column for *The Times*.

Warne and Waugh appeared at a press conference in Adelaide the morning of the story's appearance in *The Australian*. Both read out statements in which they admitted to being 'naive and stupid', but little else. Both claimed they gave the bookie no more information than he could have gleaned from advance radio or television coverage, but refused to take further questions from the media on the issue. Neither would speak publicly about the matter again.

Their naivety and stupidity was certainly deep: all the Australia players had been warned to be on their guard following the approach to Dean Jones in Sri Lanka in 1992, a warning Jones believed everyone had taken 'on board', and both Warne and Waugh were members of Allan Border's team at Edgbaston in 1993. Moreover, as avid gamblers, both were natural targets. Waugh's special interest was horse racing and he owned a share of a trotter belonging to Australia teammate Ricky 'Punter' Ponting (who, within a few days, would admit that he, too, had been approached by a bookie at a Sydney dog-track the previous year). Waugh had once thrown his wicket away while playing a club match so he could watch a favourite running in the Golden Slipper, a major Sydney race. Warne's mentor, Terry Jenner, himself a Test leg spinner during the early 1970s, had spent two years in jail for embezzling £12,500 from his company to fund his own addiction to the gee-gees.

With Warne and Waugh saying no more, Malcolm Speed, the chief executive of the Australian Cricket Board, was left facing the cross-examination. He claimed that the bookmaker had remained in contact with the two players for 'between one and two months'. Warne himself said in his statement that the bookie last contacted him three months after their first encounter, while it would transpire that Waugh was actually in contact with him for five months.

The crucial question was: had Salim Malik approached them to throw the Test in Karachi because he knew they had already taken money? At another press conference the next day, Taylor admitted this was a possibility. 'I don't know if there is a link but there certainly could be. Shane and Mark became easy targets because they like to have a bet. They were approached for an easy dollar.'

The bookmaker was known to Warne and Waugh only as 'John'. This was a name that would become more significant with time: when the CBI report came out two years later and Mukesh Gupta's activities became known to the world, it emerged that this was a pseudonym he used. But Gupta's statement to the CBI contained no reference to him approaching Warne and Waugh in Sri Lanka. He did not allude to Warne and said his meeting with Waugh occurred during a six-a-side tournament in Hong Kong. When Mark Waugh was interviewed by the ICC's new anti-corruption unit two months after the CBI report was published, he denied that the Mukesh Gupta shown to him in a photograph was the 'John' he had dealt with. An Australian board inquiry concluded against Gupta and Waugh's 'John' being the same.

If there was anger at the feckless behaviour of the players, the public was equally incensed at the Establishment cover-up that accompanied it. The Australian Cricket Board had known of Warne and Waugh's involvement with 'John' since an unidentified journalist brought it to the attention of Ian McDonald, the team manager, who then carried out a perfunctory investigation on behalf of the board.

There appeared to be no connection between this tip-off and the one a few weeks earlier that led to the original allegations against Malik, although the Australian board must have realised the events might have been connected. If Warne and Waugh were willing to take money for information, they might have been prepared to do more; Malik's approach made more sense that way.

McDonald took unsigned statements from Waugh and Warne while they were touring New Zealand and then sent them with a covering note to Graham Halbish, the then chief executive of the Australian board. Halbish and Alan Crompton, the board's chairman, consequently met the two players in Sydney prior to the team's departure for the West Indies and summarily fined Shane Warne £3,300 and Mark Waugh £4,150 – almost exactly the sums they had received in bribes. Mark Taylor was present as Australia captain but not Bob Simpson, the coach, who was kept out at Taylor's instigation.

It was only after the players were on the plane for the Caribbean that Halbish and Crompton took their actions to the board's directors for endorsement. Some directors had already left the meeting before the matter was raised. The only record of the incident was an obscure reference in the minutes of the meeting.

Crucially and controversially, Halbish and Crompton had agreed to keep the affair quiet and persuaded the board of directors to follow suit (Malcolm Gray, who became the ICC president in 2000, is believed to have been opposed to the cover-up). The ACB did, however, inform David Richards and Sir Clyde Walcott, of the ICC, both of whom happened to be in Sydney, again on condition they kept the matter secret, which they did. So much for rulers ruling.

It only emerged later that Waugh was contacted again by 'John' while on tour in the West Indies. Phoned in Jamaica, Waugh immediately terminated the relationship.

When the matter became public in 1998, Crompton dismissed suggestions of a cover-up as 'ridiculous', but admitted that secrecy had been adopted partly because the public might have assumed something worse was involved. Speed endorsed this view, saying the fines were kept quiet to 'protect the reputation of Australian cricket and the international game' and because the public might make the 'wrong mental leap'.[4] It was yet more disastrously misguided thinking.

In their way, the administrators' behaviour was no less hypocritical than Warne and Waugh's. The Australian board felt the ICC should have conducted its own inquiry into Malik, yet wanted the world governing body to connive at its own cover-up on Warne and Waugh. The ICC, with breathtaking nerve, felt that it was no more its job to expose Warne and Waugh's wrongdoing than it was to expose Malik's. 'We felt the way ICC was constituted, we could not inform Pakistan,' Richards said. 'We were of the view that the onus was on the ACB to disseminate the information.'[5]

The Pakistanis took umbrage at the double standards exercised by the Australians. Waugh and Taylor had attended the Pakistan inquiry promising to tell the truth. Neither had been asked about 'John', but nor had they volunteered anything about him either. While Waugh appeared terrified into silence, Taylor, a man famed for his integrity, was more duplicitous, insisting, 'We've got nothing to hide.'

Justice Malik Qayyum, a prominent Lahore High Court judge who headed the inquiry, was particular damning of Waugh. 'If he did not have a legal obligation, he had a moral duty to bring it to our notice, and it casts doubt on his credibility,' he said.[6] Qayyum demanded Warne and Waugh come back to Pakistan to give further evidence, but in the end his court arranged a special hearing in Melbourne. Warne and Waugh were questioned closely about the Singer World Series but nothing new emerged.

The Australians launched their own inquiry under Rob O'Regan QC, his brief all matters from 1992 onwards. He interviewed more than 70 people, in camera, and in two months published his report. Familiar incidents were given a thorough going-over and there was some significance in the detail. Waugh's bookmaker had indicated to him that 'he had players from around the world in various international cricket teams providing him with information'.[7] This may have been standard bookie-speak, and 'John' may or may not have been Mukesh Gupta, but it sounded remarkably like Gupta's pitch to Sanath Jayasuriya and Dean Jones.

O'Regan was withering in his condemnation of the Halbish–Crompton fines. 'In my opinion this punishment was inadequate. It did not reflect the seriousness of what they had done ... I do not think it is possible to explain their conduct away as the result merely of naivety or stupidity. They must have known that it is wrong to accept money from, and supply information to, a bookmaker whom they also knew as someone who betted on cricket. Otherwise they would have reported the incident to team management long before they were found out...

'In behaving as they did they failed lamentably to set the sort of example one might expect from senior players and role models for many young cricketers. A more appropriate penalty would, I think, have been suspension for a significant time.'[8]

It also transpired that Taylor himself was approached for information by a bookmaker in Pakistan even while the Qayyum inquiry was going on. Evidence was gathered that a match between a World XI and an Indian XI in 1992 may have been fixed, details of which were kept within a 'secret chapter' for the ACB's eyes only. The report confirmed what many already suspected, that contacts between bookies and players rarely made the tour reports, even when the tour managers knew about them.

The walls of secrecy were near impregnable.

PUBLISHED IN THE wake of Cronje's downfall after lying unnoticed for several months following a military coup in Pakistan, the Qayyum report confirmed that the network between bookies and players was extensive and sophisticated by 1994, the year in which Hansie Cronje became South Africa captain.

The most suspicious activity the inquiry uncovered related to matches played in the twelve months up to Pakistan's tour of South Africa and Zimbabwe in 1995, which broadly meant Salim Malik's reign as captain. There were suggestions, though, that corrupt practices preceded and survived Malik's time in office. Suspicions were voiced that as early as 1992, players had deliberately underperformed. Haroon Rashid, the Pakistan coach, thought matches were still being thrown as recently as December 1997. Aamir Sohail alleged Wasim Akram had feigned injury in withdrawing at the eleventh hour from Pakistan's World Cup quarter-final against India in 1996, thereby helping India to win.

Akram's response was a firm and detailed denial. He said he tore an intercostal muscle in his side during the previous match against New Zealand. 'There was no chance of being fit for Bangalore, despite three daily cortisone injections …We decided to keep this from the public because we didn't want to give the Indian team a psychological boost. That was a big mistake; we should have come clean about the injury so that the public would not get sucked into ridiculous theories about bribes.'9

Qayyum demonstrated that by the mid-1990s a system was in place by which matches could be fixed, if that was the aim. Key players possessed mobile phones which could be used to communicate with bookmakers; Intikhab Alam testified that the Pakistan board 'had arrived at the conclusion a long time ago that these mobiles were used by players to maintain contact with the bookies'.10 Qayyum cleared the team as a whole but had no doubt as to what broadly had gone on: 'The allegation that the Pakistan team as a whole is involved in match-fixing is just based on allegation, conjectures and surmises without there being positive proof. As a whole, the players of the Pakistan cricket team are innocent'.11

At the time it appeared, the Qayyum report was the most thorough investigation into match-fixing there had been, but it was another flawed inquiry.

The judge's efforts were dogged by government interference and it is believed he came under political pressure to soft-pedal his recommendations. Strong circumstantial evidence would emerge to support this theory. It related to an even more sensitive investigation by Justice Qayyum into allegations of corruption by Benazir Bhutto that had resulted in him sentencing the former prime minister to five years' imprisonment. Abdul Rahim, deputy director of the intelligence bureau, claimed that Qayyum was pressured into his verdict by officials acting on behalf of Nawaz Sharif's government; Qayyum was even summoned to a meeting with Sharif himself. Rahim said the judge's office, home and mobile phone calls were bugged during Bhutto's trial and that he was under threat of dismissal if he did not come in with the desired verdict.12

During the course of his year-long match-fixing inquiry, Qayyum interviewed more than 70 cricketers and bookmakers, but the investigation was poorly resourced. Except for one legal adviser, he worked alone: no policemen or detectives were put at his disposal and the intelligence bureau helped for just two days. Despite the management's suspicions about the use of mobile phones, no one's telephone records were scrutinised. These might have been revealing. Qayyum bemoaned that there was no system in place to deal with the problem. 'There was no legislation on match-fixing, no rules and regulations that this commission could go by. In effect, this commission had to start from scratch.'[13]

Many players made generalised allegations; some changed their statements or contradicted those of others. A picture emerged of a host of matches that might have been rigged and of frequent contacts between players and bookmakers, but confirmed instances of match-fixing were few. 'A number of people were quite uncooperative ... This commission felt a lot of the time that most of the people appearing before it were not telling the truth, or at least not the whole truth. Even more regretful was the attitude and statements of those who said they had not even heard of match-fixing. Some appeared tutored.'[14] But if the players were reluctant to confirm the rumours, some officials were more forthcoming. They believed match-fixing had gone on.

However, some observers felt Qayyum was reluctant to draw obvious conclusions from overwhelming circumstantial evidence. 'The government message to him was: "Don't paint too bleak a picture." I think he realised he could have done the game a lot of damage had he found a lot of players guilty.'[15] Outside the bounds of the report he admitted, 'I am convinced that some of the Pakistani players are involved in match-fixing. They deliberately threw a few games.'[16]

He took action against a few. Salim Malik was banned from cricket for life and fined £12,500. He was found guilty of attempting to bribe Warne, Waugh and May, and further suspected of fixing the match against Australia in the Singer World Series: Salim Pervez, a gambler who mixed freely with the players, testified that he paid Malik and Mushtaq Ahmed, the Somerset leg-spinner who in some batsmen's estimation was even more versatile than Shane Warne,

£70,000 to ensure Pakistan lost. But, unable to locate another book-maker whom Pervez said accompanied him to Sri Lanka, Qayyum withheld judgement.[17]

Mushtaq Ahmed himself narrowly avoided a life ban. Javed Miandad testified that Mushtaq confessed to him of his involvement in match-fixing, and Mushtaq's own testimony was far from convincing. 'When Mushtaq Ahmed appeared before this commission, he seemed to know already which match we were going to ask him about,' the report read. 'And he blurted out, "I was OK in that match".'[18] Qayyum barred him from holding responsible office and fined him £3,750. Mushtaq was saved by his own good bowling fig-ures in the match in question: he took two for 34 from his ten overs. Malik's contribution, 22 off 51 balls, was less ambiguous.

Wasim Akram faced various charges but none were upheld. The most serious, that he paid a junior player, Ata-ur-Rehman, around £1,300 to bowl badly in a one-day match in Christchurch (Ata con-ceded 44 runs in nine overs in a low-scoring game), became mired in confusion as Ata-ur-Rehman kept changing his story. There were allegations that Ata, described by one journalist as 'a simple boy', had been intimidated; he went into hiding at one point.[19] Ata said Wasim told him the Christchurch match had been fixed through Zafar, a neighbour of Wasim's in Lahore. Wasim rejected all these claims and denied knowing Zafar was a bookmaker. Qayyum also investigated the kidnapping of Wasim's father and concluded that it was not car-ried out by the mafia.[20]

Though nothing specific was pinned on Wasim, Qayyum said he felt he was 'not above board'. 'He has not co-operated with this com-mission. It is only by giving Wasim Akram the benefit of the doubt after Ata-ur-Rehman changed his testimony in suspicious circum-stances that he has not been found guilty of match-fixing. He cannot be said to be above suspicion. It is, therefore, recommended that he be censured and kept under strict vigilance and a further probe be made either by the Government of Pakistan or by the cricket board into his assets.'[21] Wasim was fined £3,750 and barred from captaining Pakistan again; but no probe was forthcoming. Ata-ur-Rehman was given a life ban for perjuring himself.

Four other players – Waqar Younis, Saeed Anwar, Akram Raza, and Inzamam-ul-Haq – were censured and fined £1,250, all for withholding evidence or not telling the whole truth. 'Waqar Younis ... said he had not even heard of anyone being involved in match-fixing.' Inzamam, as thunderous in his hitting as he was forgetful in his running between the wickets, similarly seemed to suffer from amnesia. 'They both needed stern prompting to speak true and even then it is doubtful they spoke the whole truth.'[22] Some of the players appealed against their punishments, without success.

Afterwards, Malik was aggrieved. 'Everyone agrees one man cannot fix a match,' he said. 'It needs five or six men. Yet I am the only one found guilty.' Though not banned, Wasim lost almost as much in prestige. One of the most talented cricketers the game had seen, and possibly the greatest left-arm pace bowler ever, he found himself permanently tarnished. For years he had been earmarked as Imran Khan's natural successor, a born leader. Yet in the end, he was disbarred from ever leading again.

6

THE MANY IDENTITIES OF MK GUPTA

Hansie Cronje's rise in international cricket was swift, in hindsight too swift. He had barely been playing Test cricket a year when he was appointed vice-captain to Kepler Wessels. Wessels was already well into his thirties when South Africa returned to the Test fold – a short-term appointment to head a young and inexperienced team.

Cronje was the heir apparent, a good enough player to command a place and an astute tactician. The local press billed the captaincy succession as a contest between Cronje and Jonty Rhodes, but in fact there was no contest. 'It was clear from the beginning that Hansie would one day take over from me,' Wessels said.[1] As if confirmation were needed, Cronje stood in when Wessels was injured in Australia early in 1994 and, in no small part through his tactical nous, led the side to a famous 5-run win in Sydney.

In fact, the path to the captaincy was so open for him that it caused resentment among others in the team, who thought his relationship with Wessels too cosy. But this perception was false. Wessels and Cronje may have known each other since Cronje was a child, but there was a twelve-year age difference between them and they had played little cricket together. They may have had things in common, but they were not particularly close.

When Wessels informed the South African cricket board that he intended to retire after the 1994 tour of England, it looked as though Cronje's moment had arrived. But then a curious thing happened. When it came to the England tour, and Cronje's chance to seal his promotion with as many impressive performances as he could muster, he suffered a horrible collapse of form. He forgot about his duties helping Wessels. 'Hansie ended up a total introvert during the latter stages of the English tour,' Wessels recalled. 'It was when I realised this that I started relying less on him.'[2]

The situation was so dire that Wessels was forced to abandon his retirement plans and stay in charge for a one-day tournament in Pakistan. This proved a disaster for the team under their new coach, Bob Woolmer. They lost all six matches but one problem at least appeared solved: Cronje recovered enough self-belief for Wessels and others in the South African management to believe the transition in leader could now go ahead. Cronje actually finished as the leading run-scorer in the tournament. Wessels duly announced his retirement and Cronje was put in charge for South Africa's home series against New Zealand and Pakistan.

It was an almost unavoidable predicament. Power had come easily to Cronje, and a dangerous power at that, as few in or around the South Africa team knew much about the pressures and pitfalls of international sport. Cronje had played in all but one of South Africa's seventeen Tests since their return to competition. He was as experienced as anyone. But why did no one heed the warnings of the likes of John Blair, or scrutinise his character? Time would show that Cronje had insufficient respect for the game's traditions.

But, as we have seen, he took over the job at precisely the time corruption was sweeping the game. The South Africans had a glimpse of this in Pakistan in late 1994. One night Wessels had a drink with some of the Australians and they told him about the approach made a few weeks earlier by Salim Malik. Wessels discussed the matter with Peter Pollock, the convenor of selectors, but neither thought it much of an issue. That could be taken as an indication of how few people had an inkling of the problem, or of South African naivety, or both.

Talk of throwing games reached more ears than Wessels'. During South Africa's last one-dayer, in Faisalabad, Cronje went up to his captain when Pakistan were struggling in a run-chase. Wessels recalled, 'Hansie came to me with a huge smile on his face. He remarked that if we ended up winning that match, people would really think that it had been fixed ... I don't know why he ever said that.'[3] In Cronje's version to the King Commission he claimed that the team had joked about the fact they thought Pakistan had been throwing the game. Wessels could remember no such talk. Cronje claimed Wessels told him about the offer to the Australians, but Wessels denied speaking to him about that too.

Perhaps this incident helped colour the opinions Wessels expressed in a trenchant newspaper column that became notorious for its unwillingness to praise Wessels' 'protégé' and successor. Before Cronje's exposure, Wessels' comments were customarily treated as an amusing diversion, if not sour grapes, as Cronje built up an enviable set of results as captain. And when the Indian police went public with their claims, Wessels was one of the few in South Africa not to dismiss them out of hand. 'This thing is rife in cricket,' he cautioned, '...and the biggest mistake we could make would be to try and sweep it under the carpet without an investigation.'[4]

Cronje found the job of captain lonely, but as his position became more secure, so his desire to flex his muscles became apparent. During his first three years in charge, the bonds between himself and Woolmer, the coach, and Ali Bacher were gradually loosened, while Cronje's own power over his players noticeably grew.

The relationship with Woolmer cooled for several reasons. One was that after about two years, Woolmer found his message was losing its force with the players. This was not an uncommon phenomenon: the challenge facing all coaches is to keep coming up with new ideas which invigorate their players. But he did try to innovate; in fact, some thought he was too keen on gimmicks and this in itself caused problems with Cronje.

Meanwhile, Bacher was also subtly undermined. Imtiaz Patel, Bacher's right-hand man at the board, detected Cronje's passion for control. 'He would often just make a fleeting remark, like, "Don't you think Ali has too much power?", changing the topic shortly afterwards,' he recalled.[5]

With the players, it was easier for Cronje to impose his personality. Probably without ever expressing it in as many words, he demanded total loyalty and obedience, and seemingly got it in most, if not all, cases. He was not an orator, preferring to establish control through a zealous approach to all aspects of preparation. Following it himself to the letter, he expected his players to follow suit, although few managed to keep up with the punishing, unreasonable schedules. It was as though Cronje were back in Bloemfontein, where everyone trained all year round, through freezing winters, driving themselves to ever greater levels of performance, whether it be running on the road, sprinting on the track, or pumping iron in the gym. By highlighting the inadequacies of others, Cronje stifled opposition. Jacques Kallis, who came into the team in 1995, said Cronje 'never sort of stood down to anyone'.[6] Ray McCauley commented, 'He hates criticism.'[7] Woolmer described him as the 'epitome of the dour Afrikaaner'.

Cronje alleviated the spartan regime by occasionally displaying to his men what he called his 'naughty side'. This usually took the form of practical jokes that were not particularly funny, unless this was what passed for Afrikaner humour. It usually involved some sort of cruelty being inflicted on the victims. Cronje had practised such pranks at school; one, during a cricket tour of Natal, involved him arranging 4.00 a.m. wake-up calls for all his teammates and the coach, though not, of course, himself. Perhaps his most famous target was Paddy Upton, South Africa's fitness trainer. During the 1996 World Cup, Cronje slipped him a couple of sleeping tablets and delighted in watching him pass out on the grass when Upton should have been on duty during a match. These japes were usually taken in good heart by targets such as Upton, but the theme was always the same: Cronje had to be shown coming out on top.

Cronje's problem was that he did not really know where to draw the line. He wielded power for so long that he could not imagine it ever being taken away, however he behaved. Early in his career when he won a man of the match award in a one-day international at Cape Town, he found himself on the same podium as the country's president, FW de Klerk. When Cronje took receipt of his prize, he put his arm around the president and shaped to pour champagne over him. He was abruptly stopped by Wessels. 'No, Hansie. Stop,' he said. 'You can't do that. It's the Prez. Stop it.'[8]

When he was in the mood to tease, Cronje had the knack of keeping his voice at its customary monotone pitch, making it all the more difficult for others to know when he was being serious and when he was not. But how convenient was it for others to say they had not taken his behaviour seriously because they knew him to be a joker? It was certainly an excuse inordinately used. Was it possibly that he was a good liar and they extremely dense?

Cronje had been given power but wanted more. Wessels, who continued playing successfully at provincial level for another four years, regretted giving up the captaincy so soon. 'Maybe I should have stuck it out a little longer with the national team,' he said. 'The guys were very young.'[9]

BY HIS OWN ACCOUNT Hansie Cronje was first approached by a bookmaker in January 1995 in Cape Town, only three months after becoming South Africa captain. He was 25 years old.

Years later, Cronje was unsure precisely who this man was. He claimed the man, 'an Indian or Pakistani', described himself only as

'John'. This would lead to some confusion. Cronje drew a distinction between this man and Mukesh Gupta, with whom he would have extensive dealings and whom the Indian police would say used the pseudonym 'John'. Was Cronje trying to conceal that Gupta and 'John' were the same man? He might have had his reasons for separating them. If he admitted to knowing Gupta as far back as 1995, it might have raised questions about the extent of these dealings and led to the terms of reference of the King Commission being broadened.

Back to Cape Town 1995. Introducing himself as 'John', the man approached Cronje shortly before the best-of-three final against Pakistan in the Mandela Trophy. 'I was approach by an Indian or Pakistani man, who described himself only as John,' Cronje told the King Commission. 'He offered an amount, I think about $10,000 [about £6,700], for the team to throw the game. I subsequently discussed this with Pat Symcox. We agreed we should not even put it to the team, and that was the end of the matter. I did not approach any other players.

'I recall that when I walked onto the field for the match, I was asked by Salim Malik [the Pakistan captain] whether I had spoken to John. It was evident to me that he knew about the approach I had received. I felt ashamed and embarrassed and, wishing to avoid even talking about the matter, merely nodded. Before the second one-day final in Johannesburg, I was again contacted by John who asked if anything could be done in respect of the second game. I told him I was not interested.'

That Malik clearly knew 'John' as well, and Mukesh Gupta told the Indian authorities he had had dealings with Malik, lent further credence to the idea that 'John' and Gupta were one and the same.

Cronje was more interested in 'John's' proposal than his statement implied, as he subsequently admitted under cross-examination. He had only been captain for a little time, but was tempted by Gupta's offer. 'I wish I could say I told him to get lost, or jump off the building,' Cronje said, 'because if I had my life would have been very different ... But I didn't. I said I would go back to my room and think about it.'[10]

It was a decisive moment in Cronje's life and he made the wrong call. He would later try to rationalise his mistake, and in the process gave a convincing explanation as to why so many players were persuaded to provide 'harmless' information. 'It is such a big temptation as a 26-year-old [sic] to be on the road [and] somebody comes to you, offers you 50,000 US for a little bit of tiny information which can be useful to him. And all you have to do is supply him that tiny piece of information which is not going to affect the way you play, it's not going to affect the way you captain, it is not going to affect the outcome of the game. It is not going to affect anything to do with the game – it is very, very tempting to say, "that's the information you need".'[11]

Cronje possibly called on Symcox, as opposed to any other teammate, because he saw the big off-spinner, now nearing the end of his career, as someone with a straight-talking, devil-may-care streak. Here was someone, Cronje thought, who might be willing to throw a game. Symcox told his young captain to reject the idea. 'Hansie called me to his room ...and we chatted about the match and a few things. Then he said he had been made an offer to lose the game and wanted to know whether he should put it to the team. I told him I thought it was a bad idea. My advice was not to worry about it and just get on with the game. I said I thought we could beat Pakistan anyway and we should just concentrate on the cricket.'[12] Cronje admitted that had Symcox agreed, they would 'probably have gone through with it'.

Cronje's team may have concentrated on the cricket, but it does not appear that their opponents did. The Cape Town final was the occasion that finally provoked Rashid Latif into his public protest against Salim Malik's conduct.[13]

Cronje's equivocation was an open invitation to 'John' to try him again, but by Cronje's own account he never did. 'I never spoke to him again,' he said. Unless Mukesh Gupta was 'John'. In which case, he did.

Two years later Mukesh Gupta entered/re-entered Cronje's story. They then had several encounters in swift succession as South Africa and India paid each other reciprocal tours between October 1996 and February 1997, though before this happened another bookie, known only as 'Sunil', also appeared on the scene. According to Cronje, 'Sunil' befriended some of the South Africa players during a tournament in Sharjah in April 1996 and approached Cronje to fix matches during the tour of India. He and Cronje had gone out to dinner on occasion. What had they spoken of? 'It was cricket, it was politics, it was television and it was whatever blokes talk about normally,' Cronje said. But Cronje stated he turned down his offers to fix games.[14]

It was towards the end of the series in India that Gupta made contact, during the third and final Test in Kanpur. He checked into the Landmark hotel where the teams were staying and asked Azharuddin, whom he already knew, to introduce him to Cronje; he wanted to be presented as a diamond merchant. Accordingly, on the evening of the third day, Azharuddin phoned Cronje. 'He called me to a room in the hotel and introduced me to Mukesh Gupta,' Cronje said. 'Azharuddin then departed and left us alone in the room.'[15]

The accounts of Gupta, as given in India's CBI report, and Cronje differ slightly but significantly. Cronje claimed Gupta, whom he said was also known as 'MK', had asked him if South Africa would give wickets away on the last day of the Test to ensure they lost: 'He asked me to speak to the other players and gave me approximately $30,000 in cash to do so.' Gupta said he asked Cronje what he thought the outcome of the Test might be – South Africa's position was precarious – and Cronje had replied that South Africa would lose. Gupta said the amount he paid Cronje was $40,000. The discrepancies perhaps suggest Cronje tried to play down being given a lot of money just for information. Was it actually a downpayment on future favours?

Cronje, who had now been an international cricketer for almost five years, found the prospect of the money irresistible, but asking his teammates to throw a match, he claimed, was harder to contemplate (though he had already managed to broach the subject with one player, Symcox). Cronje led Gupta to believe he would talk to his players. 'This seemed an easy way to make money but I had no intention of doing anything,' Cronje said. 'I did not speak to any of the other players and did nothing to influence the match. In the event, however, we lost the Test. I had effectively received money for doing nothing and I rationalised to myself that this was somehow acceptable because I had not actually done anything.'

South Africa lost the match heavily, as they were always likely to do given the situation on the third evening, when India led by 330 with five second-innings wickets in hand. They were left the almost impossible task of batting ten hours to save the game and the contest was all but over when Cronje went out at 29 for three after the early loss of Gary Kirsten, Herschelle Gibbs and Daryll Cullinan. He hit an aggressive 50 to top-score the innings. Defeat sealed South Africa's first series loss in four years.

At the end of the India tour Cronje smuggled the money Gupta had given him back to South Africa, and later took it to England where he deposited it in his bank account in Leicester, thereby breaching the foreign exchange rules of South Africa and India.[16]

Taking this money would ultimately prove fatal to his career. Whether the outcome of the Kanpur Test was arranged or not, Gupta must have now thought he had Cronje firmly on his side. And, sure enough, the day after the Test finished, he was back to him again. To the intense annoyance of the South Africans, a benefit match had been tagged onto the itinerary. They had been in India a long time and were anxious to get home, and this extra fixture in Mumbai (which, to make matters worse, was accorded full one-day international status) felt like an unnecessary and unwanted imposition. Gupta asked Cronje whether his team would be interested in throwing the match. Cronje agreed to see what he could do.

'By that stage we were exhausted, it was the end of a long and arduous tour, and a number of key players were suffering from injuries,' Cronje said four years later. 'MK asked me to convey an offer of $200,000 to the team to throw the match. It was a long time ago and I cannot recall the exact sequence of events…'.

In the face of such a large offer, Cronje's reservations about approaching his players seemed to evaporate. He apparently approached some of the senior players first and it was quickly agreed that the offer must go before the whole team. One of those Cronje spoke to beforehand, on the flight to Mumbai, was Derek Crookes, a few months older than Cronje but a much less experienced player. 'I asked him if he was joking,' Crookes said. 'He said I should think about it overnight.'[17] Crookes turned him down but others were tempted by the riches on offer for underperforming in a contest for which few had an appetite.

'A team meeting was held the evening before the match, attended by all the players in the squad,' Cronje said. 'I conveyed the offer to the team, which rejected it. I recall, in particular, that Andrew Hudson, Daryll Cullinan and Derek Crookes spoke out strongly against it. It was agreed that the decision had to be unanimous or not at all.

'After the meeting a few players remained behind and we chatted about the matter. We were curious to see whether the offer could be increased. I telephoned MK and told him the team was not interested but asked whether he was prepared to increase his offer to $300,000. He replied that this was too much but that he would increase it to $250,000.'

'The team was unhappy about the match having official one-day international status,' Symcox said. 'It was at the end of a very tough tour and everyone wanted to go home … It was the first time any of us, especially myself, had this sort of thing thrown at us [clearly his conversation with his captain nearly two years earlier escaped his mind] … Some guys, including myself, said it was a lot of money and we should look at it. Some guys were for it, some against.'[18] He confirmed that Andrew Hudson, Daryll Cullinan and Derek Crookes led the opposition.

'In any other circumstances such an offer would not have been entertained,' David Richardson said. 'It was the one and only occasion in more than eight years of international cricket where such an offer was discussed in a team environment.'[19]

According to Gupta, Cronje did not actually convey to him that the South Africans were unwilling to go ahead with the deal until 3.00 a.m. on the morning of the match, which suggests that the meeting among the interested players went on very late.

Cronje added, 'The next morning before the match, there was a very brief meeting at which it was confirmed that the offer was rejected. When Mr Woolmer, the coach, heard about the offer he was very angry about it ...I then telephoned MK and told him that the offer was rejected. No money passed hands. I did however tell him that the team was sub-standard because of the number of injured players. I received no benefit or offer of payment for this information.'

Cronje, it must have been obvious, was keen to accept the offer; he would hardly have put it to his players otherwise. Woolmer remembered him saying, 'If we took the money we could put it together and buy a house at Fancourt for us all to share.'[20] In time, Cronje would indeed buy a property at Fancourt, but alone.

Some of the players were actually pleased to be approached. Cullinan said they had listened to opponents from the subcontinent 'openly bragging of the money they have made [from bookmakers], the cars they have received. There is talk about providing information but it goes further than that at times.'[21] Richardson stated, 'We had heard that other teams had been approached and when we got this offer we thought, "We're one of the big boys at last".'[22]

The match itself was doubly frustrating for the South Africans, because not only did they have to play it, but they lost it anyway. Cronje, feeling the pressure of the long tour, Gupta's persistence and his own frustrated craving to take the money, was at breaking point. 'The game was a farce and Hansie pulled the team off when the crowd pelted us with water bottles,' Woolmer recalled. 'At the supper break, Hansie was so upset because the game was going against us … that he threw his plate of food down so hard on the floor that the chicken rebounded onto the roof of the dressing-room. The sight of the chicken stuck to the roof was amusing, but the captain's temper was such that he left for the washrooms where he smouldered out of control and in tears.'[23] Cronje said he was 'very annoyed with myself' for not taking the money.[24]

Having turned down the offer, the South Africans knew that the matter must not get out, or that if it did, they must say they never seriously considered it. Cronje had told them that if they accepted the offer, no one must ever know about it; for Crookes, this was one of the reasons he objected. He was unwilling to keep anything from his wife.[25]

It was suggested some of the players swore each other to secrecy. Even under questioning during the King hearings, they gave away few details of their discussions, especially about the meeting among senior players. Most claimed amnesia and only under intense pressure would Cronje even name as senior players who might have been at the meeting Richardson, Symcox, Kirsten, Brian McMillan and Fanie de Villiers. 'It may put people in a bad light and after five or six years [actually four] I may be incorrect in naming players,' he said. The senior players (whoever they were) clearly gave the offer serious consideration, although before the King hearings the general impression was that Cronje's phone call to Gupta asking if the offer could be increased was a 'joke'. Symcox testified that $250,000 was 'quite a lot of money, you know, especially when you divide it by the rand'. No one except Cronje made reference to the presence of 'Sunil' in Sharjah.

Despite the players' efforts, the matter did come out. Colin Bryden, cricket correspondent of the *Sunday Times*, South Africa's leading newspaper with sales of 450,000, heard of the story and wrote about it the week after the Warne–Waugh story broke. The article appeared under the heading, 'Proud South African Cricketers

Hit Match-Fixers for Six'. Bryden spoke about the offer to Cronje, who said that it was basically laughed off, adding, 'The sooner it [i.e. match-fixing] is sorted out, the better.'

What was striking was that the South African board showed so little interest in the matter. The official tour reports, prepared by Woolmer, the coach, and Robert Muzzell, the manager, made no reference to the episode. Ali Bacher himself claimed before the King Commission not to have known anything about the offer until Jonty Rhodes told him of it the day Cronje confessed, though Woolmer said he had mentioned it to Bacher in dispatches and meetings. Cronje confirmed that Woolmer had mentioned it to the board.

Bacher even claimed never to have seen the *Sunday Times* article or had his attention drawn to it, which seems astonishing for a man in his position at a time when match-fixing, thanks to the Waugh–Warne story, was on everyone's agenda. David Richardson used to refer to the offer during after-dinner speeches (though presumably not to how close the team came to accepting it).

Subsequently, after he had completed his evidence to the King Commission, Bacher admitted in a newspaper interview that he had indeed spoken to Woolmer and Cronje about the Mumbai offer. 'I did engage in a fleeting conversation with Hansie which probably lasted no more than five to ten seconds. There was, however, no mention of countries or amounts involved at any stage,' he said. 'I acknowledge, in hindsight, that I should maybe have pursued the matter, but at the time, that was totally unthinkable.' Like almost every other administrator, Bacher could not comprehend that his players might have had any truck with bribery. 'If the bookmakers can get to Hansie Cronje, they can get to anybody in world cricket,' was his excuse.[26]

What Bacher also did not want to admit, of course, was that – contrary to the impression he cultivated – he and Cronje were not on good terms. There was, in fact, little communication between them. For his part, Bacher seems never to have properly considered the feelings of his players: he was simply too busy shoe-horning them into an even more crowded tour schedule to consider whether they were actually fitted for the task. His obliviousness and his failure to act proved a grave deficiency.

When India made their reciprocal tour during the winter of 1996–97, Mukesh Gupta followed: he was in Durban for the first Test and Cape Town for the second. Now he asked Cronje to provide information in respect of both games, on which Cronje understood he wished to place bets. 'I understood that MK would pay me an (unspecified) amount if he won anything. The amount would depend on his winnings. In respect of the first Test, I supplied him with the team selections and a daily forecast. In respect of the second Test, I was only asked to tell him when and at what score we would declare. I did this.' In exchange for this information, Gupta transferred £33,300 into Cronje's bank account in Bloemfontein and five days later paid him another £13,900.

Perhaps sensing that Cronje had almost won over his team in Mumbai, Gupta asked him to speak to his players about throwing the third and final Test in Johannesburg, offering the talismanic figure of $300,000 – the sum they had sought in Mumbai – should they agree, but Cronje refused. Cronje later claimed that none of the matches in this series – South Africa won the first and second Tests and the third was drawn – were fixed or manipulated.

However, according to Gupta, Cronje 'assured' him South Africa would lose the third Test. Gupta believed that it was because this assurance failed to materialise that Cronje lacked the courage to meet him again. Cronje phoned to apologise and promised South Africa would lose some matches in the one-day triangular tournament that was to follow. He promised exact information but again was unable to deliver. His information proved incorrect and Gupta (so he claimed) suffered huge losses. How much Cronje could do is unclear but he was seemingly still eager to add to his earnings. Perhaps, after what had happened with the Mumbai one-dayer, Cronje felt it too risky to go back to his players and propose that they now throw a Test. He risked jeopardising everything if his contacts with bookmakers or punters were shown to be too intimate. When Gupta challenged him about this, Cronje said he had been powerless. 'India had played so badly and missed so many chances that he could do nothing about the result.' The relationship was breaking down.

Cronje and Gupta spoke several months later, during a quadrangular one-day tournament in Pakistan. Cronje claimed that it was at this point that he terminated the relationship, saying he felt guilty doing what he knew to be wrong, but if the relationship really did end there, it was more likely because of the losses Gupta had sustained. Uncertain who was causing him losses, Gupta began pruning his list of contacts.

7

AZHARUDDIN

What perhaps went wrong for Hansie Cronje and Mukesh Gupta in South Africa early in 1997 was that someone else was already fixing the matches. India lost four of their six qualifying matches; South Africa won all six of theirs and went on to win the final between the sides by 16 runs. India's four qualifying defeats included a first-ever loss to Zimbabwe. Among those playing for India was Mohammad Azharuddin, whom Cronje said introduced him to Mukesh Gupta in Lucknow.

AZHARUDDIN WAS arguably the most gifted cricketer to be caught up in the scandal. At the time he received his life ban from the Indian board he had scored more than 6,000 runs in Tests, more than 9,000 in one-day internationals, and played in more one-dayers than anyone in the game. His personal wealth was estimated to be greater than any other player's. How much was earned honestly, and how many more runs he might have scored had he always tried, was impossible to say.

There were many parallels between his story and that of Cronje, which may explain why they felt such an affinity for each other. Why, when they had so much going for them, did they risk losing everything?

Their upbringings were very different. While Cronje enjoyed privileges, Azhar grew up in a crowded suburb on the wrong side of Hyderabad. He was polite, devout and gauche, an unassuming Muslim in a predominantly Hindi society. His grandfather inculcated in him a sense of right and wrong, and a love of cricket, an interest fostered further at school. With a bat in his hand he stood out for his lazy elegance, powerful wrists and superb timing.

In 1983, the year India won the World Cup, he turned 20 and started work as a clerk at the State Bank of India. But unlike that other bank clerk, Mukesh Gupta, he was never to be trapped behind a desk. His future lay on the cricket field. The following year Azhar uniquely scored centuries in each of his first three Tests against David Gower's England side. He captivated his audiences. Sunil Gavaskar proclaimed him 'God's gift to Indian cricket'. Azhar himself remained modest. 'It's God's blessing,' he said.

Religion and morals were cornerstones of his life and contributed to his promotion to the Indian captaincy in 1990 when the board faced a players' pay revolt. He promised to re-establish the old sporting standards, though in other ways his character left him ill-suited to the job. 'He set about tackling his new responsibilities with the modesty that is a refreshing trait: the devout Muslim probably believed in just praying extra hard and leaving his young team to play to the best of their resources. Such a style was disastrous to begin with, but soon enough Azharuddin learned to assert himself as captain.'[1]

The Indian players were not badly paid by 1997; they received about £1,900 per Test and £1,400 for every one-dayer. But Azhar found it hard to leave his modest upbringing behind. An Indian journalist, Ayaz Memon, was struck by this when the team played a series in New York shortly before Azhar became captain.

'One day I met Azhar hanging out in the lobby alone,' Memon wrote. 'I was setting off to buy an "authentic" Polo shirt for a friend. "I will come along," said Azhar. "I love Polo too." We stepped out of the hotel, and I was about to hail a cab when Azhar stopped me. "How far is it?" he asked. "Around 20 blocks," I said. "Why waste dollars on a cab?" he asked. "Let's walk."

'It took us 45 minutes of brisk walking to reach the destination. Once inside the "authentic" Polo shop, Azhar was agog. We spent almost an hour there, I picked up the shirt for my friend, but Azhar had chosen nothing. "Too expensive," he said, much to my astonishment.'[2] There are uncanny echoes with tales of Cronje's miserliness.

Those close to Azhar detected a change in him from around the time he became involved with Dawood Ibrahim's 'Muslim underground' and met Sangeeta Bijlani, a former model and minor Bollywood actress.

The Bollywood film industry was perhaps the mafia's favourite area of extortion. The underworld was suspected of funding many films, only ten per cent of which were money-spinners. Movie executives became targets as the underworld set out to recoup its losses. The Indian government offered protection to those who approached the police, but in most cases producers and stars hired their own bodyguards. Of course, contacts between actresses and cricketers were not necessarily suspicious: two former West Indies captains, and the new India captain, Saurav Ganguly, were all romantically linked with Indian film stars. Unusually, Azhar abandoned his wife and children and married his actress.

To the disquiet of colleagues, Azhar did little to hide the affair. Ali Irani, the Indian team's physiotherapist, spoke out, not only about the relationship but also Azhar's 'other activities'. 'In 1994, I gave a confidential report to the secretary of the BCCI [Indian cricket board] in which I mentioned that when a team meeting was going on, Azharuddin, who was captain of the team, was speaking to Sangeeta Bijlani on the phone,' Irani stated. 'Azharuddin came to know about this and our relationship soured. It became worse in

1995, when I told him not to divorce his wife to marry Sangeeta Bijlani. In fact, I did not attend his wedding.'

Azhar moved to Mumbai and started filling his wardrobe with expensive designer labels. 'I like to spend money,' he said. 'I like to wear designer clothes. If I earn a rupee I will spend it and if I earn a crore I will spend that also.'[3] On another occasion, he commented, 'What's wrong in having Armani suits or Rolex watches? Is it wrong? I have earned all that through hard work.'[4]

His income was alleged to have reached staggering proportions. A commissioner of income tax disclosed that Azhar once declared annual earnings of more than £2.5 million; he also estimated his total worth at around £25 million.[5] According to CBI investigators, Azhar and his wife owned two properties in Hyderabad, two penthouse apartments in Mumbai and four plots of land in various parts of India. He also possessed five cars. Investigators suspected that two properties may have been given to him by bookies Shobhan Mehta and Mukesh Gupta.[6]

Azhar's remarriage to a Hindu provoked a public outcry. The affair was exploited by Hindu fundamentalists and for a time he came under intense media scrutiny. It was at precisely this period that he became involved with Mukesh Gupta.

Azhar had only met Gupta by chance. Ajay Sharma had wanted help from Mukesh Gupta with buying a car; in exchange for £250, he promised to introduce Gupta to Azharuddin. The meeting took place at the Taj Palace hotel in Delhi in 1995. Ostensibly, the meeting was to discuss Azhar's efforts to raise funds for a fashion show and charity cricket matches, but it appeared he immediately agreed to fix games. Azhar would use a locker at the hotel to deposit payments from bookies.

The deal that was struck was unusual. Again according to the CBI, Gupta paid Azhar £80,000 as an advance against what was clearly intended to be several 'arrangements'. 'Azharuddin promised MK that he would provide the exact information as to when India would win or lose.' Sharma, who also introduced Gupta to another

Indian cricketer, Ajay Jadeja, was paid £8,000 for setting up the meeting.[7]

The first Gupta–Azhar meeting took place in 1995 but, if Azhar's version was to be believed, it was late 1996 before they fixed their first match together. It was unthinkable that after being paid so much, Azhar would have been required to do nothing for so long. They could have manipulated matches during the 1995–96 season, when India hosted a tour by New Zealand and participated in one-day tournaments in Singapore and Sharjah, both of which were lost.

Nor might Gupta have wanted to overlook the World Cup on the subcontinent early in 1996. One of the most controversial decisions of the tournament was Azhar putting Sri Lanka in to bat in the semi-final at Calcutta. Sri Lanka scored 251 for eight and India, batting under the floodlights, feebly collapsed. They were 120 for eight and doomed to defeat when a crowd riot brought the game to an undignified halt and led to the match being awarded to Sri Lanka. Azhar was heavily criticised for what he did and India's exit contributed to his sacking six months later.

The first match Azhar confessed to fixing with Gupta was during the Titan Cup tournament, which took place during South Africa's tour of India. Azhar admitted that, with the help of two teammates, he ensured a qualifying game against South Africa at Rajkot was lost. Azhar scored 9, Jadeja 26 and Mongia 3 during an Indian batting performance *Wisden* described as 'lame'; South Africa, thanks to a half-century from Jonty Rhodes, won with ease, despite illness ruling out two regulars. Irani had no doubt about Jadeja's involvement with Azhar. He said Jadeja had once told him in 1996 not to talk about 'such things', 'as he was no longer into it'. Irani 'suspected that Jadeja made this statement to him because by that time Jadeja probably knew that Azharuddin had confided to him [Irani] about match-fixing.' Jadeja has vehemently denied any involvement in match-fixing.[8]

There were also suspicions about Azhar's behaviour in the Titan Cup final against South Africa. A police surveillance operation had traced a call between Azhar and Anees Ibrahim in Dubai on the morning of the match.[9] A number of bugged calls led police to believe it was intended that South Africa should win the game, but they actually lost, inspiring Mumbai's commissioner of police, Rakesh Maria, to think that the South Africans were not beyond suspicion themselves. 'South Africa has been involved from the beginning,' he was quoted as saying after the Hansie Cronje affair broke. 'What is Cronje talking now? Utter rubbish! This Titan Cup final ... totally fixed,' he said. 'Totally fixed.'[10]

The Titan Cup possibly marked the start of Azhar double-crossing Mukesh Gupta. Sharma confirmed that complications arose between the two men during this tournament. Was Azhar now working for Anees Ibrahim? What had they spoken about on the phone?

Police uncovered evidence implicating several India cricketers, whom they said took between £160,000 and £200,000 during the tournament.[11] The turnover on the final alone among Mumbai bookies was estimated at nearly £7 million. But if some made money, Mukesh Gupta and Anil Steel were apparently not among them. Gupta said they incurred heavy losses and the story of Steel's insolvency got around. Asked why it happened, one bookie explained, 'Counter-fixing. He'd paid to fix a match but somebody didn't follow instructions.'[12]

Gupta immediately asked Azhar to make amends. He demanded information on the India–South Africa Tests that followed. Azharuddin correctly forecast that the Ahmedabad Test would not end in a draw and India would lose in Calcutta, but more problems ensued when the India team went to South Africa. Azharuddin started using intermediaries to communicate with Gupta: first Irani, whose reservations about the whole exercise were allayed with bribes from Gupta, then Bijlani herself, who relayed predictions to Gupta by phone. (Bijlani herself, like her husband, denies any involvement in this operation.) Most turned out false. Irani said Steel 'gave me money for Azhar on a number of occasions ... Azhar would ring me or tell me in advance that "John" would be sending money.'[13]

Irani accepted 'large amounts of cash on behalf of Azharuddin', some transactions being as high as £16,000 to £24,000. For rendering this service, Azhar paid him between £400 and £800.

Gupta said it was because of Azharuddin's inaccuracies that he turned to Cronje, though the timing of the meeting in Lucknow was curious if Gupta was solely thus motivated: according to Gupta's own account, Azharuddin had just provided him with accurate forecasts for the Ahmedabad and Calcutta Tests. Moreover, Azharuddin was the man Gupta turned to for help in liaising with Cronje. It must be likely that Gupta would have sought the help of the South Africa captain anyway.

Gupta's disaffection with Azharuddin would have been real enough by the end of the tour of South Africa, which concluded with a triangular one-day tournament also involving Zimbabwe. The longer the one-day tournament went on there, the more probable it would have seemed that the Indians were in league with another bookie. Azharuddin physically withdrew from Gupta, using intermediaries to communicate with him rather than doing so himself. Why?

Not that everything worked out. An unnamed Indian team official described how when India beat Zimbabwe to reach the final, Azharuddin's disappointment was plain. 'He scored two runs in the match and someone authoritatively told me he had placed bets,' he said.[14] Sunil Dev, the tour manager, wrote in his tour report to the Indian board, 'I would like to mention that once a player retires as a captain he should also retire from the team as a player. No army can be commanded by two generals, no company can be run by two managing directors.'[15] Azharuddin had been replaced as captain by Sachin Tendulkar the previous year.

Azharuddin and Mukesh Gupta stayed in contact for several months until Gupta, apparently convinced Azharuddin was betraying him, terminated the relationship.

Azharuddin admitted to police to 'perhaps' fixing another match with Mukesh Gupta several months later, during the Asia Cup in July

1997. It was the subsequent Sahara Cup in Toronto that appeared to be the final straw. Azharuddin's information again proved inaccurate, and Gupta suspected he was misleading him. 'MK thought that either Azharuddin was perhaps involved with some other bookies at that time or he did not have the requisite number of players to fix a match.'[16] The split came just weeks before Gupta and Cronje spoke for the last time. Did Gupta suspect that Azharuddin and Cronje, who were on friendly terms, were working together for someone else? Gupta, who estimated he had paid Azharuddin around £145,000, demanded he return some of the money. He said he managed to recoup £48,000.

Irani, who as physiotherapist to the India team forged close ties with several players, seemed to confirm Gupta's fears. He told investigators that Azharuddin had once told him that 'as he was doing matches with Anees Ibrahim, he could not do [them] with anyone else'.[17]

If Azharuddin was trying to hoodwink a bookmaker, he would not be alone in that; Cronje would do the same. Indeed, one of the most striking features of the scandal was the number of cricketers who thought they could outwit the criminal fraternity. Few, if any, made it pay.

Many of India's matches in 1997 came under suspicion. Immediately after playing in South Africa, they toured the Caribbean. They lost the Barbados Test after being dismissed for 81 chasing only 120. Inderjit Singh Bindra, the president of the Indian board, claimed the game was thrown; his theory was supported by Irani. There was also speculation about a one-day international in St Vincent, which India, chasing 250, lost after collapsing from 201 for three with eight overs left. When Azhar was overlooked for a subsequent one-day tournament in India, it was rumoured he had been omitted on disciplinary grounds.[18]

Azhar's admission that he fixed only two matches for Gupta was regarded as a 'dilution of the actual facts' by the CBI, given the money he received. He denied any involvement with the mafia, but

CBI investigators were convinced it was 'explosive documents' showing financial transactions between Azhar and underworld figures, plus photographs of him with one of the suspects in the 1993 bomb blasts, that finally led to his confession.[19] 'We have established his connections with the D company [Dawood Ibrahim gang] beyond doubt,' one tax official said. '…We have proof of numerous financial transactions.'[20]

The CBI said that it clearly established that Azhar took money from bookies and punters to fix matches and was approached by the underworld to fix matches for them. 'It is clear that Azharuddin contributed substantially towards the expanding bookie/player nexus in Indian cricket. He received large sums of money from the betting syndicates to "fix" matches. There is also evidence which discloses that he roped in other players also to fix matches, which resulted in this malaise making further inroads into Indian cricket.'[21] Madhavan, the Indian cricket board's investigator, concurred: 'He was the captain of the Indian team for long and let down the country and the cricket-loving public in a despicable manner.'[22]

Azhar's behaviour on and off the field inevitably aroused suspicions, though most of these were voiced privately, even after the publication of the *Outlook* article in 1997. Sachin Tendulkar, who captained India between 1996 and 1998, later admitted to the CBI that he had felt Azhar had not always been putting in 100 per cent. 'He suspected that he was involved with some bookies.'[23]

AZHARUDDIN, HANSIE CRONJE and Mukesh Gupta all tended to play things down. Azharuddin said he only fixed two matches with Gupta, despite working for him for more than two years. During this time Gupta said he paid him more than £140,000. According to Cronje, his dealings with Gupta were confined to a few weeks in 1996 and 1997. The money he received was less than the money Gupta said he paid him.

Gupta, a reliable witness according to India's CBI, was probably least trustworthy when it came to money. He claimed to be 'almost broke' by 1996 through fixes not working out, and it appears to be true that Anil Steel, his partner, became insolvent the following year. However, Gupta had a motive to exaggerate his financial troubles because tax inspectors were ready to charge him for any undisclosed income.

In February 1997, at the very time his relationships with Azhar and Cronje were in difficulties, Gupta opened a jewellery shop in an exclusive area of Delhi which police valued at £1.6 million. A couple of years later he was living palatially with his wife and two children in a three-storey house in Defence Colony worth about £400,000. When tax officials raided his premises, they found evidence of betting, numerous bank accounts and hundreds of thousands of pounds of undisclosed income. Gupta told police he had acquired his wealth through property deals and 'gifts from abroad'.

Gupta claimed to have given up all links with bookmaking and gambling in May 1998, yet was seen sixteen months later sitting in the pavilion at Galle during a Test match between Sri Lanka and Australia.[24]

Gupta's importance has been exaggerated by the wealth of detail he volunteered to police in the aftermath of Cronjegate. He was, according to Delhi's crime branch, the biggest bookie in the city, but across Asia there were plenty of other fixers like him. Indeed, a truly big fish would never have dared reveal so much. The story of Mukesh Gupta's dealings with Cronje, Azharuddin and others was just one small piece of a mighty, shadowy jigsaw.

8

WAS THE 1999 WORLD CUP FIXED?

Hansie Cronje's reign as captain had two years to run, but by 1998 there were already signs of his relationship unravelling with South Africa's cricket establishment.

Early that year, while they were sitting in the coffee shop of the Hilton hotel in Sydney, Bob Woolmer, with three successful years as South Africa's coach behind him, was informed by Ali Bacher that he had lost the confidence of the players. It was a verdict that left him 'breathless'.[1] Asked who was unhappy, Bacher declined to say. More disconcerting still, Woolmer knew that Bacher could only have received such information from Cronje himself.

In his autobiography, Woolmer subsequently identified Cronje as the main figure. Cronje wanted a stricter regime than the coach and disagreed with him about aspects of practice and fitness training. Woolmer had also heard rumours that Cronje asked other senior players if they were in favour of a switch to Eddie Barlow, a former South African allrounder who had been a candidate for coach when Woolmer got the job. However one looked at it, and even if

Woolmer was coming to the end of his usefulness to the team, Cronje's behaviour was ruthless – and once again highlighted the power wielded by the captain.

Bacher told Woolmer he should step down after the World Cup in England in 1999 and that he would be recommending such a course to the board. In terms of Woolmer and South Africa preparing for the World Cup, the breach between coach and players could not have come at a worse time.

That was one flashpoint. Then, later that year, Cronje effectively ruptured his bond altogether with Woolmer, further undermining South Africa's World Cup preparations. The incident occurred during the Commonwealth Games in Kuala Lumpur in 1998, the first time cricket had been included. Cronje had been invited to speak at a coaching conference and used the occasion – as did Barlow – to criticise Woolmer's methods, 'in a way...', Woolmer recounted, 'quite disgraceful'.[2] Cronje was kicking Woolmer's long-term plans into touch at a most delicate juncture and ensuring that their relationship, already in a delicate state, would never heal. 'Apparently my name was mud ... I had no choice but to soldier on until June 1999,' Woolmer recalled.[3] No wonder he said of Cronje, 'There were times when I thought I could not trust him.'[4]

By now Cronje was a very different man from the one who had taken on the captaincy. He was a loner, often eating in his hotel room without company, a man who found it increasingly difficult to be 'one of the boys'. In the six months leading up to the World Cup a number of people noticed a darkening of his mood. They included his mother, as well as the Noakes–Woolmer partnership. Bob Woolmer wrote, 'Hansie's face is like a book: when he is cross, he has very frightening facial features ... he smoulders ... he used to roar in torrents.' He also referred to his 'moods, tantrums and troubled states of mind'.[5]

After the scandal broke, Woolmer elaborated on Cronje's autocratic manner. 'Recently colleagues have said he is money-driven. I would add that he loves to get his own way, does not tolerate sloppiness and hates losing an argument. Only once in our association did he apologise for being out of order, and only when he was pressurised to do so. Hansie had some serious mood flare-ups. As coach I was someone to whom he could turn to vent his frustrations. He hated poor preparation and would look for someone to take the can.'[6]

Cronje's tempestuous behaviour behind the scenes could not have been more at odds with the picture of unity and discipline his team presented on the field. Having prepared at a training camp in Bloemfontein, they looked a better drilled outfit than ever as they crushed West Indies 5–0 at home and then won away in New Zealand.

But in the dressing room tensions were reaching breaking point. First, during the early days in New Zealand, a row erupted between Cronje and the South African board over the board's quota system for 'players of colour', recently introduced under government pressure to show national sports teams as more representative of the 'Rainbow' nation's diverse racial mix. Cricket was not the only sport to which the quotas were applied. Three non-white players were taken to New Zealand: Herschelle Gibbs and Paul Adams, both Cape Coloureds, and Victor Mpitsang, a black African.

After the first one-dayer, Cronje, supported by Woolmer, dropped Gibbs from the next two games, for which all-white teams were selected. It would be suggested that both believed the quota system only applied to Tests, but it seemed odd that neither Cronje nor Woolmer should have been aware of the proper situation and, if that was the case, even odder that a heated dispute at a meeting between Cronje and the board should follow.

Speaking of the incident later, Cronje claimed, 'I grew up in a totally different time and era in South Africa, call it post-apartheid, where everybody was equal and everybody had equal opportunity, and I didn't see any reason why people should be judged differently.'[7] But this was patently false. Cronje grew up before South Africa underwent its seismic political shift, and even after sweeping legislative changes, there remained a real danger of ethnic groups being denied equal opportunity, which is precisely why the 'quota' system had been introduced.

If Cronje had simply made a mistake, there was no need for any argument. The only plausible explanation was that he personally objected to the quota system and by selecting an all-white team was attempting to defy the wishes of the board and the government. The meeting broke up with Cronje tendering his resignation, a decision he was talked out of 24 hours later by 'friends'. Who these people were was unknown, though Woolmer apparently remained supportive of Cronje's point of view, a loyal act given Cronje's recent conduct towards him.

As the World Cup approached, Cronje was a more powerful figure within South African cricket than ever.

ONE QUESTION LEFT unanswered by South Africa's King Commission into the Cronje affair concerned his dealings, if any, with bookmakers during 1998 and 1999. These years did not fall within the Commission's terms of reference and Cronje was in no rush to enlighten anyone about what may or may not have happened. He issued a simple denial that he had done anything wrong during this period, maintaining he had had no contact with any bookmaker. But it was hard to believe that once the bookies had succeeded with such a prominent Test captain, they would have left him alone without a struggle. After all, he must have made a ready target for blackmail after taking Mukesh Gupta's money.

There was no shortage of speculation as to what might have happened in these two years. There were strong rumours that the bookmakers influenced the England–South Africa Test series in 1998, which South Africa lost 2–1, having led after three games. By winning in Nottingham and Leeds, England achieved their first victory in a five-match series for eleven years. It was a major upset.

There were no specific allegations that Cronje or any other South African deliberately underperformed, but it was alleged that one of the umpires might have taken a bribe. The deciding game in Leeds was engulfed in controversy, as umpire Javed Akhtar, flown in from Pakistan, made a host of errors which on balance heavily favoured the home side. Of ten lbw decisions, nine were given by him and eight of those were against South Africa. Akhtar's decision-making was a talking point long before England ran out winners by 23 runs. Cronje, the leading batsman in the series for either side with 401 runs at 66, was restrained in his post-match comments, refusing to make excuses for the defeat and congratulating England, although many thought South Africa deserved to take the series. Cronje would deny the match was fixed. 'I never thought there was anything strange. I was fuming because again we were unable to finish off England in England.'[8]

During the match, Ali Bacher was suspicious enough to telephone a subcontinental bookmaker he had met two or three years earlier to ask whether he thought it possible that the umpire had been 'bought'. Bacher later publicly identified the bookmaker only as 'Mr R', though it was believed the bookie's name was 'Raju'. It was interesting to note how Bacher's mind was working at this time, four months before the South African *Sunday Times* published its story about the Mumbai offer on which Bacher was so slow to act. According to Bacher's account, his source told him that Akhtar had 'possibly' been bought, but when they next met, in India eighteen months later, the bookie reminded him of his phone call and alleged, 'The umpire was on the payroll.' He added that one of Karachi's biggest bookmakers had flown to Leeds a few days prior to the Test to ensure his 'client' complied. It was believed that the bookie was Hanif Cadbury, the Karachi bookie who had moved to Johannesburg.[9]

Akhtar angrily rejected Bacher's accusations, made public in the week following Cronje's downfall. 'It's all false,' he said. 'There have been mistakes in the past, mistakes in the present also, and mistakes still being made, but it's totally false, not for money. Whatever mistakes happened over there [in England] were genuine mistakes, not for money.' He denied ever being approached by a bookmaker.[10]

The World Cup in England in 1999 became a rich field for Cronje conspiracy theorists. There were three main points that supported their thesis. The first was that South Africa, the pre-tournament favourites, narrowly lost out to Australia, the eventual winners, in the semi-finals. The match was actually tied, Australia progressing on superior run-rate from the second phase in which they had beaten South Africa in another thriller, the turning point of which was Herschelle Gibbs, a joint-accused with Cronje in the Indian match-fixing case, dropping Steve Waugh as he spilled the ball in premature celebration.

The second point was that South Africa inexplicably lost to Zimbabwe in the first phase after winning all their other games. They had already qualified for the next phase but it was still important they beat Zimbabwe because losing would mean them carrying two fewer points forward to the second phase. Their batting capitulated feebly. Cronje himself was yorked for nought by Neil Johnson, one of six wickets lost before South Africa's total passed 40.

Third, Cronje personally had a very poor tournament with the bat, mustering only 98 from eight innings, which included ducks in the two crucial games with Australia, though the second was patently the result of a poor umpiring decision.

During a five-week tournament, a captain will make hundreds of decisions, any one of which could have had far-reaching consequences. It would be surprising, therefore, if some of them could not be viewed in hindsight with suspicion as to their motives, especially when the person in question later admits to taking money from bookmakers.

Nevertheless, Cronje did do some curious things, aside from his bizarre attempt in the opening fixture to receive radio communications with Woolmer via an ear-piece while India were batting. The technology was immediately banned by the ICC. Among his strangest acts was batting himself at number three against Pakistan, a higher position than he had occupied for two years because of his fragility against pace. Shoaib Akhtar, the fastest bowler in the competition, duly dismissed him in quick time. Then, in the Edgbaston semi-final, he took himself off after bowling one cheap over in favour of a tired Steve Elworthy, whose next two overs cost 16. Cronje was in the habit of bowling himself sporadically in one-dayers, but this seemed perverse. Most striking of all, in the same semi-final match he held back Lance Klusener until there were less than six overs of South Africa's innings remaining.

That South Africa progressed so far was in large part due to the muscular commando-figure of Lance Klusener, whose powerful swipes through the on-side had time and again bailed out his side after the failure of the upper order (Cronje was not alone in his shortage of runs). Klusener turned matches against India, Sri Lanka, England and Pakistan, and it was not his fault the Zimbabwe game was lost. He was left unbeaten on 52 from 58 balls. Going into the semi-final, his record was an astonishing 250 runs off 214 balls and the practice was established that he would go out to bat at the latest at the fall of the first wicket once the final fifteen overs of the innings had begun.

However, on this occasion Shaun Pollock was sent in once a wicket had fallen after the 35th over; Klusener did not arrive until the 45th over, by which time 39 runs were required from 31 balls. He smashed 31 off 14 to put the scores level in the last over but a mix up with last man Allan Donald led to a run out and the game being tied – and thereby lost. What would have happened had Klusener, rather than Pollock, gone in four overs earlier?

But this was not an isolated incident. Cronje's treatment of Klusener had long been one of measured detachment. Klusener had broken into Test cricket during the 1996 tour of India, taking eight wickets in an innings in his first match, in Calcutta, and a few weeks later adding a maiden century in Cape Town. It was a sparkling start to a Test career but Klusener subsequently struggled to find a meaningful role. Cronje, it was suspected, was frustrated that Klusener was not prepared to work on his fitness as hard as himself, and he had preferred to throw the ball to others and to bat others higher in the order. That only changed after Klusener sustained a foot injury in England in 1998 and concentrated on developing his brutally powerful hitting. But, as we shall see, there was also a mutual distrust between the two, which may have been based on Klusener's ability to detect Cronje's true nature.

Whatever the explanation for South Africa's World Cup failure, it proved an almost unbearable trauma for many in and around the team to come to terms with. It took some months to get over and, according to Pastor McCauley, Cronje himself never recovered. He implied that the disappointment contributed to Cronje's subsequent self-destructive behaviour in India. Cronje himself said he bet £1 on South Africa at 4–1 to win the tournament, the first time he had bet in his life.

Others preferred to lay the blame squarely on Cronje's shoulders. Tim Noakes referred to a growing distrust of innovation among the team and a series of blunders by South Africa's captain 'on and off the field' that 'cost this country the tournament'. He added, 'We had the best coach and the best team in the world. If Cronje had backed Bob Woolmer, we would have won the tournament. Instead, he undermined him … Why did he remove all the influences in the team so that he became the captain, coach and primary selector? He had carte blanche to do what we wanted. The United Cricket Board will rue the day they didn't put controls in place to ensure their captain was honest.'[11]

Even before Cronje's downfall, Noakes was outspoken in his criticism of the players. 'There was absolutely no defensible reason why the 1999 South Africans should have lost in England,' he wrote. 'The unpalatable truth remains that the team had actively to lose before Australia could win. Perhaps the basis for that defeat will eventually be acknowledged…'.

Though he did not specifically accuse anyone of corruption, his comments were nevertheless an interesting insight into the vulnerability of the modern player. 'The foundation of any such shortcomings lies in the persisting failure to address, in a creative manner, the cancer of modern international cricket,' he said, 'the overwhelming emotional demands made on young men who must be away from their stable home environments repeatedly and for prolonged periods during their formative years.'[12]

BOOKMAKERS WERE surely active at the World Cup. A former Indian actress familiar in cricketing circles was reported as saying that she had heard that games before the semi-final stage were fixed, and the CBI report contained a reference to the India–Zimbabwe group match at Leicester.[13]

The CBI report also alleged that a fixer-punter called Ajay Gupta paid Azharuddin's hotel-bills in Delhi and gave him £16,000 to underperform, along with two other teammates, in a one-dayer against Pakistan in Jaipur two months before the tournament; also, that during the World Cup itself, Gupta and his associates travelled to England and provided Azhar with a mobile phone and paid for his shopping at Harrods.[14]

There was, moreover, the case of an opening bowler allegedly offered £14,000 to bowl a wide with his first delivery of a group match who was still weighing up the offer when he ran in to bowl. In fact, the ball was good. This story rapidly did the rounds among the players and when I heard of it, sought out the player in question during a match at Canterbury the following year. After hanging around in the car park for a couple of hours, I finally got to put the question. With a smile, he denied such a thing ever took place. When another player subsequently told me about the incident, I told him I had already unsuccessfully tried to substantiate the story. 'Ah,' he said. 'Of course. He would have denied it to you. You're a press man.'[15]

Rumours were attached to Pakistan defeats. One was in the first phase against Bangladesh, one of the biggest upsets in World Cup history; another to India in the second. The result of the Bangladesh game meant nothing to Pakistan: they had already qualified for phase two as group winners and could not carry points forward from the game as Bangladesh were already eliminated. The match was well and truly 'dead'. When Pakistan played India, however, they were not yet certain of reaching the semi-finals, and defeat meant they had to beat Zimbabwe in their last second-phase tie to seal their place.

Concerns were also expressed that the final, a one-sided match which Australia won in less than 60 overs, might have been rigged – based, it seemed, on talk that players might have been socialising the night before. No supporting evidence has ever been produced. The most suspicious event was Wasim Akram's decision to field first, but only with the hindsight that Pakistan being bundled out for 132 provided. Beforehand, Steve Waugh, the Australia captain, thought the pitch good for 260.

The manner of Pakistan's defeat to Bangladesh at Northampton was striking. This time they won the toss and chose to bowl, even though the pitch was a used one and expected to turn later. Akram justified the decision by saying that his side had batted first in four earlier games and they needed practice batting second. When Bangladesh batted, Pakistan conceded the high number of 40 extras, including 28 wides; when they chased 224 to win, they lost three wickets to run-outs. One Test captain is alleged to have said, 'I couldn't stop laughing, it was so suspicious.'[16] Pakistan rarely looked like making a game of it and the final margin – 62 runs – was not even close.

As losers, Pakistan took £2,000; had they won, they would have received £4,000, which meant the difference between winning and losing worked out at around £200 per man. The odds on a Bangladesh win were 33–1. One of the reasons given by the Qayyum report for the involvement of Pakistan players in match-fixing was poor remuneration. At around this time they typically earned about £45,000 per annum, while the figure for their Australian counterparts could be more than £250,000.[17] The Pakistan team, too, received little in the way of win bonuses, thus reinforcing the financial incentive to throw matches. Lord Condon's report highlighted the fact that during the World Cup the players 'received a low single figure percentage of the proceeds'.[18]

Sarfraz Nawaz, who spent several seasons at Northamptonshire, attended the game, possibly the most colourful event to be staged at a ground hitherto synonymous with the quiet attrition of the county circuit. Before it was a few overs old, he predicted to committeemen that Bangladesh would win. Sarfraz said that Pakistani friends of his in Northampton had been in Allan Lamb's restaurant, the Jade Pavilion, the night before the game, and had overheard a conversation among players and reported back that 'something was happening'.[19] Sarfraz said, 'At 11.00 a.m. I told people Pakistan would lose. They were shocked. The committeemen said it was not possible. I said, "You see".'[20]

Many Pakistanis might not have minded had their former compatriots won; Bangladesh were campaigning for Test status and Akram, in his post-match television interview, said he was 'happy' for his opponents and thought they deserved to play Test cricket within a couple of years. But Gordon Greenidge, once the West Indies' flamboyant opener and removed as Bangladesh's coach after the tournament, urged caution: 'I think people are forcing it to happen a lot sooner than it should.'[21] But the next year, largely on the back of this victory, Bangladesh's ambition was fulfilled.

Richard Pybus, Pakistan's English-born technical coach, who was sacked several months later, said, 'I have no idea if some of the players were got to before the [Bangladesh] game but I saw nothing of it. We played abjectly, but we had already got through and it is easy to believe the guys were flat. They played poorly against not very good opponents. That's happened through time immemorial. But there was not a hope in hell that the India match was fixed. The guys played flat out and lost.

'They had absolute tunnel-vision about winning the World Cup until the final. We lost the final because half the Pakistan Cricket Board turned up and disrupted our practice. The manager was pulling people out to talk to guests and during the match half the cricket board was in our changing-room. Mushtaq Mohammad [the coach] and myself could not sit on the balcony. The pre-match talk and warm-up were ruined. It was laughable. We lost because the atmosphere around the team changed.'[22]

India's coach, Anshuman Gaekwad, also denied the result against Pakistan was manipulated. 'I went to the Pakistan dressing room and the players were very depressed by the defeat.'[23]

It was alleged that pressure was applied to the players before the tournament by bookmakers insisting they owed them a favour after they had lost money on a Pakistan–England game in Sharjah the previous month.[24] That game took place after India and Pakistan had already qualified for the final at England's expense; it was a dead game which Pakistan were expected to win. Their unexpected defeat by 62 runs led to some bookies in Mumbai incuring losses running into hundreds of thousands of pounds. From the underground network, suspicions were immediately voiced that the game had been 'fixed' by rival bookies, and an instruction was sent out by one of Dawood Ibrahim's aides that no bets should be paid. 'I was receiving numbers of calls from Bombay [from punters] that the match was on the wrong track,' he said. 'They were smelling a rat and the bookies were cheating them. So I telephoned all the bookies and told them to forfeit the match. You can ask every bookie in Bombay and he will tell you this is a fact.' He alleged Shobhan Mehta, a prominent Mumbai bookmaker, had masterminded the 'fix', a charge Shobhan Mehta's family denied.[25]

It was claimed a feud subsequently broken out among the bookies that culminated in the death of the infamous Hanif Cadbury. Cadbury was found dead in Johannesburg on 16 May, two days after the World Cup opened. There were conflicting accounts about his death; some said he was shot many times and his body hacked into pieces; others, that he had been strangled.[26] At the time the *Daily News*, one of Pakistan's leading newspapers, carried a report under the heading, 'Bookie Hanif Cadbury Killed in South Africa'. The report read, 'Sources attributed the death of the 33-year-old Hanif to a conflict between two bookmaking giants mainly operating in international cricket', before quoting an unnamed former Test cricketer as saying that Hanif's 'most recent involvement [in bookmaking] included the Sharjah Cup where the most powerful bookie of the region lost over Rs400 million [£6.4 million] in the wake of Pakistan's defeat to England'. The article continued, 'He hinted that Hanif's murder might have taken place at the behest of the mafia chief as the deceased belonged to a rival group.'[27]

Rashid Latif, the wicketkeeper turned whistle-blower, said, 'The immediate word in Karachi's stockmarket and among the bookmakers was that he [Hanif] had fallen victim to rivalries among major bookmakers of the subcontinent over match-fixing.'[28]

But there were other theories. Friends claimed the death was linked to a jealous business rival and police sources said Cadbury had been robbed on his way home from a casino carrying a large amount of money that he had won. But the Mumbai bookies were in no doubt: 'Hanif Cadbury refused to part with his profit and he was killed.'[29]

After the Sharjah tournament was over, Javed Miandad resigned as Pakistan's coach. Publicly, it was said he had fallen out with players over the distribution of prize money, but he later admitted that he quit because he believed his team threw a match. During the England match, Miandad 'had received a phone call from someone apparently reliable and whom he did not want to name, who said that the match was fixed'. When Miandad was told that five players had taken money to throw the game, he made Akram talk to the man. Miandad said that during the interval between innings, he was furious at the team for allowing England to recover from 40 for five to total 206. 'He further went on to state that before he knew what was happening, five of his batsmen were out.'[30] Pakistan were all out for 144 with nearly ten of their 50 overs unused, Angus Fraser taking three wickets and Mark Ealham four.

Wasim Akram confirmed that the man on the phone was Dawood Ibrahim, who presumably wanted to halt what he had discovered was afoot. Ibrahim asked Akram to make the players take an oath on the Koran, but Wasim did not do this 'because [the] Holy Koran was not available on the ground at that time'.[31]

Whatever happened beforehand was, of course, no guarantee that anything untoward happened at the World Cup itself, but apart from widespread suspicion about some matches, allegations were also made about the relationship between certain players and an Indian gambler called Ratan Mehta, who was in England at the time of the tournament.

Mehta may or may not have tried to fix World Cup matches. The evidence against him is circumstantial and flimsy and he vigorously denied ever being involved in match-fixing. But he did mix in interesting circles. It appeared he went around giving the impression he was close to players. There was evidence he was known to Cadbury and a number of the Indians alleged to be involved in the conspiracy involving Hansie Cronje.[32]

A large man in his early thirties, Ratan Mehta was a familiar figure at grounds around the world and was sighted in the players' enclosure in Toronto three months after the World Cup. Mehta owned a restaurant and nightclub in Delhi to which he liked to invite cricketers and Bollywood starlets. 'Small-time actresses used to hang around the cricketers, creating an aura of mystique about Ratan.'[33]

Mehta found discretion an elusive quality and a witness claimed to overhear Mehta boasting in London clubs that he had 'fixed' things.[34] 'I saw him taking calls every couple of minutes. It was actually quite annoying. He appeared to be taking bets via Dubai ... He's got a reputation as a "fixer" in India but I was surprised he appeared to be fixing a game as big as a World Cup match.'[35] But it was possible, if not probable, that Mehta was just a compulsive gambler – boastful, indiscreet and incapable of the subterfuge necessary to 'fix' matches and keep the fact secret.

During the World Cup, Mehta's elder sister, Mona, was detained for allegedly running a betting ring. She later said, 'After my case, in which I was harassed, our confidence is low. I am not a bookie. A little betting goes on here and there. But it's innocuous. Ratan has [bet] as well.'[36] Asked why Mehta claimed to know Wasim Akram, she replied, 'My brother may have done that to show off. He doesn't know Akram that well.' Akram himself denied knowing Mehta, while admitting, 'I may have met him in a hotel lobby.'[37] According to the CBI report, Mehta had on occasions sought the 'judgement' of Pakistan players on matches in which they were involved and had at times given them 'small gifts'.[38]

But the player to whom Mehta appeared to be closest was an Indian, Ajay Jadeja. Jadeja, who would be banned for five years for match-fixing, was a descendant of the legendary cricketer-prince Ranjitsinhji, but although he was a regular in India's one-day team, he never progressed beyond being a marginal member of the Test side. He lived the kind of life that rarely saw him out of the gossip columns. He was romantically linked with the daughter of a Cabinet minister, attended celebrity parties in Delhi and gave a striking display of affluence, owning two houses and an office in the capital plus land in Mumbai and a village on the Delhi–Haryana border where Kapil Dev had set up a landshare scheme among Indian cricketers in which Azharuddin was also involved.

Kapil Dev, who was 'like a father' to Jadeja, admitted to knowing of Jadeja's association with 'certain dubious persons' and felt that his choice of friends 'was not always as it should be'.[39] Even Jadeja acknowledged this. The CBI report stated, 'Asked about his association with bookies/punters, Jadeja … said that he had made certain mistakes in his career and was ready to pay the price.'[40] But he denied knowing Mehta was a punter.

It took the CBI months to investigate the labyrinthine connections between bookies and players. Their efforts to unravel them continue even now. Typical of the web of intrigue were the allegations surrounding Mehta. A man called Sanjiv Kohli, who owned restaurants of his own in Delhi and was also a punter, was alleged to have told the CBI that Mehta had phoned him from Sri Lanka in 1997 claiming to have 'fixed' the Pakistan team to lose a one-day match there; he wanted Kohli to provide £40,000 to fund the 'fix'. Kohli declined on the grounds that as Sri Lanka were already favourites, there was no point. When Mehta returned to India he demanded £32,000 from Kohli to pay the Pakistan players, but Kohli declined, saying he had made no money out of Mehta's information. Another Delhi gambler, Pawan Puri, confirmed this story to the CBI and believed Jadeja and Mehta had fixed games together.[41]

Mehta rejected the allegations, saying Kohli wanted to malign him because they had argued over financial matters, but admitted to having stayed in the same hotels as the Pakistan team on several occasions.

Puri also described attending a party with Mehta in Delhi a few months after the World Cup. Puri had picked up Mehta in his car around 11.00 p.m. On the way Ratan Mehta asked him to phone a Mumbai bookmaker and place a bet for him that the Test between India and New Zealand in Ahmedabad would end in a draw. Puri was surprised at this, given that after three days New Zealand were precariously placed, but carried out the request even when the bookmaker advised him against it. Ratan Mehta denied a bet was ever placed, saying he had simply asked Puri to find out odds. Puri said that at the party itself Mehta had got drunk and bragged of inside knowledge about the Ahmedabad Test and placing bets with other bookies.

The next morning India surprisingly chose not to enforce the follow-on in Ahmedabad, and New Zealand went on to escape with a draw. Sachin Tendulkar, India's captain, told the CBI that the decision not to enforce the follow-on was taken jointly by himself, Kapil Dev – who was now India's coach – and two players, Jadeja and Anil Kumble. Others corroborated his account but Tendulkar conceded other forces could have been at play. 'On being asked whether anybody could have influenced this decision, since the bookies in Delhi allegedly knew one day in advance that the follow-on will not be enforced, he [Tendulkar] accepted that it was possible.'[42]

When the CBI studied phone records, they discovered Jadeja was called 193 times in Ahmedabad by one bookmaker before or during this game. The same bookmaker had spoken to him on numerous other occasions during New Zealand's visit.[43]

From the earliest days, rumours had abounded. One Indian board official publicly announced before the one-day series that the bookies had determined it would sit at 2–2 after four matches. He was proved right.[44]

SEVERAL WEEKS AFTER the World Cup, Pakistan's sports ministry asked Justice Qayyum to include the tournament in his ongoing investigation into match-fixing. Qayyum duly broadened his terms of reference to include Pakistan's games against Bangladesh and Australia; the India game he ignored. Then, mysteriously, after three days, he came under political pressure not to look into the World Cup after all. 'Initially I was told I should look at match-fixing without restrictions,' Qayyum said. 'Then I was asked to withdraw. This was very unusual. Of course I was surprised. Anybody would be surprised if you are asked to do something and then told not to three days later.'[45] No explanation was given for the contradictory instructions, although there may have been political motives behind the original request. There had been allegations that former prime minister Nawaz Sharif and his aides had bet millions of pounds on Pakistan defeats.

A few days before the Qayyum report came out in May 2000, Salim Malik was secretly filmed by the *News of the World* admitting, under questioning about the Bangladesh game, 'Yes, something happened there.' He also implicated players who were still in the Pakistan side, but these names were not revealed by the newspaper.[46]

Tauqir Zia, the head of the Pakistan Cricket Board, later went back to his government and asked for an inquiry into the World Cup. He denied he was acting under pressure from the international cricket community, though allegations about Pakistan's part in the tournament had been renewed. Shortly after Lord Condon's interim report into match-fixing was published in May 2001, it was announced that a Lahore High Court judge had been given two months to investigate the World Cup and allegations made against umpire Javed Akhtar.

9

THE ENGLAND CONNECTIONS

Six weeks after the World Cup, evidence emerged of an attempt to fix a Test match in England. Chris Lewis, the England allrounder who made the last of his international appearances the previous year, said he had been approached by two Indian bookmakers, posing as businessmen, offering him £300,000 to recruit England players to fix the outcome of the Test against New Zealand at Old Trafford. The men denied the allegations.

The case created confusion and controversy for the England and Wales Cricket Board (ECB), which had been drawn into the scandal to nothing like the same extent as their counterparts in Pakistan, India and Australia. The most explosive element of Lewis's story was that the men who came to him claimed that three England players had taken bribes in the past. In the wake of the Warne–Waugh story, Surrey allrounder Adam Hollioake had publicly admitted that on the eve of his first match as England one-day captain in Sharjah in 1997, he had received approaches from bookies but had turned them down.

South Africa's newspapers report Hansie Cronje's disgrace. The previous day he had confessed to the South African cricket board that he had taken money from an Indian 'bookmaker', despite earlier denials. In a phone call to Ali Bacher he admitted: 'I haven't been entirely honest with you.'

Cronje was covering his trail even at a 'confessional' press conference in Cape Town. A statement read out on his behalf by Sports Minister Ngconde Balfour (left) claimed he had not received money.

The cricket world was stunned when it emerged Australia's Mark Waugh and Shane Warne (right) had taken money from an Indian bookmaker calling himself 'John' for information about pitch and weather conditions. A few weeks later, Pakistan's Salim Malik tried to bribe them to under-perform. But what was the real identity of 'John'?

Cronje wanted to be the most powerful figure in South African cricket. To this end, he contributed to the removal of Bob Woolmer as coach. 'He played the stock market,' Woolmer said. 'Cricket was not his only source of income.'

Left: Wasim Akram was fined and barred from captaining Pakistan after a report was produced by Justice Malik Qayyum in May 2000. Wasim was deemed 'not above board'. The judge added: 'He has not co-operated with this commission ... He cannot be said to be above suspicion.'

Below: Mohammad Azharuddin, the India captain, caused outrage by leaving his family for an actress, Sangeeta Bijlani (left). He spoke to her on the phone during team meetings and allegedly used her to relay predictions to a bookmaker. Why did Bollywood actresses play such a prominent role?

Above: Salim Malik was banned for life after being found guilty of attempting to bribe three Australian players to play badly in Pakistan in 1994. Many matches during his year as Pakistan captain came under suspicion.

Ali Bacher (left) and Jacques Kallis arrive for the King Commission hearings. Bacher later admitted his testimony was incorrect. He had learned of the bribe offered to the South Africans in India in 1996 at the time it happened and not in April 2000.

Above: Pieter Strydom (right) and Henry Williams (second from right) were both targeted by Hansie Cronje. The South African captain tried to lure them into match-fixing during the tour of India in 2000. Strydom declined but Williams agreed.

Opposite: Herschelle Gibbs' evidence to the King Commission was flawed. He claimed he forgot about the deal struck with Cronje – £10,000 to score fewer than 20 in a one-dayer in Nagpur – yet twice reminded his captain of the arrangement

when they were batting. In the space of twelve months Gibbs was fined for this deal, breaking a team curfew and a drugs offence.

Opposite: An Indian bookmaker alleged that in 1993, India's Manoj Prabhakar (right) introduced him to the then-England vice-captain Alec Stewart (left), to whom he paid £5,000 for information. In July 2001, after Gupta refused to testify, the ECB formally cleared Stewart of any wrong-doing.

Right: Chris Lewis contacted the England and Wales Cricket Board within hours of being offered £300,000 to fix the Old Trafford Test in 1999. Yet the ECB did not contact the police until after the match was over. Police described Lewis's conduct as 'impeccable'.

Rashid Latif of Pakistan was one of the few to publicly speak out about the corrupt practices of his fellow players. It cost him his place in the team and, for a while, his liberty. Latif also accused the ICC of ignoring his correspondence about match-fixing.

The evidence of Delhi bookmaker Mukesh Gupta was central to India's CBI inquiry that shocked the world. While the cricketing fraternity maintained a conspiracy of silence, Gupta provided investigators with a wealth of detail. 'We found no reason for him to lie,' the CBI said.

Right: Judge Edwin King offered to give Hansie Cronje immunity from criminal prosecution if he told the King Commission the truth about his dealings with bookmakers. Unconvinced by Cronje's performance, he declined to do so. It was usually others, not Cronje, who exposed his misdemeanours.

Below: Lord Condon (left) and Malcolm Gray had the task of guiding cricket into safer waters. They wanted to clean up the past but their priority was safeguarding the future with a raft of preventative measures. 'It's not just a matter of catching the crooks,' Gray said.

No one had alleged an England player had actually accepted money to underperform before.

Faced with this startling development, the ECB was slow to respond. Clearly reluctant to take the allegations seriously, perhaps partly because they first appeared in a Sunday tabloid newspaper, administrators gave the impression they would prefer to do nothing.

One passage from Lord Condon's subsequent report could have been written with them in mind. Discussing the way national boards had coped with the match-fixing scandal, he wrote, 'Resolute action by some has been diluted by others who have procrastinated and missed opportunities to deal with the problem. National pride and embarrassment have certainly hindered a more collaborative and coordinated approach to dealing with the problem.'

In their unwillingness to face unpleasant facts the ECB undermined the honest attempts of a player to help them. Few players had ever volunteered information on match-fixing; Lewis's treatment guaranteed few would venture to follow his example. That Lewis was by nature a loner did not help, but police said he conducted himself impeccably throughout. Not knowing of the troubled history of Lewis's relationship with the establishment, they were perplexed at his treatment.

Lewis had severely strained his relations with the authorities by dismissing the England selectors as 'full of shit' following his omission from the World Cup. The previous year, I had done an interview with Lewis in which I discussed with him the extent to which his career had been blighted by racism, albeit perhaps subliminal. He was reluctant to play the race card but nevertheless left me in little doubt that he had experienced racism at times. Equally, though, his career had contained a litany of missed opportunities on his part. He was a gifted cricketer in all departments save one, self-belief, and was inclined to emotional outbursts. One of the 'businessmen' who approached him said Lewis spoke about being made to feel an 'outcast' from the England team.[1]

The basic elements of the story had a familiar ring to them.

Lewis's interlocutors, Aushim Khetrapal and Jagdish Sodha, moved in the twilight world of the Bollywood film industry. Sodha was in his early fifties and distributed cult Hindi films overseas. Ten years younger, Khetrapal was a sports promoter who claimed to have arranged upwards of 200 events, ranging from squash, snooker and cricket tournaments to junior tennis academies. One of his proudest boasts was that he gave Ajay Jadeja his first big break securing him a sponsorship deal with Liberty Shoes.[2]

Khetrapal rarely sat still for long. A few months after the Lewis episode, he claimed to have turned to acting, with parts lined up in several movies; he was also involved with a television news programme and had completed a music album.[3]

But the role of bookmakers also held a fascination for him. An Indian journalist described sharing a journey with him: 'All along the drive to Delhi, Khetrapal kept asking about the bookie I had met, where he lived and how he operated. In between, he told me how betting was essential for the development of cricket. "It is only when big betting comes to a sport that it becomes big. The only thing wrong here is that players are throwing away matches. They should not sell the nation. Otherwise betting will generate a lot of money for the game. It is not a bad thing. It will do more good than harm."'[4]

Khetrapal claimed his purpose in going to England was to revive plans for a benefit match in India that had hit difficulties. 'Two days before a Sri Lankan team was to arrive, they were told not to come even though they had signed an agreement,' Khetrapal said. 'This put us in an embarrassing situation with ESPN [the broadcasters] and sponsors. The Punjab board gave us dates till August 9 to get the players again. To make this happen, I went on July 30 to England.'[5] Khetrapal planned to raise a New Zealand side or a West Indies one, and had set up meetings with the two captains.

Again, according to Khetrapal, soon after arriving in England he and Sodha split up. Khetrapal went to Leicester, where the New Zealanders were playing their last warm-up match before the Old Trafford Test, and talked to the captain, Stephen Fleming, 'about various contracts, including coming to India'. Then he met Brian Lara, who was on his way to play golf in Scotland, at Heathrow, after which Khetrapal shared a hotel room with Sodha at a nearby Holiday Inn – perhaps a curious thing to do given that they said they had only first met waiting for their flight three days earlier.[6] Telephone records suggested that while he was in England, Khetrapal contacted Sanjiv Chawla, the man alleged to be Hansie Cronje's 'spymaster' who lived in London.[7]

Khetrapal claimed that it was because the discussions with Fleming and Lara proved inconclusive that he and Sodha then turned to Lewis. Sodha had a friend in Harlesden, Gopal Patel, whose cousin, Kamlesh Patel, was an acquaintance of Lewis's (Lewis had been brought up in Harlesden). Lewis described Kamlesh as 'somebody that I've known from time to time, that I got tickets for games from'.[8] Gopal had suggested Lewis might be able to raise an English side for the benefit match. Kamlesh was duly contacted and got in touch with Lewis on 2 August.

That is the account as given by Khetrapal and the Patels. However, it differs in many particulars from Lewis's version. The most telling discrepancy was that Lewis said Kamlesh first phoned him about a week earlier than this, saying he had friends coming over from India and that 'he had a business proposition that he wanted to discuss'. His friends were in 'entertainment'.

So, according to Khetrapal, the meeting was a chance one; according to Lewis, it was planned well in advance. If it was premeditated, Khetrapal must have known Sodha before they met at the airport. The whole story started to look much more like a conspiracy. There was seemingly no doubt as to which version the police believed.

Lewis agreed to meet the businessmen to talk about their 'proposal' in the room above Kamlesh's newsagency at 66 High Street, Harlesden that evening, three days before the Old Trafford Test. When he arrived, he found five Asian males waiting for him. These were probably Khetrapal, Sodha, Kamlesh, Gopal and Narendra

Patel. Lewis recalled that there was someone called 'Jatesh' involved, but this may have been Jagdish Sodha.[9]

It seemed Khetrapal did most of the talking. Again, there were two versions of events, one Khetrapal's, the other Lewis's. Perhaps neither was invalid, in the sense that talk of a benefit match (Khetrapal's version) may have led into a discussion of darker deeds as conversation in the crowded room dropped to the level of whispers (Lewis).

According to Khetrapal, he outlined his credentials as match promoter. He asked whether Lewis could raise an English team. Lewis appeared reluctant, plausible enough given that he would have doubted whether he had the clout to recruit players: he was no longer in the England side, nor would he ever be again. It was logical, though, that someone in Lewis's position might not want to look a gift horse in the mouth. He enjoyed the trappings of wealth and through the use of an agent, Gareth James, had negotiated lucrative terms at Surrey and Leicestershire. He drove an expensive Mercedes convertible and enjoyed wearing the latest designer clothes.

Khetrapal claimed Lewis's reaction to his invitation to raise a team was, 'What is in it for me?'[10] Khetrapal told him that the team would be paid nearly £7,000 plus expenses, and Lewis himself a co-ordination fee; Jadeja was co-ordinating the Indian team on the same terms.

Lewis only ever talked about the offered bribe, though he implied other matters were discussed first. 'They wanted me to provide them with information as regards pitch conditions and how I thought the game would go day to day. They also wanted me to contact players and see if they were interested in performing to order, for money.'[11] He said £200,000 to £250,000 was on offer for a one-day international and £300,000 for a Test.

He added, 'I was obviously shocked ... £300,000 is an awful lot of money. I wondered how they could actually afford that much.'[12] When his story appeared in the *News of the World*, he described how he 'nearly fell off his chair in shock' when the true nature of the 'proposal' became clear.[13]

Lewis said he was asked to recruit 'two or three' key England players to underperform at Old Trafford. Alec Stewart and Alan Mullally were both mentioned as possible targets. Stewart, as wicketkeeper, could drop vital catches, and Mullally could bowl wide of the wicket (in fact, although Stewart was to play, Chris Read had been selected to keep wicket). 'When they initially asked me to fix the match, they suggested that I should talk to these people [Stewart and Mullally] ... [They] didn't suggest that these guys were involved in any way, they just suggested that these were a couple of people that I should try to tap up.'[14]

But the biggest shock was yet to come. By way of encouragement Lewis was told that Test cricketers from several countries, including England, had taken bribes in the past, and he was given the names of three England players who had allegedly done so. 'They are all famous players, hero-worshipped by millions of young fans in this country. Khetrapal said dozens of top players were at it – so why didn't I just come onside? ... The amounts the three received went into "thousands". I was told everybody was at it, including players from South Africa, India and Pakistan. He told me that one of the three – a batsman – had received a "substantial figure" to get himself out deliberately during a one-day international against Australia.'[15]

Lewis would add, 'He didn't say what it was for, whether it was fixing matches or information or anything.'[16] The three England players were described as 'close friends of Lewis', each of them having played regularly for England in the previous four years.

'At the time I actually just listened. The conversation was actually left where they would call me the following day to see what my reaction was. I then left the meeting and called my manager [agent] and my solicitor directly after and told them exactly what was happening.'

The next day 'Jatesh' called Lewis three times on his mobile phone – this was confirmed by phone records held by Scotland Yard – and tried to persuade him to agree to the proposal. Then Kamlesh Patel called and asked him to join them for a drinks party, as 'Jatesh and the others were leaving the country'. Khetrapal rang him even after he had returned to India. In the end Lewis switched off his mobile. He said that in the course of 48 hours he received many calls. When Khetrapal and Kamlesh Patel rang, he could hear other voices in the background in a way that suggested they were acting at the behest of others.

It would transpire that a day or so earlier in Leicester, Fleming had received a similar approach regarding the same Test match. He, too, rejected the offer, which he reported to John Graham, the manager of the New Zealand team, and Chris Doig, the chief executive of New Zealand Cricket. The ICC was also informed. Lara never reported any meeting with these Indian businessmen to his national board.

On 4 August, about 36 hours after their meeting with Lewis, Khetrapal and Sodha flew back to India.

ALTHOUGH THE MATTER effectively ended there for Fleming and Lara, the story had only just started for Lewis.

The morning after his visit to Kamlesh Patel's newsagency, Lewis informed the England and Wales Cricket Board of what had happened. 'We called the board at 9.00 a.m. I expressed to them exactly what had happened. I gave them full details at that time of everything. I also informed them that the said people were actually still here in the country and which hotel they were actually staying at,' said Lewis.

The facts of the case were plain: an attempt had apparently been made to fix a match on English soil, a match that was to start in two days' time; aspersions had been cast about the integrity of three England players. These were serious matters and Lewis had recognised them as such. Lewis commented, 'The ECB have consistently told players that if they are ever approached to go to them and they will handle it and that was exactly what was done – a matter of hours after I spoke to this chap.'[17]

Either that day or in the days immediately following, Simon Pack, the ECB's international teams director, held a meeting with Lewis at which the incident was discussed at length. What passed, especially in relation to the three players alleged to have taken bribes, would become a subject of heated dispute.

Lewis said he merely conveyed to the board the fact that the names of three players had been mentioned. 'As regards to how true what was being said was I don't know,' he stated. 'I had no information regarding whether an England player was actually taking a bribe … Whether those things are actually true or not is down to the ECB and the police to actually prove … The ECB chose not to hear those names … I told them what had been said and the reply was that this was hearsay and they didn't want the names.'[18]

Astonishingly, a week was allowed to pass in which the Old Trafford Test took place with only four officials at the ECB – Pack, Tim Lamb, the chief executive, the chairman Lord MacLaurin and Gerard Elias QC, the chairman of the disciplinary standing committee – aware that the game might be the target of a conspiracy.

After the match, according to Lewis, the ECB suggested to him the matter perhaps ought to be referred to the police. 'I was told a week later by the board that it was probably in our best interests to report it to the police which I did and after a period of perhaps a week or so had many meetings with the police. I gave my full account and recollection of what had actually been said during that meeting [in Kamlesh Patel's house].'[19]

In response to Lewis publicly complaining about the way the matter was handled, the ECB gave a very different version of events in a lengthy statement by Lord MacLaurin:

I am absolutely satisfied with the way in which matters have been handled, particularly by the international teams director … [I am] satisfied that there is no foundation whatsoever in the idea that those involved at the board were not interested in the information that was made available by Chris Lewis ... To suggest that the board did not seek to establish immediately from Chris Lewis the names of the England players allegedly involved as soon as this information was divulged is unbelievable...

Of course, precisely what was said at this initial meeting cannot be proven for there were no witnesses to it, but a detailed computerised record made shortly after the meeting shows that the establishing of identities (which Chris Lewis remained reluctant to divulge to the ECB) was a key feature of it.

Lewis's nervousness and reluctance to divulge any names to us at the time was perhaps understandable (he has repeatedly referred to his concern for his safety), but the meeting ended with the hope and expectation that he would be able to tell us names in due course and as trust developed over the next few days. In the end, this hope did not materialise.

Second, there is no truth in the allegation that the ECB did nothing about the information it had received or that there has been some form of cover-up. Lewis was made aware of the importance that the board attached to sharing the information with the ICC (and later with the police), although records make clear Lewis's reluctance for this to happen ... Lewis was informed that the matter would have to be referred to New Scotland Yard whether he liked it or not. To his credit, on August 18 he accompanied the international teams director to St John's Wood police station and has cooperated with the CID investigation since then. With the matter now in police hands, and notwithstanding Lewis's continuing sensitivities over security, the board took the decision to inform the ICC in strictest confidence of all that it knew, and did so on August 20.[20]

Even by the board's own account, the police were not contacted until seventeen days after Lewis first reported the matter and eleven days after the Old Trafford Test had finished.

Lewis admitted that he had no desire to be publicly linked to the naming of three players as the recipients of bribes. 'If my name had come out, my career in the game would be over. I also genuinely would have feared for my life. If I had helped smash a multi-million pound betting ring, I don't think they would be happy with me. Do you?'[21] But he strongly rejected the suggestion that he was unwilling to hand over the three names in private to the right authorities.

Lewis and the board also fell out over how the story, which appeared in the *News of the World* about a month after the Lewis–Khetrapal meeting, came into the public domain. For Lewis himself to sell the story made no sense; nor was he paid for the article, though he was for one with the same newspaper after the Cronje scandal broke. Lewis himself hinted that it was down to an ECB leak, a charge MacLaurin dismissed as 'unrealistic and untrue'. MacLaurin added that apart from Lewis, his agent and the police, ten people knew of the matter – six officials at the ECB and four at the ICC. In fact, the evidence, which included details contained in the newspaper that could only have been known to the police at the time, firmly pointed to Scotland Yard leaking the information with the aim of moving forward their investigation.

Had the Cronje story not broken, almost certainly nothing more would have been heard of the allegations against the three England players. The police were primarily interested in the attempt to rig matches, and their investigations focused on whether the law had been violated. As under Indian law, there was no obvious criminal activity involved in a player accepting a bribe in return for information or underperforming.

The police questioned all the England players involved in the Old Trafford Test. It was believed that they questioned no one in connection with the alleged bribes. 'I spoke to one of three players supposed to have taken bribes,' said David Norrie, the cricket correspondent of the *News of the World*, who knew their identities. 'He said he had not been questioned. When I told him he was one of the three, there was a 30-second silence.'[22]

Only after Cronje's exposure did the ECB announce it had found no evidence of malpractice against any England cricketer. Gerard Elias issued a statement saying that there was 'no evidence whatsoever to justify the bringing of disciplinary charges in relation to betting and/or match-fixing against any member of the England international squad, past or present'. The board met with Lewis for two and half hours but it was another six hours before the announcement was made. No details were given of what investigation was undertaken by the board over the course of the previous eight months.

Lewis's behaviour at around this time was instructive. He was clearly angry and bitter. He felt he was being portrayed by the board as accuser rather than ally. Shortly before Elias's verdict was made known, Lewis accused the board of 'leaving me to sink'. He even briefly withdrew from the Leicestershire side until it was acknowledged he had done nothing wrong. Such an undertaking was never fully forthcoming. He accused the ECB of mismanagement, as did his agent. One of the police officers involved in the case described Lewis's behaviour throughout as 'impeccable'.

The ECB had closed the file on a matter that could never be considered finished. Had the South African board or police investigated Cronje's affairs in March 2000, they would probably have come up with nothing. But a month later his career was finished. If authorities did not look, they were not going to find.

Khetrapal, meanwhile, had problems of his own. Shocked to discover his meeting with Lewis had made the newspapers, he contacted Jagmohan Dalmiya, the ICC president, for assistance. Khetrapal claimed to have known Dalmiya for at least ten years. They had organised several tournaments together; Khetrapal claimed they were sufficiently intimate for Dalmiya to have dined at his home on several occasions. But Dalmiya couldn't help him. On 22 October 1999 he wrote back to Khetrapal saying that he objected to his comment 'that I have known you for years and that we shared a certain bond'; he insisted they had not worked together since the Asia Cup in 1990–91, an event that 'left extremely bitter memories ... neither have I worked with you for any venture nor have I been aware of your activities'.[23]

Scotland Yard detectives twice visited India, on the second occasion interviewing Khetrapal and Sodha. They also arrested and questioned the three Patels. Sanjiv Chawla was arrested and released on bail. A file was passed to the Crown Prosecution Service that contained allegations about a number of 'bookmakers' but nothing that incriminated England cricketers; the Inland Revenue was, however, believed to be making inquiries into the affairs of certain players.[24] In June 2001 the investigation was closed, but there was still no move on the part of the ECB to produce a report on the case.

10

THE HOTEL PARK ROYAL

n April 2000 the Delhi police laid charges against Hansie Cronje and four other South Africans of criminal conspiracy relating to rigging matches and betting, but the case slowed to a crawl as Cronje's exposure triggered a nationwide investigation by India's Central Bureau of Investigation. The full story of the plot in which Cronje became entangled thus remained incomplete, while throwing up some intriguing connections between the principal characters.

However, many details emerged following the arrests of four of the main suspects: Kishen Kumar, a failed actor from Mumbai; Rajesh Kalra, a printer from Delhi; Sunil Dara, a Delhi bookmaker; and Sanjiv Chawla, also originally from Delhi, who ran a garment store in Oxford Street in London, where he had lived since 1993. All were around their late twenties or early thirties.

Kalra was arrested the day before the Delhi police went public with their claims against Cronje and it was believed his statement led to Cronje and company being charged. Kumar was arrested the following week, after leaving hospital suffering from stress. Chawla was questioned by Scotland Yard detectives eight months later in relation to the Chris Lewis affair and was believed to be the 'Sanjay' whose conversations with Cronje were bugged by the Delhi police. All three denied being involved in match-fixing.

Kumar was the common link.[1] Kalra and Chawla were unknown to each other until they met in London around September 1999, a meeting which Kumar probably facilitated. 'We struck an instant rapport,' Kalra said of Chawla. 'He kept coming to Delhi.'[2]

Kumar and Chawla had known each other since childhood. Raised in Jangpura, a poor district of Delhi, they had enjoyed few privileges. Kumar said that neither of them had had a television in their home.

Kumar's life was transformed by the success of his elder brother, Gulshan, who through his own enterprise developed into the biggest music tycoon in Bollywood with an empire estimated to be worth more than £60million. On the back of his wealth, Kishen lived comfortably and pursued an acting career that, despite his brother's best efforts, failed to take off. Then, in August 1997, Gulshan was murdered while leaving a temple, shot in the street by three assailants, another victim of the mafia's extortion campaign in Bollywood.

On his brother's death, Kishen moved to Mumbai to take over Gulshan's business interests and enjoy even more of his wealth. But this simply made Kishen, too, a mafia target. He was to be threatened and shot at by thugs associated with a rival gang to Dawood Ibrahim's.

Chawla's family originated in northern Pakistan, migrating to India around the time of Partition. In 1953 they moved to Jangpura and set up a garment business that developed into a sizeable operation; by the end of the century it was producing 25,000 items per day, mostly for export to the United States, and had fixed assets worth £800,000. The family lived in a large house in an upmarket suburb of Delhi, employing a servant and a driver.

Sanjiv declined to join his father and two brothers in running the business and left to set up an import–export garment business in London from a small shop in Oxford Street. The store sold cheap, non-Indian clothing. 'The ambience of the shop does not give the impression of Chawla being a man who can trade in thousands of pounds,' one eyewitness suggested.[3]

This was Chawla's only known employment. When the scandal broke, Rajiv Khurana, the company secretary of the Commercial Clothing Company, said of Chawla, 'I don't think he has that sort of money [to fix matches]. He drives around in a broken-up BMW.'[4] Khurana, who owned another clothes shop in Oxford Street, appeared to be the power behind the business. Someone working in this other shop said Chawla sometimes came to him asking to borrow a couple of hundred pounds. Chawla lived in a flat on an estate in Hendon.

But Chawla made several overseas trips and his father said his son moved in high society. He knew some well-known Indian cricketers and was apparently familiar with some cricket officials. 'Sanjiv is a deep water fish. He has been around for a while in the world of cricket betting, so I guess you make friends along the way,' Kalra was reported as saying.[5] One who knew him described him as 'more interested in gambling on cricket … definitely not what is commonly termed a bookmaker'.[6]

Even when Chawla was in London and Kumar pursuing his acting, the two friends remained in contact. When Kumar went to London or Chawla returned to Delhi they would look after each other. 'Whenever I go to London he treats me very well,' said Kumar. 'He arranges for my telephones and cars there. And whenever he comes to India I meet him there too.'

Rajesh Kalra arrived in Delhi the same year Chawla left. He had grown up in a town south-west of Delhi and arrived with little to his name except a degree in psychology. He set up a printing business and within a few years had acquired a good deal of wealth and many trappings of middle-class respectability. 'He was near broke … He came to Delhi empty handed. We are probing how he made so much money in such a short period,' a police source said.[7] Had he not been in police custody at the time, Kalra would have married in April 2000.

But Kalra also acquired a reputation as a big player in underworld gambling. His name was linked to a police raid on a gambling den in Calcutta in 1997. Police described him as 'arguably the biggest cricket betting operator in Delhi with worldwide links including London, Dubai and Mumbai'.[8] His primary task was to liaise with punters.

Kumar and Kalra had known each other three years. 'When I met him and took him as my friend, he had no criminal record,' Kumar said. 'I have thousands of friends and I don't think that there is anything wrong with having friends. If they do anything wrong, I cannot be held responsible.'

POLICE BELIEVED THIS group held several meetings towards the end of 1999. After Kalra and Chawla met in London, further gatherings were alleged to be held in India between Kumar, Chawla and two Delhi bookmakers, Manmohan Kattar and Sunil Dara. This quartet 'held several meetings in Delhi and Mumbai to discuss and chalk out the match-fixing gameplan'.[9] Police said Kattar and Dara played a 'pivotal' role.

At these meetings Kumar and the two bookmakers allegedly agreed to pool money. Kalra estimated the total sum raised was between £265,000 and £335,000, though the final plan may have involved numerous Indian bookmakers fixing several matches for a total of more than £1.5 million. Police believed a 'massive' amount of money was converted into foreign exchange and sent in late 1999 or early 2000 to a London bank account.[10]

There was speculation that Kumar would face a charge of raising money by illegal means and Chawla, if extradited to India, one of illegal currency dealings. Kumar denied being involved in attempts to fix matches or raising money to bring fixing about. He said, 'I did not put my money in betting', adding that he was 'too busy to indulge in such things'.[11] Released on bail, he claimed the police had 'threatened me to name some people falsely ... or else they would show me as having links with underworld gangs ... the Delhi police cooked up a false story to create an atmosphere of hatred and prejudice against me'.[12]

ONE OF THE MOST intriguing questions is how this group ever came to have their names linked with Hansie Cronje. If they were, indeed, planning to fix matches, how did they know the South Africa captain might be vulnerable to an approach?

There was no solid evidence, but many circumstantial connections.

Kumar, Kalra and Dara mixed in some interesting circles in Delhi, circles Chawla joined when he was over from London. All of them attended the exclusive gymnasium at the Hotel Park Royal. One of Chawla's brothers, Gagan, was a member there too. Among others who frequented the gym were Indian Test cricketers Manoj Prabhakar and Ajay Jadeja. Kumar and Kalra knew them all, though Kumar played down the relationships with Prabhakar and Jadeja. 'I have met them once or twice in the sports club ... and a few times at parties,' he said.[13] There were also suggestions that Chawla knew Azharuddin and had helped him pay for a wristwatch.[14]

Jadeja and Azharuddin were active players but Prabhakar was potentially no less useful just because he was retired. 'Retired players who have a close rapport with the team have come in handy as a link between members of the team and the syndicate,' one underworld source said. 'We cannot go into the dressing room or even to the hotel where the team is staying. But a former cricketer has access and has friends in the team.'[15] Prabhakar had become managing director of Naturence, a cosmetics firm, and used Kalra's printing business to produce brochures and talked to Chawla about exporting his products to London.[16]

These three players all knew Mukesh Gupta, as, perhaps even more significantly, did Dara. 'He was an associate of MK,' a CBI official said of Dara, who may have been the 'Sunil' that Cronje and other South Africa cricketers had got to know in Sharjah and India in 1996.

The group could have known Cronje might be willing to fix matches from a number of sources. Though discreet, Mukesh Gupta might have intimated his dealings with the South Africa captain to Dara, if not Prabhakar; and to Azharuddin, if not Jadeja. If he was indeed the 'Sunil' Cronje spoke about, Dara might have known from his own conversations with the South Africa captain that he might be susceptible to an offer despite turning down his own approaches in 1996.

Equally, the initiative could have come from mafia connections. Had the group been under pressure to get involved in match-fixing? Or had they been encouraged by Ratan Mehta's claims of intimacy with players at the World Cup? It was understood that he was known to certain members of the group.[17]

At some point, someone identified Cronje as a good target. Whoever it was, they were badly mistaken. As one bookie said, 'He was a disaster waiting to happen. He did not know how to handle it. He did not have the mindset.'[18]

LATE IN 1999, not long after his first meeting with Rajesh Kalra, Sanjiv Chawla allegedly started telephoning a man in South Africa called Hamid 'Banjo' Cassim.[19] Police said the calls dated from around October or November; Cassim said they began during South Africa's home Test series with England, which opened in late November.

Cassim, a tall, burly, shaven-headed man, was in his mid-forties. He was of Asian extraction and lived in Fordsburg, an Asian enclave of Johannesburg, where Hanif Cadbury had also resided before his death. There, Cassim owned a store called Sweet Junction, which supplied foodstuff to street-hawkers. He was a keen cricket follower and known to many of the India and South Africa players. Cassim described himself as their close friend; others dismissed him as a hanger-on. The truth probably lay somewhere between.

He had been a self-confessed cricket groupie since meeting the touring Indians in 1992–93 through his sister-in-law, who knew Ali Irani, the physio. Cassim had been invited to Irani's hotel room, where he met Kapil Dev.

Cassim came to idolise Kapil Dev. He took him out to dinner and introduced him to his family. 'We became very good friends,' Cassim recalled. 'He invited me to Bloemfontein to watch one of the games and from that time onwards we kept in regular contact.'[20] This friendship enabled Cassim to get to know other India and South Africa cricketers. 'All the Indian players are my friends,' he once said. Azharuddin recalled, 'The entire team came to know him.'[21]

Cassim claimed to have been a kind of Mr Fixit for the players. He had done various jobs since leaving school at sixteen: he had helped run his brother's snack shop and a cousin's pharmaceutical business, and owned his own electrical shop before opening Sweet Junction. For the Indian players he arranged vegetarian food and private medical treatment when they did not want their board to know they were unfit. He provided electronic goods at cost-price and when the house of Alan Hudson, the South Africa player, was burgled, presented him with a video recorder free of charge. He played a part in Kapil being presented by a local businessmen with a BMW car in recognition of reaching 400 Test wickets, and recruited South Africa players to appear in benefit matches for retired Indians.

Cassim claimed it was common practice among visiting players to contact him. 'I would attend games, visit them at their hotels, take them out for meals. Some even ate at my house,' he said.[22] In return, he had received gifts. 'They all call me Maamu, "Mother's brother",' he said with pride.[23] Cronje was more blunt: Cassim was a 'regular hanger-on ... always handing out biltong for team members and asking for tickets'. He added, 'I am also aware that Hamid is a friend of Mohammad Azharuddin.'[24]

According to Cassim, Sanjiv Chawla first telephoned him because he was about to come to South Africa to watch the England series and had heard Cassim was well connected to the players. Chawla had wanted to know whether Cassim could introduce him to the South Africa team.

Cassim agreed to help because that was what he always did; he claimed there was nothing unusual or sinister in extending the hand of friendship. 'If you call me from India and say, "Look, I'm coming to South Africa," it's my nature to look after you,' he said. '… To me it was nothing unusual.'[25]

Investigators acting for the King Commission may have been unconvinced. There were discrepancies over how long Cassim and Chawla had known each other. Recalling their conversations, Cassim said: 'He kept calling me and saying, "Hamid, I met you in 1996." But I still say that when I saw him for the first time [in 2000], I never recalled his face.'[26]

Cassim not only insisted he had not met Chawla before, he also claimed to know nothing about his business. 'In the time that I spent with him as well as the telephone calls that I had from him,' he said, 'I gathered the distinct impression that he was more interested in gambling on cricket and most definitely not what is commonly termed a bookmaker.'[27] On another occasion he insisted, 'I'm definitely not a punter or a bookmaker … I was aware of Sanjay Chawla being a punter because he told me. He said, "Look, I put on an occasional bet," and whenever he called me, he wanted the weather report in South Africa and I gave it to him.'[28]

Nor did the South African police discount Cronje already knowing Chawla. Chawla was known to have visited South Africa before, and Clive Lloyd, the manager of the West Indies team, claimed to have seen him in Ali Bacher's VIP box during their 1998–99 tour; Bacher's response was that he had thought the man was a businessman, not a bookie.[29] They were suspicious at the speed with which the relationship progressed. Asked whether he thought Cronje was dismissive.[30]

11

SATAN DICTATES TERMS

The fifth and final Test between England and South Africa at Centurion in January 2000 looked dead in more ways than one. It was meaningless in that South Africa already led the series 2–0; it had also stalled on the home team's first-day score of 155 for six. There had been three days of rain since. No other result but a draw seemed possible.

On the fourth afternoon there were discussions among match officials, South African board representatives and the two captains, Hansie Cronje and Nasser Hussain, about whether something could not be laid on for the crowd. But a one-day match on the final day was ruled out because Test and one-day cricket in South Africa were backed by different sponsors. Asked by English journalists whether he would entertain the idea of setting up a finish on the last day, Hussain had laughed off the idea: '… And lob-ups and stuff? No!'

But that evening Cronje received a call on his mobile phone from a man identifying himself as Marlon Aronstam. Aronstam told the South Africa captain he was involved with a company called NSI.

What he did not say was that this company was a sports betting firm and he himself was a professional gambler involved in the betting business for nearly 20 years. Aronstam owned racehorses and had recently paid a former cricketer to provide him with information. The relationship had not worked out. 'I decided he wasn't worth what I was paying him because he only worked when it suited him,' Aronstam said. 'I wanted him to fly to Zimbabwe to look at a pitch during a Test series and he told me he was busy.'[1]

'We chatted for a while,' Cronje recalled. 'Marlon said that he was a cricket lover and wanted to see action on the field. He said that my image as a captain was poor and that I was being perceived as a conservative and negative captain. We also spoke about my recent form, which had not been good: I had had two ducks in a row. Marlon urged me to speak to Nasser Hussain, the English captain, about an early declaration to make a contest of it, saying this would be good both for me and for cricket.'[2] But what Aronstam proposed – that each side forfeit an innings to set up a fourth-innings run chase – had never been done before: county teams had done so, but never Test sides. Aronstam told Cronje that if he could produce an outright result (i.e. not a draw), then he would donate around £5,000 to charity and give Cronje a gift.

Once again, the grapevine seemed to have worked its mysterious magic. 'I do not know where he [Aronstam] got my cellphone number and I had not previously heard of or spoken to him,' Cronje said.

Within hours Aronstam was inside Cronje's hotel room in Sandton City, Johannesburg. Aronstam wanted Cronje to call Hussain to his room but he refused: 'I did not want him to be involved.' Aronstam pursued his argument in favour of setting up a contest the next day. 'He genuinely sounded as though he wanted to see a cricket contest and I was not asked to influence other players, to perform badly, or to influence the result,' Cronje said.

Cronje could have left it at that: an outlandish suggestion he briefly considered and then rejected. But he did not. As Aronstam was about to leave the room, Cronje stopped him and asked how money could be made from cricket. 'The ball's in your court,' Aronstam replied. At this point, Aronstam alleged, Cronje offered to throw a match. Cronje said, 'The impression I gave was that were South Africa to have qualified for the final [of the one-day triangular that followed the Centurion Test] then I was prepared to talk about it.' Again, according to Aronstam, though Cronje denied it, Cronje stated that a few players were needed to fix a game and named Herschelle Gibbs, Nicky Boje and Pieter Strydom as willing to co-operate. Aronstam was stunned.[3] 'I couldn't believe it. I was shocked. We hadn't even known each other for an hour…'.[4]

Cronje spent 'quite a lot of time' thinking about Aronstam's offer. Then, at breakfast the next morning, Cronje told his players he was considering setting up a finish. 'It took a little bit of convincing because some players were keen to keep going,' he commented. 'There were mixed views … Some members were opposed and others were in favour.'[5] In fact, most, if not all, were unhappy. Jacques Kallis was strongly opposed and said his view was shared by the majority of the team.[6] Cronje sent a text message to Aronstam's mobile: 'Be patient. Working on it. Possible game.'[7]

At the ground in Centurion, Cronje tried winning England round to the idea of a run-chase. The weather had improved and a full day's play was in prospect. While the teams warmed up, he approached Alec Stewart, Hussain's predecessor as captain, on the steps to the dressing room and asked if England might be interested in chasing 270 in 73 overs if both sides were to forego an innings. Stewart replied, 'I think that would be too high. We might go for 250-odd.' But he relayed Cronje's offer to Hussain.[8]

Five minutes later Cronje approached Hussain and offered a more generous target of 255 in 73 overs. After speaking to the England coach, Duncan Fletcher, Hussain declined. 'We needed to have a look at the wicket. I did not know what it was going to do after a few days under covers,' he said. Cronje believed his efforts had failed: 'The England team and management seemed reluctant and I called Marlon and left a message that there would be no declaration.'

The Test resumed, with South Africa still batting, but after 45 minutes Hussain sent a message to Cronje via South Africa's twelfth man that he was 'open to another offer and willing to take it'. A few moments later Hussain left the field to check what the target would be. It was agreed England should chase around 245; as it happened, they were left 249 in 76 overs. It was a very generous offer.

Once news got out as to what Cronje had done, there was widespread astonishment. Many viewed his efforts to make a game of it as commendable. However, for England to forfeit their first innings, as umpires Darrell Hair and Rudi Koertzen ruled on the day, contravened the Laws of Cricket. To get round the problem, Tim Lamb, chief executive of the England and Wales Cricket Board, conveyed a message to Hussain and Cronje that evening that England's non-existent first-innings should be deemed declared at 0 for no wicket, despite it never having commenced. Reports came in of claims of match-fixing from Indian bookmakers, who perhaps knew a fix when they saw one, but Cronje's reputation was such that no one in the Centurion press box took them seriously.

Having achieved what he intended, Cronje attempted to capitalise on the change in events. He asked Strydom, who was playing his first Test, to place a £5 bet on his behalf on South Africa to win. Strydom duly tried to do so, and also asked a friend to wager the same for himself, but learned later that bookmakers had suspended betting.[9] Cronje messaged Aronstam again: 'We have a game.' But Aronstam, too, was unable to place a bet.[10]

England won by two wickets off the first ball of the last scheduled over, but were never really stretched. Stewart and Michael Vaughan, who scored a match-winning 69, did not decide to go for the runs until England had reached 190 for four, by which time they needed only a further 59 from 11 overs.

At the post-match presentations Cronje's players sat on the outfield utterly devastated. Before details of the Aronstam deal came to light, Daryll Cullinan reflected, 'I would like to think that Hansie was acting in the interests of the game and doing something for the public, but it totally went against the guy I know. I have known him for 15 years and played under him for seven and it seemed an odd decision. He wasn't in the habit of giving anything to the other side, or making a game of it.'[11]

Cronje, of course, did not publicly admit that night to the lengths he had gone to set up the run-chase. I was so surprised by what he had done that I put back my return flight to London to speak to him, and others, about the day's events. After attending the press conference, I returned to Sandton City to await Cronje's arrival at the hotel. Two hours after the England players had returned, many of the South Africans, including their captain, had still not come back. Unlike many other players, Cronje never showed up in the hotel bar that evening.

I contacted him next morning and we agreed to meet outside the hotel lifts in a couple of hours' time as he was then leaving for another appointment. When I buttonholed him, our arrangement had clearly already slipped his mind; he seemed puzzled as to what I was doing there. He appeared unwilling to talk but then he usually was, so I thought nothing of it. I put it to him that his adventurousness of the previous day had been a reaction against forever being labelled dull. He insisted it was not. He also insisted he had never revised his offer to England. This took me by surprise, as I had already spoken to Hussain and Stewart and heard their sides of the story. 'My first offer was my only offer,' he maintained. I was so taken aback I went back to Stewart to check I had not made a mistake. Unable to come up with an explanation for the differing accounts, I agreed with my desk not to run a story. Cronje, in fact, was still receiving widespread praise for what were seen as his efforts to enhance the image of the game. Minutes after the game finished, Ali Bacher, as one-track as ever, had declared, 'We are very proud of our country.'[12]

When the full story came out, Cronje still claimed to have played to win. 'The match delivered a genuine result and was in no way manipulated,' he said. But so generous was his declaration, the cricket did not need to be manipulated. Hussain felt differently. England's victory had been 'ruined'. Another England player, Michael Atherton, wrote, 'looking back, it is easy to see that Cronje's bowling changes and field placings … were designed to prevent the draw'. 'It will always be remembered,' added Hussain, 'as the Test that was fixed.'[13]

I later discovered two reasons why I had not seen Cronje around the hotel that final evening. One was that he had another meeting with Aronstam, who handed him a leather jacket and £800 in two cash amounts. 'I believed this to be the gift he had spoken of,' Cronje said. But the money Aronstam gave him was not in recognition of what had occurred at Centurion (from which Aronstam had been unable to benefit), but a deposit on future information. This, Cronje duly provided during the triangular one-day series that followed. Aronstam insisted that all it amounted to was Cronje's assessment of pitch conditions,[14] although a 'particularly accurate' forecast on one Zimbabwe total earned Cronje an extra £300.[15] Aronstam regarded his outlay as a drop in the ocean; he said a professional gambler could earn ten times the money from one match alone.[16]

The other distraction that evening was a meeting arranged by the 'hanger-on', Hamid Cassim. Cassim had taken a phone call from Ali Irani telling him that Reena Desai, an Indian film actress, was arriving in Johannesburg; Irani asked him to pick her up from the airport. During the drive, Desai had told Cassim that she would like to meet Hansie Cronje and Jonty Rhodes. Cassim said he would see what he could do. The final evening of the Centurion Test was when the meeting took place. Rhodes had not been playing, but Desai met Cronje, Gibbs, Lance Klusener and Shaun Pollock.

What was interesting about this meeting was how Cronje behaved in front of the film star. Cassim said it was the first time he ever heard Cronje talk about 'money on matches'.[17]

It must have made a bizarre scene. Here was the South Africa team, still absorbing the shock of losing a Test for reasons most could not comprehend, being introduced to an attractive celebrity. 'Guys, this is Reena, she's come over from India and was most anxious to meet some famous sportsmen. Reena, this is Hansie, our captain, Shaun, Lance and Herschelle…'. And there was Hansie, the man who never gave the other side anything, smiling and chatting enthusiastically, as though handing a Test on a plate to the opposition was something he did every day. And then he moved onto his favourite subject, money. But this time it was different. It was not stock markets, but the volume of money gambled on matches. Nor did he seem to mind if the 'hanger-on' heard him.

He seemed to be showing off in front of his Bollywood actress. How very unoriginal.

Two DAYS LATER CRONJE met Cassim again at the Wanderers in Johannesburg, shortly before the first match in the triangular series. Cassim stopped him on his way to the nets and said he had someone else he would like the South Africa captain to meet. Cassim also said that if he had known Cronje was going to declare at Centurion, he could have 'made himself some good money'. Cronje replied, 'Why didn't you ask?'[18]

By his own admission, it was this encounter with Cassim – rather than the subsequent one with Sanjay – that marked a fatal moment for Cronje, the moment that led directly to his downfall three months later. 'Since that day, in a moment of stupidity and weakness, I allowed Satan and the world to dictate terms to me, rather than the Lord,' he wrote in his original confession. 'Hamid called me almost four times a day from then on.'[19] Cassim's explanation for the frequency of calls was that Cronje had promised him a T-shirt, which he eventually picked up from Cronje in Sandton 'at a quarter past twelve in the night'.

Ten days after that, Hamid 'Banjo' Cassim drove to Johannesburg airport to pick up Sanjiv Chawla. He took him back to his shop, where they shared a meal. Chawla then left for Durban, where South Africa were to play Zimbabwe, Cassim following a day later. Cassim would give the impression that it was Chawla who was interested in contacting Cronje, but Cassim himself phoned Cronje's number 28 times the day Chawla arrived in South Africa.[20]

Chawla implicitly denied everything that others allege followed. His solicitors issued a statement saying he never met Hansie Cronje or spoke to him on the telephone.[21] One of his brothers insisted he was never known as Sanjay.

Cronje's version of what happened in Durban was different. 'Hamid was at the hotel when we [the team] arrived. He introduced me to a man known to me only as Sanjay, who he said was from London. I was not told he was a bookmaker and thought he was a punter.' According to Cassim, the three of them met in Chawla's room for about ten minutes during which time Cronje and Chawla spoke of team selection, batting orders, bowlers and pitch conditions. At that point, five matches remained to be played in the triangular series. While they talked, Cassim said he watched cricket on the television; he heard the others talk about 'scores, pitches, players'.

Cronje said the conversation was broader than that. 'Hamid and Sanjay indicated that Sanjay wanted me to supply them with information, but did not specify what information. They also said that I could make a lot of money if we would lose a match. I said that I was not prepared to do it unless we were assured of a place in the final … I was spinning them along as I do not think that I had any real intention of throwing a match.' But only two weeks earlier he had apparently volunteered to throw a match in the same tournament for Marlon Aronstam.

Shortly before the meeting ended, Cronje says, Chawla handed him some money. There were different versions about how the money was presented, how much there was and what it was for. Cassim said it was taken out of a safe and handed over in an envelope; Cronje said it came in a mobile phone box. The amount that became widely accepted was $10,000–15,000, but this stemmed from Cronje's written confession, and, as we have seen, Rory Steyn saw Cronje revise this figure from $20,000–25,000. Cronje said he never knew the precise amount. 'I did not count the money, which was kept in a filing cabinet at home together with my prize-money from the World Cup, the Kenya tour, and left-over sustenance allowances ... and travel allowances for what proved to be an abortive benefit tour to the sub-continent.'[22]

Cronje later admitted the money was downpayment on $100,000 (about £67,000) that would be his if he fixed a one-day match. When he and Chawla parted, he says, the matter as to whether he would fix a match had not been fully resolved, presumably due to Cronje's insistence that he would only throw a game if it was 'dead'. 'Sanjay handed me [the money] in case I changed my mind,' he stated. According to Cassim, Chawla had said, 'Keep this and we'll talk later.'[23] Cassim, who claimed he was surprised Cronje took the money, returned to Johannesburg once the meeting was over.

South Africa surprisingly lost the match to Zimbabwe by two wickets but went on to reach the triangular final without the luxury of a 'dead' game.

'It was not initially my intention to throw any games or to fix results: driven by greed and stupidity, and the lure of easy money, I thought that I could feed Sanjay information and keep the money without having to do anything to influence matches,' Cronje said. 'In fact there was no manipulation of games or results [in the triangular tournament] in South Africa, and I supplied no information in respect of the matches in South Africa.' Except, of course, the 'particularly accurate' information in respect of a Zimbabwe total he passed to Aronstam.

The claim that Cronje received money from Chawla for the relatively innocent exchange of 'information and forecasting' did not come from himself. Nor did it appear in his written confession or at his press conference in Cape Town. It originated at Ali Bacher's own press conference the same day. Bacher later admitted, 'The phrase "information and forecasting" was my own guess as to what Cronje had received the money for.' Bacher also surmised that Cronje had been blackmailed by Sanjay: 'The guy said if you change your mind ... if you don't cooperate, I'll run to your board.'[24]

It may not have been blackmail, but Cronje knew he was now trapped. In his first meeting with Sanjay, the conversation had touched on South Africa's forthcoming tour of India. Cronje recalled, 'I told him that maybe [in] the first one-day international in India I could see what could be done, thinking that if we could get the match out of the way, we'd get rid of them [Sanjay and Cassim] and could then focus purely on cricket.'[25] He added, 'I realise now that the purpose of the payment was to "hook" me for the Indian tour.'[26]

And it did.

12

CRONJE AND SANJAY IN INDIA

ndia was of special significance for the new South Africa. Politically, a cricket tour by a South Africa team could never be an ordinary tour; history decreed otherwise. South Africa owed black nations a great deal and had to be seen repaying its debts.

A few months after South Africa were readmitted to the ICC in 1991 following the collapse of apartheid, Pakistan's tour to India was cancelled because of tensions between Hindus and Muslims, and an ideal opportunity had presented itself for a goodwill visit. A South Africa team led by Clive Rice duly travelled to India to play a series of one-day matches. The flight into Calcutta was said to be the first from South Africa ever to land in India and the team's arrival met with the special blessing of the Marxist government of West Bengal. Thousands lined the route from the airport to the players' hotel and the opening encounter, watched by a crowd of 90,000, was marked by the symbolic release of doves.

In terms of winning and losing, the tour meant next to nothing. Results were irrelevant. But the situation nine years on was very different. India had not been beaten in a home Test series for more than ten years and if the South Africans were to aspire to Australia's unofficial world Test championship crown, they needed to end that long unbeaten run. South Africa's tour of India in 2001 was one on which winning and losing should have meant a great deal.

But South Africa's captain viewed things from a more complex viewpoint. He had been on the 1991 tour as a development player and was perfectly aware of the diplomatic implications of any visit to India. But then in 1996 he had returned to the country and succumbed to the bookies' overtures, taking bribes worth more than £50,000 and being offered another bribe on behalf of the team worth £200,000. Only a few days before leaving for this latest tour, he had twice suggested to other 'bookies' that he might be willing to throw matches. Cronje's tour of India in 1996 had been shameful. The mission of 2001 got off on completely the wrong foot.

One of the worst aspects of his behaviour was that he not only stooped so low himself but used his position to encourage two of the least experienced and most impressionable members of his party into literally gambling with their futures for the sake of a few thousand pounds. Herschelle Gibbs and Henry Williams admired Cronje, would have followed him anywhere and done anything for him. If he was prepared to do something, however questionable, so were they. He took advantage of this and it led to both losing a great deal in terms of prestige and self-regard. Gibbs was a good enough player to resurrect his international career, though precariously; Williams was not. What was more, they were the only two non-white members of the whole party. It was perhaps the blackest mark of all against Cronje's conduct.

SANJIV CHAWLA REACHED India at about the same time as the South Africa team. It appeared he had left England by 19 February, the eve of the first Test in Mumbai. He checked into the Taj Palace, the hotel in which the teams were staying, and for the next three weeks appeared to shadow the South Africans' movements. He stayed in their hotels in Bangalore, where the second Test took place, and Kochi, the venue for the first of five one-dayers. It was alleged that in Mumbai and Kochi he gave as his home address Kishen Kumar's residence in Bandra. Kumar rejected suggestions that he paid Chawla's bills in these places.[1]

Chawla, his family and friends vigorously denied he went to India to contact cricketers. His brother Gagan said his sole purpose in being in Delhi was for the birth of Gagan's son, on 8 March. Kishen Kumar said Chawla came to India to buy a shop in Mumbai. But the evidence provided by Rajesh Kalra, the printer-bookie, to the police, and Hamid Cassim and Hansie Cronje to the King Commission, portrayed a different picture. Chawla and Cronje, it was alleged, had recently met at a hotel in Durban and money changed hands. Chawla, as we know, denied any such meeting ever took place.

It was further claimed that Chawla made many calls from India to Cassim in Johannesburg – Cassim himself put it at about 20 to 30 – asking for help in contacting Cronje, help that Cassim duly supplied.[2] One piece of evidence suggesting a link between Cronje and Chawla was that both men phoned Cassim from the Taj Residency in Kochi on the same day, the eve of the first one-day international.[3]

One minor mystery that would attach itself to the early days of the tour was the precise role of a Mumbai woman called Yasmeen who reportedly had links with the underworld and was thought to be known to the South Africa team.[4]

Cronje claimed he was continuously harassed by phone calls from Sanjay and Cassim; they rang him at all hours of day and night, as they had during the one-day series in South Africa.[5] 'In the build-up to the Tests, the pressure on me increased. I received calls on a regular basis from Hamid and Sanjay. Even when the cellphone was switched off, calls would come through to my room as late as two and three o'clock in the morning. I felt increasingly trapped. I had already taken money from Sanjay and it became increasingly difficult to resist his requests to speak to other team members and manipulate results.'[6]

Cronje was indeed trapped, because without admitting his culpability to his own cricket board or the police – an act that would have led to his certain disgrace – there could be no escape. If Sanjay was to be satisfied, Cronje's only option was to fix matches, or at least appear to fix them.

However, it was far from certain that Cronje's portrayal of himself as cornered victim was entirely accurate at this early stage of the tour. This was a claim he made after his exposure, when it might have been to his advantage to shift the blame for what had happened onto the shoulders of others. So, while it may be true that Sanjay and Cassim gave him no respite, it may also be the case that when contact was renewed at the start of the tour, Cronje remained eager to earn the considerable sums on offer. The money he had received in Durban was, after all, a downpayment on almost £70,000 available to him if he could fix the result of a one-day match. A similar amount may have been available if he could arrange the outcome of a Test. If he pulled off a number of fixes, he stood to make a small fortune. If the Indian police were right, there was a plan to fix several matches for a total of more than £1.5 million. Cronje's share was potentially considerable.

In his original statement to the King Commission, Cronje claimed he was initially reluctant to recruit players to help him fix matches: 'I initially had no intention of involving other players and thought that I could satisfy Sanjay by accurately forecasting outcomes. Sanjay was not satisfied with this, and pressured me to speak to some of the other players to manipulate results.'

But the facts suggest a great deal of pressure may not have been necessary. Only seventeen days had elapsed since the meeting with Sanjay in Durban, and only seven days since his own arrival in India, when Cronje, supposedly feeling 'increasingly trapped', first approached a teammate in the hoping of persuading him to throw not merely a one-day game (as had been discussed, but not finalised, in Durban) but the first Test of an important series. Three weeks after that, Cronje, far from doing everything in his power to distance himself from someone putting him under intolerable pressure, took receipt of a mobile phone from Sanjay, thereby cementing their lines of communication rather than breaking them.

Cronje's argument looked weaker still when it was remembered that during the India tour he remained in contact with Marlon Aronstam. Aronstam phoned him on a few occasions, 'to encourage the team to win and to congratulate us on wins but, apart from general discussions, did not request information or offer me anything'.[7]

It would only have been natural had Cronje found it difficult to approach his players. He must have feared picking the wrong person, someone who would not only reject the idea but, worse still, link a fresh approach with the collective offer put to the team by Cronje in India in 1996, and go running to the authorities. Survivors from the previous India tour included Daryll Cullinan, Gary Kirsten, Derek Crookes, Lance Klusener and Herschelle Gibbs, who at 26 was the youngest of this group. Along with the now retired Andrew Hudson, Cullinan and Crookes led the opposition that resulted in the rejection of the 1996 offer; Gibbs, as a junior member of that party, had hardly participated in the debate.

Then there was his proposal that a positive result be contrived in the Test at Centurion the previous month. How many players had got wind of what Cronje had been up to there? Nobody may have known of his discussions with Aronstam but he had asked Pieter Strydom to place a bet on his behalf.

It seemed that Cronje's teammates may have suspected something. When news broke of what had been going on during the India tour, one of them was quoted as saying, 'I never knew anything or noticed anything suspicious … I knew about Centurion but I didn't know anything about India.'[8]

Yet in the space of 30 days Cronje took near-insane risks by broaching the subject of match-fixing with as many as six teammates.

It was perhaps understandable that the first man he should have gone to was Strydom. Strydom agreeing to try to lay a bet on his captain's behalf at Centurion was in its way a trifling and harmless thing to do, but it may have suggested to Cronje that here was someone prepared to do more. Moreover, Strydom was 30 years old and had come to international cricket late; Cronje might have reasoned that his view would be that his opportunities were limited and he ought to cash in while he could. But if Cronje thought that, he was wrong.

The day before the Mumbai Test started, Cronje called Strydom to his room in the Taj and, according to Strydom, light-heartedly spoke to him about a £7,000 offer for South Africa to score fewer than 250. 'We can get 70,000 rand if we get out for less than 250,' Cronje said. Strydom knew Cronje could be a practical joker and declined the offer. He reminded his captain he was about to play only his second Test; had he played 75 or 80 Tests, he said, he might have thought about it. When he left Cronje's room he felt pleased with himself. 'I thought maybe I'd passed the test,' he commented.

Later that day, he bumped into Cronje. Cronje nudged him and said, 'How about 140 [thousand rand]?' Strydom, maybe thinking the test had not finished, declined again.[9]

Cronje did not take the matter further. 'At the time of speaking to him [Strydom] I was already racked with guilt, and his remarks about doing his best for South Africa shamed me and he in no way indicated that he was interested in receiving money,' he said. 'I did not speak to any other members of the team. Thereafter I tried to pass off the whole incident with Strydom as a joke.'[10]

South Africa, batting second after India scored 225, were dismissed for 176, collapsing badly after openers Kirsten and Gibbs shared a stand of 90. Cronje, batting at number four, was out for nought and Strydom, who came in next, for only two. Strydom later said to his captain, 'We could have made some money.'

South Africa mounted an excellent recovery to win the match by four wickets. India were all out for 113 second time around, their star, Sachin Tendulkar, contributing only 8 before falling leg-before to Cronje, who finished the match with five wickets. Pursuing 163, South Africa were given another good start by Kirsten and Gibbs before there was another collapse – Cronje and Strydom both failed again – and it needed cool work from Mark Boucher and Jacques Kallis to see them to victory.

Efforts were then made to fix the second Test at Bangalore, which took place seven days later. Cronje – 'under further pressure from Sanjay' – sought fresh accomplices. The arrangement was that if India scored 200 or more in their first innings, South Africa (meaning Cronje and anyone he could enlist) would aim to lose the match. If India scored less than 200, the deal was off.

Motivated either by the need to satisfy Sanjay, or personal greed, Cronje was now to display signs of the dangerously irrational behaviour of which John Blair, the Free State Cricket Union official, had warned. Apparently oblivious to the risks he was running, he turned to three cricketers whose taste for such an enterprise he ought to have doubted – Kallis, Boucher and Lance Klusener.

All three had played in the Test at Centurion and been opposed to Cronje's suggestion of a staged finish; Kallis later told the King Commission he was strongly against the idea. Klusener, moreover, was a member of the 1996 side that had rejected the offer in Mumbai. In his own evidence to the King inquiry, Klusener made it plain that he held Cronje responsible for that offer getting as far as a team discussion. 'Whoever received the call should have said we would have nothing to do with it,' he said. Surely the fact that his captain was relaying another offer would not go undetected by Klusener?

Perhaps Cronje never planned the approach, perhaps an opportunity simply presented itself and he took it. Either way, he was alone with them one evening shortly before the Test. Boucher and Kallis, who were roommates, had ordered too much pasta and invited their teammates to share it. Several players went to the room but by the time Cronje arrived only this pair and Klusener remained.

Cronje told them there was an offer for them all to make money during the Bangalore Test. All would later say Boucher, Kallis and Klusener rejected the idea without hesitation, but precisely how they interpreted Cronje's suggestion was less clear cut.[11] The three claimed to have viewed Cronje's behaviour as a joke but Kallis said they had told their captain 'in harsh words' that they were not interested, which suggested that the conversation actually had a serious edge to it. Cronje was uncertain what they had really thought. 'I think they thought I was joking,' he said.

Were the suspicions of Boucher, Kallis or Klusener aroused? Publicly they would insist not, but there were good reasons for not admitting to having suspected anything. Had they been suspicious, they would have been under a moral obligation to inform the authorities and that ran the risk of them being accused of squealing on a teammate. It was certainly simpler and safer to say they had suspected nothing.

The full story will probably never be known, but as a theory took hold that a teammate did indeed blow the whistle on the South Africa captain, it is worth exploring the possibility that one of these three might have been the person in question.

Kallis can almost certainly be discounted. Although he and Shaun Pollock were possibly the most gifted allround cricketers in the team, Kallis lacked – in the view of Clive Rice, who knew him well – the vision to grasp the wider implications of the game. Having gone through his schooldays in the Cape concentrating on sport rather than academic studies, Kallis lacked the native intelligence that might have made him a future captain. In short, he lacked the nous to see Cronje's behaviour for what it was, or if he did, to act upon it. In any case, when Cronje began disputing his life ban, Kallis shocked many by publicly speaking out in favour of his former captain returning to the team – and claimed other players shared his view.

Boucher was altogether shrewder. As a wicketkeeper, he was trained to take a broader view of the game, to think like a captain even if he was not one, and assess each player's actions on their merits. Even by the uncompromising standards of international wicketkeepers, Boucher played the game with an ingrained pragmatism, and no one, not even Cronje, would have found it easy to pull the wool over his eyes. Later, as events unfolded, Boucher was to display immense integrity. But it emerged during the King Commission that on the day Cronje confessed, Boucher went to Ghulam Raja, the South Africa team manager, and told him of Cronje's suggestion in Bangalore that they take a bribe. He would have hardly done this had he already spoken of his suspicions about his captain.

The case of Klusener was the most intriguing. As we have seen, relations between the two men were already cool. But the antipathy may have had more to it than a straightforward difference of opinion about how Klusener should approach his cricket.

As a person, Klusener could not have been more different from Cronje. He was unconventional and did not fit comfortably into the team on a personal or cricketing level. He had done things with his life other than just play sport in the narrow confines of white society. He grew up on his parents' sugar-cane farm in Natal and had retained the independence of a country boy. The fact that as a child he had played with the children of black farm workers, and learned to speak to them in Zulu, had marked him out with Cronje and other white members of the team, who nicknamed him 'Zulu'. At around the time Cronje began playing international cricket, Klusener was serving in the South African army. He voluntarily extended his one year of national service to three. This only served to make him more independent. He doubtless saw things in the army that he could not speak of to outsiders. But perhaps he simply bridled at Cronje's dictatorial style.

A few months after his success at the 1999 World Cup, I interviewed Klusener for *Wisden*. He had been chosen as one of the almanack's cricketers of the year. The encounter demonstrated to me just what a cool customer he was. Klusener was a notoriously reluctant interviewee; interviews were just not things he gave. I approached him while in Bloemfontein seeing Cronje. He had just finished a morning practice session. He fairly bluntly declined: now was not a good time, he said, without suggesting he had any urgent appointments to keep. But persisting, I took his mobile phone number and managed to set up a meeting in Johannesburg two weeks later.

We met in the lobby of the Sandton Sun, the same hotel in which I would fruitlessly wait for Cronje two months later. Klusener had the build of a commando and administered a crunching handshake before sitting down. Needing to draw out of him various biographical details, I tried to get the conversation flowing with small talk. It had absolutely no impact. He simply stared straight at me with piercing eyes. 'When are we getting down to business?' he seemed to be asking. For veiled hostility, only Steve Waugh came into the same category. No wonder nobody bothered interviewing him.

He told me what I needed to know, but his answers were tailored with military unfussiness. 'Of course cricket is about luck,' he said, in explanation of his phenomenal success. 'Balls go in the air and fall in gaps, but hitting does not just happen. You have to learn to improvise and be at peace with what you do.' He struck me as the sort of person who would see through any artifice. The idea that he would have interpreted Cronje's approach in Bangalore as a joke was implausible. The underlying seriousness to Cronje's jokes would not have been lost on someone with a discerning eye. Many a true word spoken in jest, Klusener might have thought.

Equally hard to countenance was the possibility that Klusener would not have made the connection between Cronje's proposal in Bangalore and the offer in Mumbai four years earlier, an offer which Klusener felt should never have been put to the team. If anyone spoke harshly to Cronje over their plates of pasta in the hotel in Bangalore, it was surely Klusener.

There was, as we shall see, circumstantial evidence that the relationship between Cronje and Klusener came under increased strain after Bangalore, suggesting that Klusener's attitude towards his captain hardened after the incident there.

Did Cronje ever suspect anyone was on to his dark secret? Following his rebuttal by Klusener, Kallis and Boucher, he said he did not approach any other players and as a result, the Test in Bangalore was not fixed.

As it happened, India, batting first after winning the toss, failed to score the 200 runs that would have been necessary to trigger the conditional fix discussed by Cronje and Sanjay. All six bowlers used by South Africa took at least one wicket, Cronje himself chipping in with the important one of Rahul Dravid, and they restricted India to 158 all out in 83 overs.

By batting two days for 479, South Africa then built up an impregnable lead, in large part because Klusener and Kallis both made nineties. Cronje, going in at 435 for five, was out for 12. They went on to complete an historic series win by bowling out India cheaply for a second time. Nicky Boje, a left-arm spinner playing only his second Test, took the match award for his 85 runs as nightwatchman and seven wickets.

South Africa thus celebrated an historic Test series win and the stock of their long-serving captain rose to new heights.

In WINNING MATCHES, Cronje was succeeding where he was supposed to fail and, in not managing to fix games, failing where he was supposed to succeed. Meanwhile, the phone calls demanding action did not let up. Perhaps by now he was starting to feel at least a little trapped. With no one apparently willing to help him fix games, he could not go forward. And going back was not an option.

Three days after the Test series finished, the first of the one-dayers took place in Kochi, the match about which Cronje had said he might 'see what could be done'. However, this now looked a distant prospect. But equally the phone calls told him he had to offer Cassim and Sanjay something.

He wriggled, but Sanjay would not let him off his hook. Cronje suggested simply forecasting how the match in Kochi might go, based on what he knew of the respective sides, the pitch and weather conditions, 'thinking that if we could get the match out of the way that might satisfy them'.[12] But Sanjay rejected the idea out of hand.

The match was almost upon them and still nothing was settled. The night before the game, Cronje's phone kept ringing but he ignored it; he knew it would be Sanjay and Cassim and he had nothing for them. But the next morning Cassim phoned again and this time Cronje answered. Cassim urged him to go ahead and Cronje must have told him he would think about it because he soon phoned Cassim back.[13]

In the interim, Cronje came up with a plan, a middle way. He decided he would pretend to Cassim and Sanjay that he was speaking to other players about fixing matches. He later admitted he had intended to do this only for the first one-dayer: 'I suggested that I would speak to some of the other players, lying to him [Sanjay] to get rid of him after the first match ... I told them we would lose and that I had spoken to other players.'[14] The names he gave were those of Gibbs, Boje and Strydom, the same three names Marlon Aronstam said Cronje gave him as potential accomplices.

Why Cronje named these three as opposed to any other players is unclear. He was perhaps closer to Gibbs and Boje than any other players in the team. Both described Cronje as their friend, though these were friendships of a rather unequal sort – perhaps the only sort of friendship Cronje was capable of forming. All his players viewed him with deference, but Cronje was looked upon by this pair – each of them, at 26, four years younger than their captain and vastly less experienced cricketers – with particular reverence.

Boje was only a marginal figure in the team. He played his first Tests on this tour and had appeared in only 23 one-day internationals in five years, but as another Afrikaner son of Bloemfontein, Grey College and Free State Cricket Union, he had known Cronje for years. Gibbs was a more regular member of the side. He was a highly gifted allround sportsman who had represented South African Schools at cricket, rugby and football, but sport was all he knew; it was said he had never read a book in his life.

One South African journalist referred to Boje as Cronje's 'faithful lieutenant', while Gibbs admitted he would do anything for Cronje, to the point that he willingly agreed to Cronje's instruction to lie to the South African board and commission of inquiry. 'I was happy to go along with whatever he asked me to,' he said.[15]

So, at last, the bookies thought they had a deal with Cronje: South Africa were to lose the first one-dayer in Kochi.

However, things went wrong because when it came to it, Cronje could not bring himself to underperform. 'We were supposed to lose the match but I couldn't go through with it,' he said. 'I decided that I couldn't not try and would give it my best shot … India won quite comfortably after [Nantie] Hayward was injured. I honestly tried to win the match, even at that stage, and believe we would have done so if Hayward was not injured.'

Events seemed to support his account and if Sanjay thought Cronje was working with Gibbs, Boje and Strydom to bring about a South Africa defeat he must have been surprised at some of the things that happened. Strydom did not even play. Then, after Cronje won the toss and chose to bat first on a superb pitch, Gibbs gave his side a magnificent start in partnership with Gary Kirsten. Both men made centuries, Gibbs scoring 111 off 127 balls and Kirsten 115 off 123. Admittedly, Gibbs gave stumping chances in the thirties and sixties that were spurned by the Indian wicketkeeper. Cronje himself went out to bat at 249 for three with seven overs remaining and contributed 19 from 20 balls.

Crucially, this late spurt took South Africa's total to 301, beyond a ceiling agreed between Cronje and Sanjay. It must have looked a pretty safe limit, for few teams score more than 300 in their 50 overs, and had South Africa scored, say, 290 and lost, presumably the bookies would have cleaned up and Cronje would have been paid. But as it was, South Africa's high total proved expensive for both parties.

Despite being faced with such a big total, India won thanks to several solid contributions. They got home with three wickets and two balls to spare. Cronje dismissed Ajay Jadeja and Rahul Dravid but conceded 48 runs in his eight overs; Boje's six overs cost 34. One of the key moments occurred in the final over when Shaun Pollock's second delivery was called no-ball by one of the umpires, even though television replays suggested he had not overstepped.

Cronje's attempted deception had misfired and he was now in

worse odour with Sanjay than ever. 'When I got back to the hotel Sanjay was upset because we had scored too many runs, and I blamed the Indian wicketkeeper for three chances that he missed, obviously not revealing that the South African players concerned had not been involved and in fact none of them knew anything about it. I did not receive any money for that match. I believe Sanjay lost money.'[16] In fact, not only Sanjay, but Rajesh Kalra too. Kalra, who alleged he and Kishen Kumar were sometimes present when Chawla spoke on the phone to Cronje, told police he and Chawla fell out badly over South Africa scoring more than 300 in this game.[17]

'Hamid kept phoning me and saying that I should speak to Sanjay, who was now worse off than before, that he needed to win some money, and that I would have to deliver something,' Cronje said. 'So intense had the incessant nagging become that I was pressured to fabricate a story that the players were angry with me for not getting their money…'.[18]

However, the ugly mood Cronje seemed determined to paint with these words was dispelled somewhat when he recounted how Sanjay wrapped up the conversation: 'He said not to worry, he would make up for it during the rest of the one-day series.'

It was not clear whether a deal was struck regarding the second match at Jamshedpur three days later. Cronje again won the toss and chose to bat, and without him South Africa would have lost more heavily than they did. He was comfortably their top-scorer, with 71 off 86 balls, and played confidently for a man short of runs until he holed out tamely in the deep. He did not bowl himself until the game, which India won by six wickets with 17 balls to spare, was effectively over.

Gibbs, Boje and Strydom all played. Gibbs batted briskly for 27 off 28 balls, Boje relatively slowly for 28 off 44, though he bowled an economical spell of one for 34 from his ten overs, while Strydom batted only briefly and was one of the more expensive bowlers, conceding 57 runs from his ten overs.

HANSIE CRONJE HAD been foolish on many occasions up to this point, but he now made his biggest mistake. He had taken risks in raising the subject of match-fixing with teammates; now he was to further expose himself to the risk of discovery by accepting a free mobile phone from Sanjay. This one act would prove his undoing.

Sanjay handed him the phone for two reasons. First, it was another means of maintaining contact with the South Africa captain. The bookie knew the number, and the player, with nothing to pay, was more likely to use it and keep it switched on. It was, in fact, a standard tactic: many players were offered or given mobile phones by bookies. Dean Jones had declined one as early as 1992.

Secondly, Sanjay may have been eager to secure his lines of communication because, after three weeks away, he was returning to England. Chawla reportedly flew to London via Moscow on 15 March, the day of the third one-day international in Faridabad.[19] The day beforehand, it was alleged, he went to the Taj Palace hotel in Delhi, where the players were staying, called Cronje from the lobby and asked if he could see him in his room 'for a few minutes'. Cronje agreed and told him he was in room 346.[20] There, Chawla handed Cronje a phone (number 98 102 94943) and said he would be contacting him on that number in future.[21] The phone was actually owned by Rajesh Kalra.[22]

If Cronje was concerned at the thought that a man whom he alleged was harassing him was now in an even better position to keep in contact with him, he did not seem to show it. The next day he saw his players in the dressing room. 'I've got some good news,' he announced. 'I've been given a mobile phone which we can make free calls on. A bloke just said, "Call who you like."' In the coming days, they would do just that. The calls would vary from Cronje's conversations with bookies to one player having phone-sex with his girlfriend.

With Cronje in India and his 'spymaster' back in London, they were further apart than they had been for some time. But they were far from alone.

13

THE PHONE TAPS

Unbeknown to Hansie Cronje, the mobile phone handed to him by Sanjay was bugged by the Indian police. Everything the two of them said was monitored and recorded. Every word Cronje uttered tightened the noose around his neck.

In one sense it was sheer bad luck that he was brought down by a police investigation apparently completely unrelated to anything to do with him; sheer luck that the blight affecting cricket was revealed for all to see. In another, it was inevitable that eventually he would be caught out. He was courting danger trying to corrupt teammates and outwit the underworld. Sooner or later, he was going to come to a bad end. That time had now arrived.

The situation arose when two Mumbai businessmen went to the police for help, saying they were receiving extortion threats.[1] Their names were never made public though it has been reliably suggested that one was Kishen Kumar but it was revealed that some of the calls came from Dubai and some were traced to an underworld figure.[2] As a result, several phones were bugged by anti-extortion officers.

Some of these phones belonged to people based in Delhi and one was registered in the name of Rajesh Kalra but apparently in the possession of Sanjiv Chawla – the one that found its way into the possession of Cronje. 'We began monitoring some phones, from which certain businessmen were receiving extortion threats,' one source confirmed. 'One of these numbers was Chawla's.'[3]

Naturally, the police were surprised to find that the conversations they monitored included some containing references to pitches and players. Once they realised what they had stumbled on they naturally sought to gather as much evidence as they could to corroborate what looked like attempts to fix international cricket matches.

'Available information with the anti-extortion cell of crime branch … revealed that some businessmen of India were in contact with certain South African players for match-fixing in the recently held Pepsi Cup one-day international cricket series between India and South Africa,' said KK Paul, the joint commissioner of Delhi police's crime division. 'As such, as per provisions of law, requisite permission for monitoring the telephone/cellphone was obtained.'[4]

The bugging began on 14 March, the day Cronje was visited by Sanjay in his hotel room, and continued for about ten days until he left India for Sharjah. During that time, more than seven hours of conversations were fed onto tapes.[5] Many of them were innocuous but those between Cronje and Sanjay, two men speaking in their second language, regarding the last three one-dayers in India, were absolute dynamite.

Their subsequent publication was a thunderbolt to Cronje, causing in him that 'horrible sinking feeling' that he would never play for South Africa again.[6] He had been caught red-handed and knew it. The complacent assumption that he would never be found out had been smashed.

The published transcripts contained a wealth of detail – thirteen cricketers were mentioned by name – and Cronje was left waging a desperate rearguard over their precise meaning. He argued that the negotiations between himself and Sanjay caught on the tapes were essentially bogus: Cronje never intended to fix matches and was simply 'stringing him along'.[7] It was an argument that was never conclusively proved one way or the other.

ANOTHER THEORY SURFACED as to how the police got onto Cronje. The day after Cronje confessed, and four days after Delhi's crime branch released its first transcripts of the Cronje–Sanjay conversations, the *Gulf News*, a Dubai-based newspaper, ran a story claiming Lance Klusener had blown the whistle on his captain.

The newspaper quoted an unnamed senior Delhi officer as saying, 'Klusener called up police following an argument with his skipper in the lobby of New Delhi's Taj Palace hotel … Following a tip-off, we decided to tap Cronje's mobile phone.'[8]

The story seemed to have been inspired by a passage in one transcript in which Cronje and Sanjay were talking on the eve of the third one-dayer in Faridabad. The conversation must have occurred within hours of Cronje taking receipt of the phone.

Sanjay wanted to confirm which players were ready to 'work' for them and Cronje – by his own account, 'stringing him along' – ran through with him the names of those supposedly willing to assist. 'Prior to the third one-day international, I had untruthfully told Sanjay that Boje, Strydom and Gibbs were involved,' Cronje recalled. 'He therefore wanted to know if they would be playing … and if further players could be involved.'[9]

The transcript ran as follows:

Sanjay: Is Strydom playing?

Hansie: Yes, he is playing. Yeah.

Sanjay: Boje?

Hansie: Boje is playing.

Sanjay: Yeah, Boje is playing … And who is playing? Gibbs?

Hansie: Gibbs and myself.

Sanjay: Yeah, what about anybody else?

Hansie: No, I won't be able to get more.

Sanjay: You won't be able to get more.

Hansie: No.

Sanjay: Okay, just tell me. But you have only four with you and not anybody else?

Hansie: No.

Sanjay: Klusener and no one?

Hansie: No. No. Impossible, impossible.[10]

No. No. Impossible, impossible. Why was Cronje's denial so firm in the case of Klusener? Did it indicate, as some suspected, that Klusener was in some way 'out of bounds' as a potential recruit? Did Klusener suspect what Cronje was up to?

The day the *Gulf News* story appeared, many attempts were made by journalists to substantiate it, without success. Indian police sources denied the story, though not too much could be read into that because they denied other things that turned out to be true. Klusener was contacted for his reaction and issued a firm denial. 'I know nothing of this entire issue,' he said. 'I have never ever had an argument with anyone. This is ridiculous. It's absolutely crazy. I did not know there was something on the go.' Asked why he thought anyone would want to implicate him in such a story, he suggested, 'It may be to drive a wedge in the team.'[11]

The story was outlandish. Even if Klusener was convinced Cronje was involved in something, it seemed unlikely he would contact the police. Surely the first thing he would have done was speak to the team management or senior officials at the South African board. And even if he – or someone acting on his behalf such as the team's security officer – had gone to the police, the police would have been reluctant to tap the phone of a foreign cricketer. In any case, they would have surely targeted Cronje's own mobile rather than one given to him by someone else. 'At no stage in this process was the telephone or cellphone of any South African player "bugged",' said Harsh Bhasin, India's High Commissioner to South Africa.[12]

What was believable was that one of the South Africa players, perhaps Klusener, had seen a suspicious-looking character hanging around the hotels, possibly trying to strike up friendships with the team, and had called on the police to get the person removed. Perhaps Klusener and Cronje argued about whether the man was entitled to hang around or not. The incident could have happened without being connected to the phone-tapping. The transcripts make clear that Cronje and Sanjay used at least one go-between.

But in journalistic circles the story refused to die. Relations between Klusener and his captain were known to be cool; it was said that by the end they were not even on speaking terms. A row, either earlier in the day on which the taped conversation took place or the previous day when they had arrived in Delhi from Jamshedpur, seemed perfectly plausible. Some sources suggested Klusener was again unhappy at being given a marginal role, though this was not obviously borne out by the facts. He had batted at number four in the first two one-day internationals (facing four balls in the first and 33 in the second) and although he bowled in neither, he was believed to have been carrying a foot injury since the first Test.

Could anything be read into what had happened in the Faridabad match? If the plan was for South Africa to lose, it failed: they got home by two wickets with six balls to spare. Cronje sent down ten overs for 69 (much the most expensive of the South African bowlers) but perhaps did most to help his team reach their target of 249, scoring 66 off 71 balls and sharing a stand of 113 with Gary Kirsten. They both fell in a collapse that saw four wickets go in seven overs before Mark Boucher and Shaun Pollock settled the issue. As for Klusener, Cronje gave him two overs, costing 11 runs, and dropped him to number seven for the slog overs at which he was so expert. He went in with eleven overs remaining and scored 6 off 16 balls.

It seemed particular suspicions were aroused by this game. When Pieter Strydom was questioned by the King Commission, he said that after the story broke, Cronje had told him, 'They [the police] were talking about the one-dayers, the third and fifth one-dayers in India.'[13]

Going by the transcripts, the next time Cronje and Sanjay spoke was on the day between the third one-dayer in Faridabad and the fourth in Baroda.[14] They had not spoken for some time – possibly two days – because Sanjay had been travelling back to England and probably held several conversations during the day. Cronje had been to the ground where the match would be played the next day.

Hansie: Okay, you are back in London?

Sanjay: Yeah, I am in London.

Hansie: I had a look at the pitch today, it can turn big.

Sanjay: It can turn big?

They talked again after. In his later account, Cronje maintained his line that he was still trying to hold off from striking any deals with Sanjay. In order to do so, he said, he now claimed that his co-conspirators were unhappy at not yet being paid for losing in Kochi, despite the fact the supposed deal had gone awry.

Hansie: No, no. They were saying that they were already doing Kochi. The other guys are already angry with me because I have not received their money, you know.

Sanjay: No. But I told you, I have already given him [presumably a go-between] altogether 60 [probably US $60,000]

Hansie: Okay.

Sanjay: And tomorrow I can deposit the money in your account. It is not a problem because of the time difference. Tomorrow itself I can deposit the money.

Hansie: Okay.

Despite this promise by Sanjay that he would pay money into Cronje's bank account, Cronje would later insist he received no money while in India.

Sanjay phoned him again to talk about the game in Baroda and they ended up discussing a script for the match in detail. If India batted first, they were to be allowed to score 300-plus; if South Africa batted first, they would not score more than 250.

Cronje pleaded that manipulating his team's performance would depend on who was bowling and asked if three Indian bowlers would be playing, spinners Sunil Joshi and Nikhil Chopra, and opening fast bowler Javagal Srinath. Sanjay would find out. He called back and said that he had been told (presumably by someone in the Indian camp) that Srinath and Joshi would play but Chopra would not. This turned out to be the case.

But yet again, the match went differently from the plot. On a good batting pitch South Africa scored 282, well in excess of their supposed upper limit, with everyone who batted scoring at a rate of around a run per ball. Jacques Kallis scored 81 not out, Gary Kirsten 72 and Klusener weighed in at the end with 14 off 9 deliveries. Interestingly, an Indian police source was reported as saying that they believed some members of the South Africa team might have got wind of a plot and aimed to sabotage it.

Cronje himself scored reasonably fast, making 26 off 27 balls; by the time he was out, at 181 for three in the 36th over, South Africa needed only to maintain a rate of 5 runs per over to exceed the supposed upper limit of 250.

The only thing that went according to plan was that South Africa lost, in large part thanks to a whirlwind opening partnership for India of 153 in 25 overs between Saurav Ganguly and Sachin Tendulkar. When Tendulkar was finally out for 122, only 27 more were needed off 29 balls, and although there was a mini-collapse, India scraped home by four wickets with one ball to spare. Cronje bowled six overs for 33.

Ironically, when I asked Raman Subba Row, the match referee, whether he had seen anything suspicious during this one-day series, he said the only incident that stuck in his mind was a dropped catch by Lance Klusener in the final over which reprieved Robin Singh, who survived to hit the winning runs.[15]

ACCORDING TO CRONJE, up until the fifth one-day international in Nagpur he had basically lied to Sanjay all along, telling him he had spoken to players when he had not and giving the impression that he – they – would tailor their performances to meet his needs. In fact, he had done nothing. He had failed to recruit anyone to help him fix two Tests and his promises regarding South Africa's totals in the one-day matches at Cochin and Baroda had come to nothing:

> During the second, third and fourth one-day games I was really only forecasting what I thought would happen, as I wanted to win the series. I received no money and tried my best throughout.
>
> The pressure on me to produce information and results was increasing. I was not only being repeatedly phoned by Hamid but also by Sanjay. I tried to deal with this by lying about having spoken to players and done things which I had not in fact done. I cannot recall all the names that I mentioned and I cannot remember all the figures and amounts. I cannot recall all the conversations, the times and dates, and what was said on each occasion. Also, a great deal of what I told Sanjay was untruthful, particularly about the involvement of other players.
>
> By the end of the tour I was under severe pressure to provide some results, and my attempts to string Sanjay along were no longer effective. He and Hamid had become increasingly upset by the fact that I had not delivered the required results, in consequence of which they had been losing more and more money.[16]

Sanjay, in fact, had become so frustrated with Cronje's erratic forecasting that he even complained about it in a call to his girlfriend.[17]

Sanjay phoned Cronje again on the eve of the final one-dayer. The transcript of the conversation began with Cronje referring to the game in Baroda – 'very close and I dropped a catch as well' – but then turned to a discussion about the game in Nagpur. With India having won the one-day series – they were 3–1 up with one to play – Cronje and Sanjay speculated whether they might alter their team. Sanjay seemed to think they would not; Cronje thought they would.

> Hansie: You must find out what team India's playing before we
> could do anything. Did you speak to Amit?
> Sanjay: Yeah, he just phoned me.
> Hansie: What team are India playing?

Sanjay: He is trying to find out but I doubt if they are going to play a weaker team because none of the players have a secure place like Ajay [Jadeja] or Azhar or Robin [Singh]. So I am sure that they would play. They would not change the winning combination.

Hansie: You think so?

Sanjay: I think.

Hansie: Okay, we must find out that first because obviously they are going to play … [names missing?] instead of Kumble and instead of Azhar, something like that, they … they are going to be much weaker you know … So you must find out what the team is before we can do anything.

Sanjay: All right OK but what if we cannot find out?

Hansie: No, you will be able to find out. I am sure you will be able to. Azhar must have an idea.

Sanjay: I cannot get through the hotel number. And if I phone anybody. I … well, I know [Nikhil] Chopra, I know Ajay [Jadeja] but if I phone them you know then it is going to be a bit suspicious because I hardly speak … to them today. I speak to them whenever I see them face to face otherwise…

Hansie: Yeah.

Sanjay: If I phone them it can be very suspicious.

Hansie: Also find out what is going on…

Sanjay: Yeah, they are in the same hotel, but you don't mention this to Azhar … because Azhar is one big mouth you know … he's going to make money out of nothing without his involvement.

Hansie: OK.

Sanjay: I am sure he is going to get a hint and is going to tell his people to put money on India.

Hansie: OK, don't worry.

Sanjay: Should I phone you back in 15 to 20 minutes?

Hansie: That's perfect.

Sanjay: Fifteen minutes.[18]

Rajesh Kalra later admitted to being asked by Chawla to phone

Nikhil Chopra and ask him if he was playing, 'probably in the India–South Africa one-day match at Nagpur'.[19] In the event, Chopra did play, one of three changes made by India; Cronje's reading of the situation had been correct.

Another conversation held later that day between Cronje and Sanjay showed plans further advanced. They discussed in which order Cronje would use his bowlers – a new development that may have been a compromise solution on Cronje's part. If fixing results or team totals was beyond him – either ideologically or because he was incapable of recruiting accomplices – manipulating minor aspects of matches was not. As captain, he could arrange these, as he was about to demonstrate.

> Hansie: I will give them [India] some runs. It is a small ground and it is a quick outfield so they must get 280 or 290.
> Sanjay: What is the minimum they should score?
> Hansie: 250.
> Sanjay: Minimum is 250.
> Hansie: Okay.
> Sanjay: If it is 249 it is off.
> Hansie: Yeah.
> Sanjay: Okay, can we make it 240 or can we make it 250?
> Hansie: Yeah, 250.
> Sanjay: And if you bat first?
> Hansie: Then we will try and get not more than 245 to 255 because it is a fast outfield and very small ground.
> Sanjay: Suppose it goes more than that. What's the target we should stand by you?
> Hansie: 270.
> Sanjay: Okay, if it touches 270, then it is off.
> …
> Sanjay: Who will bowl the first overs [for South Africa]?
> Hansie: Crookes and Williams.
> Sanjay: Who would bowl first change?
> Hansie: Klusener … Don't worry, we will be bowling with

non-regular bowlers.

...

Sanjay [angrily]: Why did you score as many as 300 runs [at
    Kochi]? Did you expect India to chase that many?[20]

Even so, Cronje did not find it easy arranging the bowling order.
Shaun Pollock, who opened the bowling in the previous four games,
was not playing; nor was Jacques Kallis, another candidate for the
new ball. But Steve Elworthy was and had opened the bowling in
three of the four earlier games. Cronje had to pointedly overlook
him in favour of Henry Williams, who was playing his seventh one-
day international and had never opened the bowling before, and
Derek Crookes, who had been told earlier in the tour by the management that he would not be opening the bowling again. Moreover,
Williams was out of action with a shoulder injury since the Kochi
one-dayer.

None of this stopped Cronje. He brought pressure to bear on
Craig Smith, the South Africa team's physiotherapist, to waive his
reservations and allow Williams to play. Crookes was also talked
round; he was 'extremely surprised' when his captain asked him to
open the bowling. 'Hansie said we had nothing to lose, so let's try
something different.'[21] But he was not suspicious, he said, because he
had opened the bowling for his province.

Thus, Williams and Crookes duly opened the bowling at Nagpur,
although it came at a heavy price for the team. Williams was clearly
unfit and only managed to bowl 11 balls before his shoulder gave way
so badly that he was forced to return home early from the tour. As
for Crookes, he was taken to pieces by the Indian openers, Ganguly
and Tendulkar. 'I started well,' Crookes recalled, 'but Tendulkar and
Ganguly are not the worst openers in the world and I ended up taking a bit of a smack.'[22] His ten overs cost 69 runs and he was surprised
Cronje asked him to continue after an expensive opening spell.

That was not the only deal Cronje and Sanjay had struck the night
before the game. Cronje admitted, 'A discussion with Sanjay took

place … during which we discussed Gibbs's score, a total of 270 runs and Williams's bowling figures. If the results were as agreed, Sanjay was to pay $140,000 [about £93,000] into my NatWest Bank account.'[23]

Very early next morning, Sanjay phoned again and urged Cronje to agree to the deal. Cronje, finally, could resist no longer. 'I gave in,' he later confessed. 'I told him that I would go ahead. I was required to ensure that Gibbs would score less than 20 runs, that Williams would bowl poorly and go for more than 50 runs during his ten overs, and that the total score should be no more than 270 runs. I was to be paid for doing this.'[24]

> Hansie: Okay, I have spoken. Yes, everything is fine. Spoken to Gibbs, and to Williams, and Strydom. Everything is fine.
>
> Sanjay: Already okay. And how many runs for Gibbs?
>
> Hansie: Less than 20.
>
> Sanjay: Less than 20?
>
> Hansie: Yeah.
>
> Sanjay: Okay. So everything is according to plan. They have to score at least 250?
>
> Hansie: Yeah.
>
> Sanjay: And if you score 270, is it off?
>
> Hansie: Okay. And financially the guys want 25 [$25,000]. They want 25 each.
>
> Sanjay: All right. Okay.
>
> Hansie: So that's 75 for those three and … What can you pay me? I do not know how much you pay me…
>
> Sanjay: You say.
>
> Hansie: If you give me … 140 [$140,000] for everybody.
>
> Sanjay: 140 altogether?
>
> Hansie: Yeah.
>
> Sanjay: Okay that's fine.
>
> Hansie: Okay.
>
> Sanjay: And we will sort something out for the previous one as well.
>
> Hansie: Okay, sure.

Sanjay: Yeah?

Hansie: All right. So we definitely are on.

Sanjay: Okay and one last thing I want to ask you … You know just in case India bat first and if they get out for less than 250 and when you come to bat in the second innings, is it possible that you could ask Gibbs to … his wicket … we will score him out and try and score slowly and not so fast so that you know … Maybe we can get out of it.

Hansie: Okay.

Sanjay: And just in case India is out for less than 250 if they bat first.

Hansie: Okay I will tell him.

Sanjay: Yeah?

Hansie: I will tell him.

Sanjay: And because if he starts scoring so early then we won't be able to get out of it.

Hansie: Okay. Not so early for the first five or six in the Indian innings.

Sanjay: Yeah.

Hansie: Okay.[25]

Cronje had not yet spoken to Gibbs, Williams or Strydom, but now, only hours before the game was to start, he went to speak to Gibbs and Williams. It seemed he never spoke to Strydom.

Gibbs and Williams were sharing a room in the hotel. Cronje knocked on their door at 5.30 a.m., entering the room, in Gibbs's words, 'with a huge grin on his face'. Williams was in the shower. He told Gibbs there was an offer for him to make $15,000 if he scored less than 20. Note that Cronje said $15,000 and not $25,000, the figure discussed with Sanjay. Gibbs found the money, and Cronje's persuasions, impossible to resist. 'I said yes. My parents were getting divorced, my father had a temporary job and I knew I would have to look after my mom for the rest of her life. I was thinking of her,' he said.[26] He spent little time debating the moral implications of the offer on the naive basis that he assumed that if Cronje found it acceptable, so would he.

Williams came out of the shower. 'Hansie told him he could get the same amount for bowling his ten overs for not less than 50,' Gibbs recalled. Williams accepted for similar reasons to his room-mate: 'I also agreed because I had a lot of respect for the captain, Hansie Cronje. If he can do something like this, why couldn't I do it?'[27]

The message that South Africa should not score more than 270 was also relayed. Williams was now obviously committed to playing and later that morning declared himself fit to take the field. As an afterthought, both players asked Cronje to try to get more than the $15,000 promised.

Once again, the plan went awry. Gibbs hit his first two balls for four and went on to lash 74 from 53 balls. Claiming that he 'forgot' about the deal, he said, 'I batted like a steam train. I kept on going. I enjoyed myself. By the time Hansie got to the wicket, I already had 30 or 40 and I asked him what we should do. Then he said just to carry on. After a few overs I asked him again, and he said one of us would have to get out.'[28] Cronje told him he himself would sacrifice his wicket. Cronje was subsequently out but Gibbs did not think it was deliberate, as he fell to an outstanding catch.

Cronje struck 38 off 31 balls and by the time he was out, in the fifteenth over, South Africa were already a staggering 126 for four. Cronje claimed that in the event he, Gibbs and Williams made no attempt to underperform once the game got underway. 'Once we went onto the field we were not able to carry out the plan,' he said. 'I know that Herschelle batted as well as he could: the offer quite clearly went out of his mind once he walked onto the field and, in fact, it was one of the best knocks I have seen ... Henry Williams, until his injury, bowled well. At lunch I told Williams that we must win the game, and that we should give our best. I tried my best ... before falling to a very good catch by [Rahul] Dravid. We not only scored more than 270 runs, but the total of 320 was South Africa's highest one-day score against India ... I do believe that once we set foot on the field, we could not go through with it and did our best – as indicated by Herschelle's unbelievable run-out to win us the game.'

Cronje said that neither he, Gibbs nor Williams received any money, adding, 'No money changed hands in respect of any of the matches in India.' The only money he ever received from Sanjay, he said, was that given to him in Durban.

THE PUBLISHED TRANSCRIPTS referred to seven Indian cricketers. In the case of three of them, their names simply came up in connection with Hansie Cronje's assessments of how games might go. With the other four however – Azharuddin, Nikhil Chopra, Ajay Jadeja and Robin Singh – there appeared to be a deeper involvement. Sanjay referred to Jadeja and Singh by their first names and toyed with phoning Jadeja or Chopra for information; through an intermediary, Chopra was spoken to. (Both Singh and Chopra have denied any involvement in match-fixing.)

Having gone public with their charges against South Africa players, the Delhi police insisted for several weeks that no Indian cricketer had been directly named in the tapes, and during that time only released transcripts that did not implicate any of them. This despite reports that Rajesh Kalra had named three Indians during questioning. The police maintained that references on the tapes to India players were 'blurred' or that the names only came up in passing.[29] The Delhi police had no wish to broaden an already complex case and it was left to the CBI's nationwide inquiry to deal with India's corrupt players.

It was only after Cronje named Azharuddin during his statement to the King Commission as the person who introduced him to Mukesh Gupta that the strategy changed. Two days later the transcript of the Cronje–Sanjay conversation on the eve of the Baroda match, in which Azhar was referred to as someone who would use match-fixing information to make money through 'his people', was released to a Mumbai newspaper.[30] The CBI report alleged that during South Africa's tour, Azhar was in phone contact with a 'bookie'.[31] They spoke at the time of the Bangalore Test and the one-day international in Nagpur, in which Azhar did not, in fact, play. Evidence also emerged of his regular phone contact with Ajay Sharma, the former India player, now working for a state-owned warehouse company in Delhi. Sharma made 29 calls to Azhar during the one-day series in India and a later tournament in Sharjah.[32] The calls followed a pattern. Sharma would call either in the two days prior to a game or on the day of the game itself. This happened for all five one-day matches in India and three of India's four matches in Sharjah. The CBI said Sharma's mobile phone use showed 'a striking spurt' during tournaments in which India played. Besides talking to Azhar, he would talk literally hundreds of times to known bookmakers. 'This leads us to believe that Sharma was feeding information from bookies to his friends in the team,' the CBI said. Asked why he phoned Azhar so much, Sharma said he rang to wish him 'best of luck' and his relationship with Azhar had been misinterpreted. Sharma also kept in touch with Ajay Jadeja, himself in regular contact with a bookmaker from Chennai during South Africa's tour. Jadeja spoke to the bookie on the eve of the first Test and on the first day of the second Test, while the bookie called him 31 times in Jamshedpur, where the second one-day international was played. Asked by the CBI why he had spoken to a bookmaker late at night on the eve of an international, Jadeja replied that he was superstitious and believed that if he did he would never be out.

WITH THE TOUR OVER, the South Africa and India teams moved on to Sharjah to play a triangular one-day competition with Pakistan. When Cronje got there, he was again contacted by Hamid Cassim. 'He indicated that Sanjay wished to resume contact with me, along the same lines as in India,' Cronje recalled. But perhaps chastened by the chaos he had caused to no purpose in Nagpur, Cronje declined. 'I had by now developed sufficient resolve to put it all behind me, and told him that I was not interested,' he said. Cronje commented that the bookie known to him as 'Sunil', whom he had met in 1996, was also around during the Sharjah Cup, asking for the odd bit of information and news on the team. 'He never paid me, or offered me any payment or benefit, nor did I receive anything from him. I gave him nothing out of the ordinary.

'The night before the final of the Sharjah Cup I received a phone call from a man, who did not name himself, who wanted to speak to me in the team-room about "a promotion". He inquired whether Lance Klusener and I would promote some of his products, and tried to set up a meeting early the next day. He also said that he was willing to give us $100,000 now, and $100,000 after the match, if we would play badly. I told him we were not interested. This was never conveyed to Lance Klusener.'[34]

In the event, South Africa lost the final to Pakistan by 16 runs. Chasing 264, they were going along nicely while Cronje was sharing a third-wicket partnership of 105 with Neil McKenzie, but he fell for a hard-hitting 79 and the innings subsided once a stand of 61 between McKenzie and Mark Boucher had been broken.

It was the last cricket match Cronje ever played as a professional.

14

THE TRUTH WILL SET YOU FREE

Hansie Cronje's account of what happened during the India tour was almost entirely based on what he told the King Commission which sat in June 2000 to establish the extent of corruption in South African cricket. At an early stage he was invited to tell the truth in exchange for an offer of immunity from criminal prosecution, an offer arranged by the prosecution team in conjunction with the director of public prosecutions, in the belief that otherwise he might refuse to answer questions for fear of incriminating himself. Cronje faced the possibility of criminal charges relating to the possession of foreign currency.

He thus had an incentive to tell the full story. Judge Edwin King encouraged him further by quoting St John's gospel: 'The truth will set you free.'[1]

But another motive was also at play. He was desperate to protect his battered reputation from further damage for fear he might be cast as pariah and never work again. He would admit to making mistakes; he could never admit to deliberately underperforming to fix a match.

Of course, he was not alone in feeling like this. Several players accused of corruption insisted their crime went no further than providing information. There appeared to be a consensus among players – and eventually the wider public – that there did exist a well-marked line between providing information and underperforming, and it was a line no player wanted to be seen crossing. Only one person, Azharuddin, would ever admit to fixing a game, and in the face of overwhelming evidence he owned up to only three offences.

It was as though on this point pivoted the debate as to whether Cronje had or had not betrayed his country. It was as though he felt that if he could escape the charge of betrayal, he retained an outside chance of rebuilding his life and career. Much time was spent at the King hearings with Cronje and his legal team resisting anyone making this charge stick, even though it appeared that in fact there were many who felt he had betrayed the South African nation regardless.

As to whether he told the whole truth to the commission, that would remain a matter of conjecture.

In the weeks after the Indian police laid their charges against him, Cronje showed himself as cool a tactician off the field as he had on it. He not only destroyed evidence at home but contacted several other figures in the scandal, warning them that the story was breaking, making sure their accounts tallied, or simply encouraging them to lie.

On the very day the Delhi police gave their first press conference, he telephoned Hamid Cassim. He also contacted Marlon Aronstam. On the night he spoke to Rory Steyn, he asked him to relay a message to Herschelle Gibbs. In Steyn's words, it was, 'Herschelle, don't worry, you're not involved. The captain says you've got nothing to worry about. Stay strong and get your mind on the game,' a reference to the one-day game against Australia in Durban the next day.[2] But Gibbs felt the pressure and two days later he was fined for staying in a Cape Town nightclub until 2.00 a.m. on the morning of a game. Cronje subsequently stayed in regular phone contact with Gibbs, urging him to deny everything.[3]

He never contacted Henry Williams direct but passed several messages through Herschelle Gibbs to 'stick to the plan' and 'not tell the truth'. He also spoke to Pieter Strydom, reassuring him that 'the furore was about one-day internationals and had nothing to do with the Tests'.[4] Strydom's response was to tell Cronje he could not lie to the commission. Cronje replied, 'It's fine. You can tell exactly what happened. Just don't mention the money.'

Cronje would always insist none of his players were involved in wrongdoing, and wanted to take the blame for corrupting Herschelle Gibbs and Henry Williams.

His strategy was consistent, at any rate. He denied everything unless incontrovertible evidence was presented to the contrary. Asked if he would have revealed his approach to Jacques Kallis, Lance Klusener and Mark Boucher had they not mentioned it to the commission first, Cronje said he probably would not have done; asked the same about the bribes offered to Gibbs and Williams, he again said, 'Probably not.'[5]

He got into greatest difficulties when he did the explaining first. In the days immediately after his exposure, statements were made by him, or on his behalf, which contained few specifics but nevertheless included claims that were later shown to be false. He said he had never attempted to manipulate any aspect of a match. He denied ever approaching a teammate about throwing a game (he actually approached six, some for a second or third time). He said he was never approached by a bookie except at Mumbai in 1996 (an offer too widely known about to be ignored). He said he had never received money for any match in which he had been involved.

In his original hand-written confession he referred only to the India tour, rather than matters that had occurred several years earlier, because he 'was only accused at that stage of the Indian tour'; he did not admit to entertaining the idea of throwing a match within weeks of becoming South Africa captain.[6] He also altered the amount of money he said he received from Sanjay; this fact was only revealed by the man to whom he handed the statement, Rory Steyn. He claimed he never touched the money Sanjay gave him; yet what was recovered was less than even his revised amount. He claimed to be finished with deception, writing, 'I'll be back. Better off than I am now, once I have been punished.'[7] Yet he continued to lie, and encouraged others to lie too.

The 40-minute statement Cronje read out to the commission on 15 June 2000 caused a sensation. We had not seen Cronje in public for weeks, and there was great interest in how he looked. He arrived at the venue for the hearings, the Centre for the Book, in the dead of Cape Town's winter, amid high security, and was ushered in through a side entrance. There was a stunned silence even before he appeared in the cavernous hall – not through the main swing doors but, as it were, out of the wall itself, through one of those doors disguised as wood panelling. He looked slightly drawn and spoke almost as if in a trance. He admitted to taking substantial sums in bribes – but he remained cautious in what he disclosed, and he certainly had had time to think his strategy through. Telling the whole truth was clearly not part of it. Under cross-examination a few days later, it emerged he had taken even more money from the bookies than he said.

The commission had subtly changed in nature from what Ali Bacher and Percy Sonn had envisaged two months earlier when, within hours of Cronje's confession, they had asked the government to institute a public inquiry. At that point Bacher had heralded it as cricket's equivalent of the country's truth and reconciliation commission. But by the time Cronje was testifying, the manner in which the evidence was given showed that that idealistic notion would never be satisfied.

The inquiry's terms of reference were frustratingly narrow. Only evidence relating to Cronje's conduct in the previous six months, and what had happened in India in 1996, was considered. If references were made to matches from other periods, Cronje's legal team quickly pointed out their inadmissibility. It was as though everyone, including the bookies, knew that from 1997 to 1999 Cronje the bad guy had taken an extended holiday.

Cronje's team won a crucial victory in refusing to accept the veracity of the published transcripts of the phone taps. Judge King allowed reference to be made to them but Cronje's team never accepted they were genuine and the prosecution team was never able to have them authenticated, despite journeying to Delhi for this express purpose. The police there refused to release the tapes because under law they had to remain sealed pending the outcome of their own case against match-fixing conspirators. It was a bewildering defeat for Shamila Batohi, the lead prosecutor.

The commission was arranged in such a way that most witnesses appeared before Cronje himself. Thus, when it came to his turn, he was able to simply confirm or deny what they had alleged. Had he testified first, he would not have known what others might say and his whole account would have been more revealing, either in what it contained or omitted. There was a general feeling that Batohi, a deputy attorney-general of Natal, who had little understanding of cricket, was less rigorous in her questioning than she might have been and missed many tricks. Asked later whether Cronje had been totally honest, Ray McCauley replied, 'Yes, he certainly answered all the questions truthfully. But I'm not sure that he's been asked everything.'[8]

No sooner had Cronje made his statement than the commission adjourned for six days. When it resumed, the first man in the stand was Dr Ian Lewis, a psychiatrist treating Cronje. He said his patient was suffering from clinical depression and under medication. Cronje was showing most of the symptoms of the disorder: depressed mood and irritability, loss of concentration, loss of pleasure and interest in things, low energy and fatigue, a sense of worthlessness, thoughts of death and dying, loss of appetite and insomnia. But Lewis said Cronje was in a position to be cross-examined and tell the truth.[9]

Cronje admitted to his relationship with Mukesh Gupta probably because Gupta was the man who had proffered the bribe in Mumbai and his name might well have come out anyway, if not in South Africa, then in the investigation already underway in India.

At one point in his statement, Cronje said it contained 'the whole truth, limited by the terms of reference'. Even then he sometimes could not help contradicting himself. He saw nothing wrong in providing information to Aronstam yet said he gave up dealing with Mukesh Gupta because he knew 'it was wrong to take money for information'.[10]

There was no doubting two things. The first was that many of the plans laid by Cronje and Sanjay certainly did come unstuck, such as the ceilings placed on the South African totals at Kochi and Baroda. But the other was that Cronje was not a complete failure, because for all the side-bets that may have gone wrong, South Africa did lose three of the five one-day matches. Sanjay could have made money on results even if he lost in other areas. Money could also have been made on South Africa scoring fewer than 200 in the Test at Mumbai, where they were all out for 176 and Cronje for nought. There was only Cronje's word for it that this aspect of the game was not fixed.

Did Cronje lie about not underperforming in India? In the Tests, both of which South Africa won, he continued his poor batting form with 25 runs in three innings, but with the ball he took six wickets at 13 apiece. In the one-dayers what he gave with the bat he took away with the ball. He scored runs heavily and fast – 220 off 235 balls in all – but in 35 overs conceded runs at around one per ball. Four of the five matches went down to the wire, just the sort of games that can be lost with one bad ball, one rash shot, one error in the field.

He said he pretended to play along with an arrangement to lose the first one-dayer in Kochi, which was indeed lost, but received no money because South Africa scored more than the agreed runs. He admitted to doing some forecasting in the next three games. For the fifth game in Nagpur, he persuaded two teammates to join him in underperforming but later claimed that all of them failed to carry out the plan and South Africa won the match. Again no money changed hands.

While Cronje might argue that he did little wrong, the fact remains that he attempted to corrupt several teammates and succeeded with two of them. In the case of the Nagpur one-dayer, he interfered with selection and distorted the natural course of the game, all to meet the demands of the bookies. Even after plans had gone awry in regard to Herschelle Gibbs's score and the South African total, he still opened the bowling with the agreed combination of Henry Williams and Derek Crookes. His handling of the game risked defeat; the fact that it was won was neither here nor there.

To all intents and purposes it was match-fixing.

Cronje, of course, tried to pass things off as a joke, his usual way of dealing with an uncomfortable situation. Pastor McCauley said Cronje had told him, '$8,200 [the money recorded from Sanjay's downpayment] and a joke had ruined his life', adding, 'there were certain people he did speak to ... but it was a joke'.[11] In his early confessions, he had merely been 'playing along'[12] with, or 'stringing along', the bookies. And to the King Commission, 'Ninety-five per cent of the time, I was stringing him along.'[13] In effect, his defence was based on the argument, 'Believe me. When I said I was fixing matches, I was lying.'

This line was flawed in more ways than one. In one breath, Cronje insisted he was fooling around with bookies, but in another maintained he was desperately fending off men who were harassing him.

How genuine were the harassment claims? There were suggestions that towards the end of the India tour this extended to threats of physical violence against the South Africa captain.[14] And yet the pestering did not stop him agreeing to return to India for a series of benefit matches between Hansie Cronje's XI and Azharuddin's XI a few weeks later (the plans were shelved following Cronje's exposure). Nor did it prevent him taking receipt of a mobile phone, or keeping it switched on, or going to great lengths to carry out the deal with Sanjay regarding the last match of the tour, in the process ripping off two teammates by offering them nearly £7,000 less than they were due. As Judge King said, the facts were 'not readily reconcilable with the notion of Cronje spinning Sanjay along'.[15]

Asked by King why he had behaved in such a way towards two colleagues, Cronje struggled for an answer. 'Maybe I was trying to cut something for myself,' he suggested.[16] King, a softly spoken, gentle man, could not hide the bite from his voice when he replied, 'May I suggest that that is exactly what you were trying to do.'

Cronje left the witness box that day sobbing uncontrollably.

It was a scene that deeply affected many South Africans, the majority of whom were already disposed to forgive a man they had once revered. 'This was something that should, after all, not happen to any idol. A sports hero is only supposed to weep when he or she is overcome by the momentous occasion of winning an Olympic gold medal and having fifty million people around the world witness, on television, when the victor's anthem is played. The only real heartache that the hero should ever know is that of coming second.'[17]

WAS CRONJE THE FALL GUY at the King Commission? This impression gained hold from the moment it was announced that the South African board would be represented by its own legal team. The board was effectively cutting adrift one of its former employees. The team spent the hearings concentrating its considerable energies on defending the reputation of the board and every player except Cronje.

King's opening appeal that the hearings must not be turned into 'any sort of revenge or witch-hunt' appeared to fall on deaf ears. As one onlooker said, 'It is hard not to equate the strategy of the United Cricket Board's legal team with a witch-hunt. They've got a target and they're after him. Everything they do points the finger at Cronje.'[18]

From behind this shield, some players were willing to plunge the knife between the shoulder blades of their former master. Pat Symcox, with little to lose in retirement, opened up by recounting how Cronje had approached him as early as January 1995 suggesting they fix a match; that Symcox had never shopped his captain in the intervening five years was overlooked. Others followed, although a few, such as Daryll Cullinan, were reduced to such inarticulacy that their testimonies were largely ignored. Not one condemned Cronje for chasing the money, and amnesia struck when it came to identifying those who had been keenest on accepting the bribe in Mumbai. On this issue, even Cronje played along.

Nicky Boje, one of those also charged by the Delhi police, said he had no idea why Cronje named him in the tapes; he had spoken to his former captain after the story broke and Cronje had told him he had just 'thrown a few names around' to placate people who were pestering him. Boje forgave him, 'I still respect him. He's still a close friend. Everyone makes mistakes.'[19]

Gibbs repeatedly lied to the South African board and commission investigators in the lead-up to the hearings, as did Williams. In effect, they did what Cronje told them and denied everything. Surely nothing better illustrated the power he had commanded over his players. Gibbs admitted, 'I was scared and uncertain, and I was protecting Hansie.'[20] It was only when Mark Boucher took him out for a drink a few days before the hearings that Gibbs was persuaded to change his mind. Boucher had warned him, 'If you don't come clean you are going to go to jail.'[21] In the event, Gibbs told the commission what happened in Nagpur and once he had done so, Williams did too.

Whether Gibbs's final account should have been believed was another matter. He claimed that once he took the field, he forgot all about the deal he had struck that morning with Cronje to score fewer than 20. But while they were batting together, he twice asked his captain what they were doing about the deal, which seemed to confirm that, in fact, the deal remained uppermost in his mind throughout.

The South African board fined Gibbs £6,000 and Williams £1,000 and suspended both from international cricket for six months. It was a six-month period in which South Africa had few commitments. Gibbs, who lost money in surrendered endorsements, was selected immediately the ban expired. He was out for nought in his first innings back but returned to being an integral member of the side.

'Agreeing to the deal was the biggest mistake of my life,' Gibbs reflected. 'It is not only me who will learn a lesson. I don't think any other cricketer around the world will ever make the same mistake. I have had a lot to think about over the past months. The ban seems to have taken forever.'[22]

But a few months later he was caught, along with a number of other players, smoking marijuana while on tour in the Caribbean. He was given another fine and ordered to undergo life-skills counselling, but some doubted whether he would ever put the disgrace fully behind him.

No other South Africa players were punished in connection with match-fixing, despite most of the team sitting on information relating to the issue for years. Their treatment contrasted with that of Kepler Wessels, one of Cronje's fiercest critics, who was not retained as a national selector.

15

THE CBI REPORT

Nowhere did the shock waves from Cronje's confession reverberate deeper than India. A country that loved cricket more passionately than any other was going to feel the betrayal keenly. But there were other factors at play. There was the role of the Indian betting industry in the affair, the 'engine-room of cricket corruption' as Lord Condon put it; and there were the long-standing rumours of malpractice surrounding India's own cricketers, rumours that had never gone away, despite two cricket board inquiries.

Almost overnight the atmosphere changed. The Indian people no longer needed convincing that their cricket was corrupt. Instinctively, they knew that all the lies and cover-ups had been just that. The nation itself had been living a lie. India was not a victim in the scandal; it was a central part of the problem. Suddenly, every rumour, however implausible, was seized upon as further proof of the game's deep-rooted dishonesty. The mood became ugly, unpredictable and vengeful. Someone had to pay for the beggaring of this vast country's broadest religion. There had to be a purge.

People who were once afraid to voice their suspicions were emboldened to speak out. Questions were asked in parliament. The press went back onto the attack with all the force their moral indignation and pent-up frustration could muster.

The witch-hunt affected many. When a stash of money was found secreted in his locker at the Gymkhana club in Mumbai, Sunil Gavaskar was branded another hero who had let his people down, even though the worst offence many suspected him of was tax avoidance. His wife explained he virtually lived out of the club and needed the money there.

For some the dangers could not have been more real. A diamond dealer was shot dead by three assassins while getting out of his car in Mumbai. He was believed to be a mafia linkman with cricketers, Bollywood stars and South African bookmakers. Among those questioned about his murder was Azharuddin, with whom he had dined two days earlier – though police sources later suggested his death might be linked to a gangland property dispute. A government prosecutor in Delhi investigating the case against Cronje received death threats.

The cricketers suspected of being at the heart of match-fixing were forced into hiding. Their cars were attacked and demonstrators took to the streets in Calcutta, Mumbai and Delhi.

Among the effigies burned was one of Dawood Ibrahim.

PRESSURE FOR A RESPONSE mounted in two areas. One was for a government-led inquiry by the Central Bureau of Investigation, a body with nationwide powers and the best organised and least corrupt officers in the country. The other was for the person who had levelled the most serious allegation against an Indian cricketer to break his long-standing silence: Manoj Prabhakar.

Prabhakar's unwillingness to speak had been taken in some quarters as evidence that he had nothing to tell. The suspicion was that his original story had simply been another publicity-seeking exercise. Senior cricket board officials stressed the importance of him going public. 'If the people who have levelled allegations are not willing to come up with the names, what can we do?' one of them said.[1]

Significant steps on both fronts occurred almost simultaneously. Hours before the Indian government ordered the CBI to mount an investigation, the sports minister publicly offered Prabhakar security if he would disclose what he knew. Prabhakar then met the home minister and privately confirmed the identity of the player who, he alleged, had tried to bribe him.

The government advised Prabhakar to 'keep quiet', presumably not to hinder the CBI inquiry, but Prabhakar had his own reasons for maintaining silence.[2] He had recently been approached by the journalist who had worked with him on his *Outlook* article in 1997 to help secretly film and record players and administrators in an effort to expose corruption. Thus, at the same time that surveillance work by the Delhi police was accidentally uncovering cricket corruption, the media was deliberately using similar methods to the same end.

The journalist, Aniruddha Bahal, was now working for an investigative news website, tehelka.com. He was frustrated by the public denials of the match-fixing suspects and believed these represented the 'cockiness of crooks who had covered their trails well'.[3] The tehelka team was convinced that the only way to catch out the culprits was to conduct a 'sting' operation.

Tehelka sought the assistance of three insiders but only Prabhakar agreed. Prabhakar's motives were easy to understand. He had long been under pressure to name his man but, as he himself privately admitted, lacked concrete evidence to back up his allegation. 'I think if we hadn't stepped in at this juncture, Prabhakar would essentially have been caught between the proverbial devil and the deep sea,' Bahal wrote. 'There would have been this tremendous pressure on him to name the team-mate … and if he had done so without any evidence, the very same media that was hounding him for the name would have strung him up from the first tree without any compunction.'[4] Prabhakar, who was not paid by tehelka, said, 'I wanted to prove that I did not lie.'[5]

The operation lasted two months, during which Prabhakar and Bahal caught eighteen witnesses – including cricketers, officials and administrators, a police chief, a television commentator and a Bollywood actress – discussing match-fixing and corruption. The interviews resulted in more than 40 hours of tapes but provided only circumstantial evidence to support Prabhakar's story. Only one former teammate, Ravi Shastri, was publicly prepared to confirm that Prabhakar spoke to him of the incident at the time. 'No one was willing to stick his neck out for cricket, or on my behalf,' Prabhakar claimed. 'Every one of those players in the tapes agrees that what I said was true. Only, no one wanted to say it openly. The reason was obvious too. Why rock the boat?'[6]

What clearly emerged from the tehelka tapes, though, was that India's management had known about Prabhakar's allegation. Azharuddin, the captain, and Ajit Wadekar, the manager, both knew. Wadekar said he had referred to it in his tour report and told senior board officials; 'Everybody knows,' he admitted.[7] No wonder Prabhakar bemoaned, 'Wadekar and Azhar have destroyed my life.'[8] Some teams, too, were evidently more deeply involved than others. The police chief was recorded saying, 'According to the bookie, it is very difficult to get through to these teams [England and Australia]. They still have that spirit that they are playing for the country ... Whereas here, our fellows are waiting like hawks.'[9]

Cronje's exposure cut short the tehelka investigation. Plans to interview bookmakers and gamblers crucially had to be abandoned, and although pains had been taken to ensure details of the 'sting' did not leak out from the operational end, nothing could be done to silence those interviewed. With public debate on the Prabhakar affair at a height, Inderjit Singh Bindra, a former president of the Indian cricket board, gave an interview to CNN television in which he said Prabhakar had told him Kapil Dev was the person who had offered the bribe. 'I have only said what Prabhakar told me,' Bindra stated.[10]

The naming of Kapil caused a sensation. He was arguably India's greatest sports icon, the man who had led India to their 1983 World

Cup triumph, an achievement unmatched in the country's sporting history. He was now India's coach and had recently called on India to stop playing for six months until the scandal was laid to rest. Even in its new-found cynicism, India had trouble coming to terms with this one.

Shortly afterwards, Prabhakar confirmed to the CBI that Kapil was indeed the man he alleged had tried to corrupt him. He publicly reiterated this at screenings of the tehelka tapes highlights. The film caused another sensation and convinced many across India that corruption was indeed rife among their sporting heroes. Those who had been duped in conversation with Prabhakar were unhappy at the deception. Some claimed tehelka had doctored the tapes; Wadekar denied he had even been interviewed. But the tapes largely spoke for themselves.

Kapil's reaction to his naming caused almost as much of a furore as the original charge. He announced he was planning legal action against Bindra for his 'wild and baseless allegations'.[11] Then, during an interview with BBC World television, he broke down in tears. 'I would commit suicide rather than take a bribe,' he said.[12] He said Prabhakar had never liked him since he was left out of Tests by Kapil during a tour of England in 1986. Prabhakar may also have grown jealous of Jadeja's preferment, with good reason. 'What is Jadeja, is all Kapil ... He cannot pass one day in the team without Jadeja,' one board official confided to Prabhakar.[13] But Kapil recovered ground later, offering unconditionally to take a lie-detector test, whereas initially Prabhakar refused.

But the impact of the tehelka tapes proved short-lived. The publication of the CBI report six months later, though it publicly confirmed much of what had been said privately on the tapes, introduced significant fresh evidence, most notably on Prabhakar's own involvement with bookmakers.

If the reaction of the Indian public to the nation's part in the scandal was one of shock, the response of the authorities was incisive and impressive. The CBI investigation turned out to be the most thorough and expert ever conducted into cricket corruption, and was widely praised. In the absence of a distinct criminal offence relating to match-fixing, an early decision was taken to involve the income tax authorities in an effort to fine offenders for holding undisclosed income or assets; such offences could incur fines equivalent to 60 per cent of the original sum. Detailed analysis of telephone, hotel and flight records was crucial in establishing links between players and bookmakers.

Dozens of cricketers, administrators, bookies and gamblers were questioned and many of their properties raided during a nationwide blitz codenamed Operation Gentleman, which involved more than 300 CBI and tax officers. Among the cricketers raided were Azharuddin, Kapil Dev, Prabhakar, Ajay Sharma and Ajay Jadeja; among the bookies and punters, Mukesh Gupta and Ratan Mehta. Kapil broke down again several times during the raids.

The officials removed papers and sealed lockers and bank accounts. They discovered evidence of undisclosed properties and land, and also of substantial sums of money being diverted in the wake of Cronje's exposure. 'We have gathered substantial and tangible evidence to prove concealment of wealth and also escaping of tax … and some kind of nexus in match-fixing … Whatever we have seen so far proves that there is a connection to match-fixing,' a government official told parliament.[14]

The raids displayed no respect for reputation or status. The president of the Samata political party, a partner in the governing coalition, was questioned 'by my own government' about her family's connection with Jadeja, and held a press conference in Delhi to denounce the 'high-handed' raids on his various properties in the city.

The players themselves emerged from their grillings maintaining their innocence. 'As far as I know there is no such thing as match-fixing,' Azharuddin said.[15] The sports minister led calls for those under a cloud to voluntarily step down until the investigation was complete. Two weeks after an interview with the minister, and with the board already sounding out candidates to replace him, Kapil Dev resigned as India's coach. He wanted to concentrate on clearing his name. Tainted players were overlooked for the team's next engagement, the ICC Knockout in Kenya. 'We thought it would be better for them to take a rest,' the chairman of selectors said.[16]

Azharuddin was in England while his properties were being searched by the CBI. He had been invited to take part in a fundraiser at the Oval and a benefit day for Mark Ramprakash in Finchley, north London. He arrived late at the tree-lined club ground in Finchley. It was a scorching day and he spent most of the afternoon in a marquee watching through sunglasses. He looked tense and refused to comment when asked what he thought about the ongoing raids. Apart from conversing in hushed tones with his wife and Wasim Akram, he said little. He did not seem to be following the CBI's advice to 'enjoy his holiday'.[17]

It made a bizarre scene, a man so much under fire in his own country in this idyll, having his hand shaken by past and present greats of the game. Whatever the trouble, he could rely on his own to stand by him.

THE CBI REPORT was flagged as a document of more than 200 pages, but in its published form was almost 50 pages fewer than that. The evidence it outlined against several India players was so exhaustive as to be almost unarguable. But some of its targets did argue. The most disconcerting protest came from a groundsman in Delhi, alleged to have been bribed to prepare a particular type of pitch, who claimed he had been beaten during interrogation. The CBI denied it.

The report was scathing about the obstruction it had encountered. 'The cricketing fraternity maintained a "conspiracy of silence" and were rarely forthcoming with specific information,' it stated. 'Not a single player, former player or official volunteered any information ... [yet] the CBI was able to collect evidence through painstaking and meticulous efforts.'[18] It was largely a bookies' report, because without them there would not have been one. 'Look at this man's [Cronje's] conscience,' Bishen Bedi, a former India captain, said. 'He couldn't sleep ... And look at our boys, enjoying perfectly nice, healthy sleep.'[19]

Subsequently, K Madhavan cross-examined those incriminated in the report as a matter of due process. They denied the CBI charges without failing to convince their interrogator of their innocence. Meanwhile, public feeling against the guilty players darkened. A leader of the right-wing Hindu extremist group Shiv Sena called for them to be hanged as traitors to the nation. 'This is the beginning of our crusade against corruption,' he said.

The Indian board banned Azharuddin and Ajay Sharma for life and suspended Ajay Jadeja for five years. Manoj Prabhakar was barred from holding office for five years and Ali Irani, the physio, was also banned. Others whose names came up during the scandal were cleared. Singh and Chopra denied any involvement in match-fixing.

In essence, Azhar and Jadeja had been deemed guilty of match-fixing; Sharma and Irani of acting as conduits between India players and bookies; and Prabhakar of approaching foreign players on behalf of bookies. 'These hard decisions have been taken after careful consideration. They will set an example for the future,' the board's president said.[21] It was later announced that Azhar, Jadeja and Prabhakar had been stripped of one of India's highest sports honours, the Arjuna award. Azhar and Jadeja both said they intended to appeal.

David Richards, the chief executive of the ICC, welcomed the punishments. 'The BCCI [the Indian board] should be commended for acting in the best interests of cricket ... Of course it is disappointing that the careers of these prominent players should end in this way, but hopefully others will learn from their example.'[22]

Kapil Dev was cleared. The report stated that there was 'no credible evidence' against him regarding the alleged bribe, no evidence he instigated the decision not to enforce the follow-on in Ahmedabad, and telephone records failed to establish suspicious links with bookmakers. He was known to be close to a bookie in

Ahmedabad and to like to gamble, but there was nothing to suggest he was involved in match-fixing.

This verdict inspired no shortage of conspiracy theories. Kapil's political affiliations were well known. He had canvassed on behalf of another ruling coalition party, the BJP, and it was noted that after the report's publication, a number of prominent figures involved in the inquiry – including two government ministers – were transferred from their posts, allegedly for pursuing the case too vigorously. Sarfraz Nawaz claimed the report was deliberately cut in length to 'let some holy cows off the hook'.[23] But Jadeja's political connections were better than Kapil's and they had done him no good. One detail that was apparently not considered by the CBI was a claim that Rushdie Magiet, the convenor of South Africa's selectors, had been told by Kapil Dev during the tour of India that Cronje was 'on the take'.[24]

No one suggested Kapil should be reinstated as national coach, or take up any other position within cricket. Nor was his name restored to the school history books from which it had recently been expunged. He remained unsmiling. 'The media refused to believe me when I said I was innocent … They first tear my clothes off and now offer me new ones to cover myself.'[25] But Prabhakar's full role, unknown to his colleagues at tehelka, was deeply embarrassing and tehelka's faith in him was not shared by all. 'His stability has been called into question,' said Lord Condon, explaining why his anti-corruption unit never sought to question arguably the greatest maverick in the whole affair.[26]

Many players and bookmakers were given a deadline by which to submit income tax returns in the light of their previously undisclosed 'earnings'. Tax sources suggested that in the case of players, these earnings for the last tax year alone ranged from £80,000 to £400,000.

CBI investigations did not stop with the report. They moved onto an inquiry into links between match-fixing and organised crime. Meanwhile, four months after his life as a cricketer effectively ended, Jadeja announced he was taking up an acting career in Bollywood.

Lord Condon said the reason it was so hard to catch culprits was that it was in the interests of neither the corrupters nor the corrupted to talk about their relationships. But thankfully for the investigators, Mukesh Gupta proved an exception to the rule.

When Hansie Cronje identified Gupta during the King Commission hearings, it triggered a hunt for him that stretched across the Asian subcontinent and beyond. At first, he could not be found. Then, one afternoon he walked in off the street and gave himself up to the CBI. If he did not tell them all he knew, he told them a lot. The CBI interviewed more than 200 bookmakers and gamblers, but Gupta was easily their star witness. Everything he said that the CBI was able to crosscheck turned out to be true.

It was because of his reliability that the CBI took the controversial decision to name in their report foreign cricketers whom he alleged he had also approached and, in most cases, bribed. The CBI did not attempt to verify these 'hearsay' claims because they viewed it as beyond their remit, but they clearly believed them to be true. 'We found no reason for him to lie about these foreign players,' a senior CBI official said.[27]

The naming of the foreigners guaranteed worldwide interest in the CBI report and global fame for Gupta. It also prompted inquiries in England, Australia, New Zealand, Sri Lanka and the West Indies to establish whether Gupta's allegations were accurate. If they stood up, the players in question faced at the least disciplinary action at the hands of their respective cricket boards. The inquiries were assisted by Lord Condon's new anti-corruption unit (ACU) and in the case of Alec Stewart, of England, run by Condon's unit itself at the request of the ECB.

An important step forward came when Gupta verbally confirmed all his allegations to Condon's unit in March 2001, but the inquiries became mired in legal debate as players protested their innocence and demanded the right to cross-examine their accuser. When Condon had still not met Stewart and his lawyer eight months after the publication of the CBI report, the ACU issued a press statement speaking of feeling 'increasingly frustrated' at the inability to agree a convenient date. Stewart protested that he had been contacted neither by his lawyer nor the ACU to set up a full interview.

The allegation that Stewart might have not co-operated with the inquiry was a matter of potential embarrassment to the ECB, whose chairman, Lord MacLaurin, had publicly stated that were any England player to obstruct an investigation he would be immediately suspended. MacLaurin had allowed Stewart to remain on tour in Pakistan when the CBI report was published precisely because Stewart had co-operated, answering the board's questions and denying receiving money from Gupta or ever knowingly meeting him. MacLaurin reiterated that his view had not changed.

In an effort to bring closure to the matter, Condon announced he had given Gupta until 1 July 2001 to 'let us know that he is willing to give evidence ... he's really got to stand up and be counted before disciplinary hearings'.[29] Condon added, 'He either travels to various locations to be cross-examined or we'll arrange for players' lawyers to come to India and in controlled circumstances let them cross-examine him about the when and the how. Natural justice demands that the players' lawyers be allowed to do that.'[30] Security was offered were Gupta to decide to travel abroad.

When the deadline passed without Gupta responding, Condon said he had advised the various inquiry teams of the position the bookmaker had taken. 'They will no doubt take this into account when they submit reports to their cricket boards,' he said.[31]

But Condon emphasised that it would be precipitous to assume the foreign players were innocent once the deadline passed. Gupta, he stressed, was not the only witness. The CBI, it appeared, had acquired evidence against foreign players from other sources that they had not been prepared to divulge. Condon confirmed in regard to Stewart, 'Gupta's evidence was not the only evidence but it was the principal evidence ... It's not just Gupta. The CBI said Prabhakar and others made statements of confirmation. An assessment will have to be made in relation to all the available evidence.'[32]

But the mercurial Gupta remained the prize witness, partly

because it was thought he had more to tell and might tell it if the time was right. 'If at any stage he is prepared to co-operate it will not be too late,' added Condon, who believed that commercial motives figured highly in Gupta's endgame plans. 'He wants to leave his options open, exploit his position and see what commercial arrangements he can make,' he said. 'But the more his motive is commercial the more people will want to test his version.'[33] Stewart, de Silva, Ranatunga, Crowe and Mark Waugh were all cleared. 'There exists no substantive evidence jusifying proceedings against Alec,' Lord MacLaurin said.

WHEN THEY FIRST came to light, Mukesh Gupta's allegations against non-Indians created a feverish atmosphere among the press, if not the public. In Australia there was a campaign to force Mark Waugh's removal from the Australia team, and in the British press the case of Alec Stewart received blanket coverage – this despite the fact that, even by Gupta's account, the worst either man was guilty of was taking money for information. No one was saying they had fixed matches. But this was now a story without shades of grey. Every perceived offence appeared the same in the eyes of the mob.

Because he wrote a column for the *Sunday Times*, I had a close relationship with Stewart and saw at first hand the enormous pressure he came under when the CBI report appeared. England were touring Pakistan at the time. Stewart first heard of the allegations when he took a call in his hotel room in Rawalpindi, venue for one of the warm-up games, from an Indian television station informing him that the CBI report was about to be published, with his name in it. The caller asked whether Stewart would mind if his replies were taped. Yes, he would, said Stewart, and hung up.

Stewart was not playing in Rawalpindi. This was fortunate in that it left him free to deal with the crisis swirling around him; unfortunate in that it made him a virtual prisoner in his hotel room while ECB mandarins in London decided what to do about him. It took 24 hours to obtain and study copies of the report, following which a number of questions were put to the England wicketkeeper in two telephone calls from Lord's. In them, he denied ever receiving money in exchange for information or knowingly meeting Gupta.

After that, the ECB issued a press release stating that as he was prepared to co-operate with inquiries, Stewart was allowed to stay on the tour. When he and I spoke privately, however, he said he would go home then if he could – 'It would suit me.' This may have been as much a comment on our spartan lives in Pakistan as a response to his more wide-reaching plight.

During that turbulent week I spoke to Alec every day, and it was obvious he felt acutely the eyes of the world upon him, even though he was not in a position to read the headlines dominating the newspapers back home. Once, when I went to room 632 of our hotel (the kind of place you hoped had seen better, more cheerful days), Nasser Hussain, the England captain, had just come in from a game of golf to see how he was. It was like hospital visiting hour. The patient looked pretty glum.

Stewart was under intense pressure to publicly respond to the allegations. He was offered money by several rival newspapers to tell his story, which he declined (whether to sell a story about not selling information must have been an easy call to make). Being forced to block all calls to his phones only reinforced his isolation. Initially he was even reluctant to write his column for the *Sunday Times*.

At first, he wanted simply to make a press statement, rather than hold a conference where he would be obliged to answer questions. In such circumstances, he feared, he might get 'tongue-tied', or journalists would try to snare him in his own semantics. He was right on the second point: after he had come down to one of the hotel's ground-floor conference rooms to speak to the press, great play was made of how he habitually referred to his denials in the past tense: 'I have already said to the ECB that I did not take money from a bookmaker', he would say, rather than, 'I did not take the money.' The press also made a lot of his equanimity in facing the potential besmirching of a reputation he had worked hard to cultivate since first playing for his country in 1989. But, like so many sportsmen, he was not someone who found it easy to express his emotions in public. Not a comfortable performer in front of cameras or media, he responded to that attention by withdrawing his personality behind a shield of cricket-speak. He was instinctively inscrutable.

My advice to him had been that if he did not hold a press conference, it would look like he had something to hide. Curiously, we were able to discuss the matter without my once asking him whether he had taken Gupta's money, or him asking me whether I thought he had. Though I had spent so much time on the match-fixing story, I could not bring myself to quiz him doggedly. He was going through hell and I had to be sympathetic rather than critical; the idea of probing seemed indecent and disloyal. Besides, we both knew that after Cronje's exposure, protestations of innocence counted for little. At one point he said to me, 'I don't know whether you believe me or not.' What finally persuaded him to speak publicly was the media barrage his wife and children were also facing back in England. The final straw was a tabloid journalist taking up residence on the doorstep of their Surrey home.

Much later, Stewart admitted the affair affected his form in Pakistan. It had been at the back of his mind throughout, he said. During the three Tests he averaged fewer than 20. He played six subsequent Tests against Sri Lanka, Pakistan and Australia for a slightly better return, before being formally cleared of Gupta's charges. Though he was naturally relieved, it was only clearance of a sort; with Gupta's failure to respond to Condon's deadline, the final verdict must have felt more like 'case not proven' than 'innocent'.

Stewart faced a future in which his name was forever linked with the match-fixing scandal. So, too, did Mark Waugh. At Lord's during Australia's 2001 tour of England, I was watching Waugh walk back to the dressing room from the nets when a heckler in the crowd shouted at him, 'Taken any money lately, Mark?' The words hit their mark: Waugh dropped his head and quickened his pace. But from such blows there could be no refuge.

16

'THERE WAS NO TALK OF CRICKET'

The men who ran cricket were unfit to deal with a corruption crisis. Many of them were former players who had fallen into administration after retirement through want of anything else to do. It was a comfortable, undemanding life, a chance to keep up with old friends. Even though they were former players themselves, their consideration for the current generation was tempered by the knowledge that players had long been yoked to serfdom.

They wanted to run the game like an old boys' club: secretive because they saw no reason to be open; reluctant to embrace change because change was inconvenient; and ignorant of commerce because there had never been much commerce in cricket. They were not corrupt because there was nothing to be corrupt for.

But the influx of money from television and the one-day boom changed everything. Within a few years cricket became big business and attracted a breed of businessmen who saw cricket as simply another marketing opportunity. They had little interest in the players either.

The clash between old and new cultures was encapsulated in an acrimonious ICC meeting at Lord's to decide the venue for the 1996 World Cup. England had submitted a bid; so had the Asian triumvirate of India, Pakistan and Sri Lanka. Only one other Test-playing country supported the Asian candidacy but through organised lobbying the subcontinent secured the majority of associate member countries and was thereby able to block England's bid. The impasse was only broken when England backed down. One English representative, Oxbridge-educated and a former amateur, described the meeting as a 'shambles'. He said, 'We endured a fractious and unpleasant meeting beset by procedural wrangling. There was no talk of anything like cricket. It was, by a long way, the worst meeting I have ever attended.'[1]

The Asian bid marched behind the rampant commercial banner of Jagmohan Dalmiya, a hard-headed Calcutta businessman who had made his fortune in construction. Dalmiya rose to prominence as secretary of the Indian board just as the potential profits from television revenue were becoming apparent. He helped make the Indian board the wealthiest in the world.

The Asian World Cup bid succeeded because it promised other countries more money than England would have given them. As soon as the tournament was secured, Dalmiya set about selling it. He had a gift for fund-raising. He auctioned the television rights for nearly £10 million – a sum hitherto undreamed of in cricket – to a new player in the market, WorldTel, and by aggressively recruiting sponsors generated total profits of around £35 million. Most of this went to the hosts under terms already agreed. The players received a fraction of this sum. England's reward for backing down was to be awarded the 1999 tournament, but it was agreed that although a larger share of the profits would go to the hosts, from now on ultimate control of the event resided with the ICC; the 2003 tournament went to South Africa, with Ali Bacher running the organising committee.

Dalmiya used the financial success of the tournament to back his personal campaign to become the ICC's first Asian president. This aim he duly accomplished the following year by continuing his policy of courting the smaller nations.

These part-players now began to take on bigger roles on the international stage. Canada, Singapore and Kenya were all added to the roster, the tournaments they staged underpinned by the lucrative television contracts that guaranteed pictures back to the subcontinent's vast market.

Control of these minor events was much prized. Kenyan officials were surprised to be invited to a meeting in London in 1995 at which an offshore company called Lancaster Holdings offered to stage and promote cricket events in their country in return for £30,000 per annum for six years. Their surprise came not so much from the amount of money offered, or that Lancaster insisted on strict confidentiality, but that anyone should be interested in involving themselves in Kenyan cricket at all, given that they had not yet been granted one-day international status. That only came a year later. Kenya turned down the offer and Lancaster staged a tournament in Singapore instead. Singapore officials were not at liberty to disclose with whom they had dealt either.[2]

The richest of these smaller venues was Sharjah, where Abdurrahman Bukhatir, who owned the ground, organised the matches and owned a television company to control the rights, reportedly earning £20 million in three years.[3]

Television contracts were fought over tigerishly. After Sri Lanka won the 1996 World Cup, WorldTel signed a deal with their national board to cover matches there for three years. It cost £3.6 million. Later, suggestions publicly surfaced that a board official had demanded a £70,000 sweetener; the board president, having grown suspicious, had secretly taped a telephone conversation in which he claimed details of the sweetener were outlined. A senior WorldTel official denied ever having had the conversation.[4]

After the Cronje affair blew up, allegations were made on behalf of an Indian television company that Dalmiya, as ICC president, colluded with WorldTel officials to ensure that WorldTel won the overseas rights to the 1998 ICC Knockout tournament in Bangladesh at a substantially undervalued figure. Dalmiya and WorldTel denied the charge.[5]

No one seriously suggested that administrators were personally involved in match-fixing. What they could be accused of was failing to take proper care of the game in their charge. Some of them suspected nothing of what was going on under their noses. Others suspected something but either did not know how to deal with it or preferred to turn a blind eye.

The Indian board was as unwilling to face unpleasant facts, or treat whistleblowers sympathetically, as their English, Australian, Pakistani and Sri Lankan counterparts, or indeed the ICC. And they had more to hide than most. Revenue investigators in the mid-1990s passed information on to them that Indian players might have received payments in connection with matches in Sharjah, and that three players were suspected of betting on matches in which they were involved, yet the board did nothing about it.[6] Five months after Cronje's exposure, the secretary of the Indian board was maintaining that match-fixing in India was 'not possible'.[7]

The CBI report was scathing about administrative indifference. 'What was the BCCI [Indian board] doing all these years?' it stated. 'In spite of their public posturing now, all the office-bearers have been negligent in looking at this problem … their resolute indifference does give rise to suspicion.

'It defies credulity to believe that the BCCI was oblivious to such rampant match-fixing. The coffers of the board started overflowing with big money coming in through sponsorship and TV rights. This should have been reflected in the performance of the Indian team but the BCCI started a process of commercialisation without any vision as to how this money could be ploughed back to ensure better performance on the field.'[8]

Perhaps frustrated at the unworldliness of the administrators,

Lord Condon joined the attack in his report:

> A compelling case is made that the ICC and the individual cricket boards could and should have done more to deal with the problem of corruption at an earlier stage. For almost half of its history the ICC was a loose and fragile alliance with a small central administration based at Lord's with limited budgets and limited powers. Naivety and no clear mandate to deal with corruption exacerbated the problem. Also the ICC staff at Lord's missed opportunities to encourage more robust action to deal with the challenge...
>
> The individual cricket boards and member countries of the ICC responded to the emerging problem of corruption with a patchwork of criminal, judicial, disciplinary and informal measures ... No single inquiry had the jurisdiction to investigate beyond its own country, players and officials. Nevertheless, a disturbing picture gradually emerged of the extent of corruption and opportunities were missed to share information and concerns.[9]

Allegations about the mis-sale of television rights in India prompted the CBI to launch another investigation, which is still on-going. This resulted in raids on the homes and offices of, among others, Jagmohan Dalmiya; the treasurer of the Indian cricket board and Mark Mascarenhas, the head of WorldTel. They all denied wrongdoing. This rumbling affair prompted Lord Condon to recommend that the ICC 'develop an internal audit function to avoid the perception or reality of misappropriation of large sums of money generated from the sale of television rights'.[10]

Dalmiya's three-year term as ICC president ended shortly after the scandal broke but he remained an important figure on the subcontinent, where he took up a prominent position on the influential Asian Cricket Council, which increasingly showed signs of a willingness to act independently of the ICC.

Soon after, David Richards, chief executive of the ICC since 1993, handed in his notice with two years of his contract to run. He said he wanted to spend more time with his family. Thilanga Sumathipala, president of the Sri Lankan board, was ousted in a coup.

Asif Iqbal stood down after 17 years as co-ordinator of cricket in Sharjah when the Indian government became the first to ban its cricketers playing at such venues. 'I am a cricketer, I deal with cricket balls not politicians,' he said.[11] An investigation into corruption in Sharjah was already underway. When the *News of the World* secretly filmed Salim Malik in May 2000, the disgraced former Pakistan captain appeared to identify Asif (without naming him directly) as a linkman, though the newspaper's attempted 'sting' operation against Asif failed when he told them they had come to the wrong man.

THE ADMINISTRATORS were eventually forced into taking steps. They admitted they could and should have done more at an earlier stage, but there could be no going back. The damage was done. The culture of the game was contaminated.

Lord Condon said that it was only after the ICC signed a television deal in 2000 covering the next two World Cups worth more than £350 million that the cricket community acquired the financial security and collective will to provide an adequate infrastructure of administration and control. The ICC finally acknowledged, too, that it had a presentational problem. It appointed its first communications manager and recruited a public relations firm to improve its image. It agreed to publish its accounts for the first time.[12]

But many of the measures taken by the ICC and national boards in the wake of the scandal barely went beyond window-dressing. There was a will to put an end to the adverse publicity but not to make a firm example of players who had stepped out of line.

The ICC had responded to the Warne–Waugh affair by setting up a Code of Conduct commission. It was chaired by Lord Griffiths, another Oxbridge-educated former amateur, whose distinguished legal career was so lengthy that he was now well into his seventies. The commission's role was to review internal corruption inquiries conducted by the various national boards.

In more than two years Griffiths never wielded the power invested in him to top up the punishments handed out by the countries. This was most striking in the case of the Pakistan players identified in the Qayyum report. Most were merely fined small sums; Wasim Akram was also barred from captaining the national side again. Griffiths could, and preferably should, have suspended some or all of them, but this would have gone against time-honoured practice. Cricket authorities never took the lead in punishing anyone. This was always done by someone else: Hansie Cronje was caught by the police, Salim Malik and the various Indians by government-led investigations. Even Channel 4, who had taken over from the BBC as television broadcasters of Test cricket in the UK, dropped Wasim as a commentator in the light of the Qayyum report's findings.

The ICC made more of a show about the Cronje scandal. It held an emergency meeting to discuss the crisis and announced plans to set up its anti-corruption unit, which Lord Condon was appointed to run up to the 2003 World Cup. The ACU was funded by the ICC but, at Condon's insistence, fully independent of it. It liaised with internal inquiries, offering advice and assistance, and carried out its own investigations.

The ICC also announced that every international player, umpire, referee, team official, groundsman, administrator and employee must sign a declaration concerning their knowledge of, or involvement in, corruption. Condon's interim report judged the process 'intrinsically flawed' and 'not worth the logistical effort'; only 21 out of 911 responses produced yes answers, only five of which led to new information.[13] Fines and bans, ranging from two years to life, were created for anyone found guilty of being involved in gambling or match-fixing. However, when the South African board assessed the cases of Herschelle Gibbs and Henry Williams, it banned them for only six months.

Condon's interim report reviewed the first eight months of his unit's work and recommended a range of measures to counter corruption in future. The recommendations focused on four areas: training and educating future generations from becoming involved in corruption; practical steps to make it harder for players to be approached by corrupters; improving pay and conditions for players, including giving them a larger stake in the running of the game; and, modernising the administration. Some of his harshest words were reserved for the ICC itself, which had to be 'more transparent and accountable'.[14] He was more sympathetic towards the underpaid and disenfranchised players. The ICC's executive board had little option but to accept the report in full, and duly did so. It was later announced that prize money at the 2003 World Cup had been increased five-fold to £3.6 million.

The report was a thorough summary of the progress and state of corruption, but doubts were expressed as to its practical value. Some of its recommendations, such as restricting the players' use of mobile phones during matches, were already widely in use. Those that threatened basic freedoms or proposed honesty clauses in contracts seemed unreasonable or unworkable. Great store was placed in the appointment of full-time security managers to travel with teams, screening hotel and flight lists for suspicious names and alerting the ACU if bookies tried to bribe players or even socialise with them. Some viewed such figures as little better than spies and Australia refused to take up the idea on their tour of England.

In South Africa, India and Pakistan the report met with lukewarm responses. Having held their own inquiries, and seen their own players punished, they felt they had already gone through the cathartic process of which Condon spoke. Mark Taylor, the former Australia captain, dismissed the report as a rehash of the 'same stuff' he had been hearing 'for the past four or five years'.[15] But reasonably enough Condon maintained that to an extent his hands were tied. Legalising gambling on the subcontinent, for example, a step that would have done a great deal to eradicate the problem, was not an option for religious and cultural reasons. Breaking the power of the mafia appeared equally impossible.

The players welcomed it. 'Only a minority of professional cricketers around the world ... enjoy a good relationship with their administrators,' a leading players' representative said. 'A significant proportion are dissatisfied with their remuneration packages. In many sports the players take about 25 per cent of revenue. In cricket, the figure is less than 10 per cent. It is no surprise some people got involved in match-fixing. It was the only way they could make the game pay them a reasonable wage ... You can draw some sort of relationship between pay and conditions and corruption.'[16]

But the conclusion that drew most headlines was Condon's belief that match-fixing was still taking place. 'It was embarrassingly easy in the past to fix matches or aspects of matches for betting coups. Most of that has stopped ... What has not stopped is a small number of people in cricket who either because they're frightened to stop, or are arrogant or greedy, are still dabbling in seeking to fix matches or events within matches.'[17] Allegations had been made to him relating to a recent ICC Knockout tournament in Kenya and a Pakistan tour of New Zealand. The ACU had taken pre-emptive action against a plot by 'known corrupters' to affect one-day matches between England and Pakistan in the NatWest Series in 2001. He believed Tests as well as one-dayers had been fixed since the formation of his unit.[18]

Equally disheartening was Condon's admission that he was not yet in a position to recommend action against players, although the ACU was carrying out a series of investigations into players, former players, umpires and others that were not in the public domain.

Both Condon and Malcolm Gray, the new ICC president, appeared eager to draw a line under the past at a press conference rubber-stamping the report. 'We should be focusing on the future,' Gray said. 'By implementing these recommendations we will be able to go forward to make sure our cricketers are not tainted in the future as they have been in the past ... it's not just a matter of catching the crooks. The main thrust of the report is showing us a way to go forward.'[19]

Condon, describing his report as a 'blueprint to put match-fixing and corruption firmly in the past', said that prevention was his main task. 'The main event is ensuring cricket never has to face this again ... We're looking back at what's happened in the past. Whatever evidence is available, we'll seek to find it and place it before the relevant authorities. But if you've got a corrupter and corrupted player, obviously neither's got an interest in talking about it … That is not to say we are not looking vigorously at past allegations but there's got to be some realism about what's going to come out.'

There was a clear impression that Condon and the Establishment were hoping that if they safeguarded the future as well as they could, the past would look after itself as a tainted generation gradually left the scene. 'We're coming to the end of a generation of people who've been involved in match-fixing who are going out of the game and I'm absolutely convinced that ICC will do its damnedest to ensure that the youngsters replacing them will not be drawn into similar practice … a very small number of current cricketers have been involved.'

Condon added another note of finality when he disclosed that he would 'gradually disengage from the process'. He had been appointed a people's peer and his work in the House of Lords would limit his future involvement with the ACU.

Gray admitted that at the outset the scandal had damaged the sport's credibility and hit attendance figures. But the crowds and television ratings had come back strongly because of some dramatic matches. 'The resurgence of Test cricket has been very fortunate for us,' he said. But Gray conceded that it would take longer to discover what sort of impact the scandal had had on younger followers. Had it left them disillusioned? Only time would tell.

HANSIE CRONJE was left with plenty of time to reflect on where he went wrong. Once a demi-god in his own land, his reputation and life were apparently in ruins. He had put his family through hell and his marriage under strain. Would he have behaved as he did had he had the responsibilities of fatherhood to consider? Without a stake in the future, he was grabbing what he could for today. It was simply all too easy. As he told the King Commission, it had seemed like 'money for jam'.

He must also have been astonished at the extent of the corruption the investigations he triggered laid bare. Or was he?

Naturally, Cronje was shocked when his name first came up, and the early days of the Delhi police inquiry, during which suspects were arrested and questioned, must have been very alarming. The hostility directed towards him from around the world, and reports that mafia groups were at the centre of the conspiracy, must also have been perturbing. When he first attended the King Commission in Cape Town, the hall was swept for terrorist devices and he arrived amid high security in case of reprisals.

Few then knew whom Cronje might accuse. In the event, he named few names, but those he did name would have been carefully chosen. His identification of Mukesh Gupta and Azharuddin presented investigators with two significant leads in their efforts to unravel the story. Did Cronje hand them to the inquiry in an attempt to divert attention from his own dilemma? If so, it worked like a dream. The Indian investigation, rather than the South African one, was soon stealing all the headlines.

Once the King Commission adjourned after ten days of hearings for the preparation of an interim report, Cronje, his family and legal team strove to draw a line under the affair. Cronje issued a statement asking for forgiveness. 'I have let down the United Cricket Board, the team, the fans and the game down,' he said. 'I am bitterly sorry.'[20] He added that he drew consolation from never having fixed a match. His father, Ewie, appealed for his son to be allowed to make a new life; he wanted to give to cricket all the money he had received from bookmakers. 'My son has acknowledged the error of his ways and asked for forgiveness. He now needs a great deal of support to continue with his life,' he said.[21] Ewie himself had personally suffered, having been forced to leave the board of the Free State Cricket Union.

That support was forthcoming. Some teammates, however, felt too angry to contact their former captain, and Bacher said he only spoke to him 'two or three times' in fourteen months.[22] But Herschelle Gibbs and Jonty Rhodes remained in close touch and there was no shortage of financial offers for Cronje to tell his story, offers he eagerly snapped up. The crassest involved a series of three one-hour interviews with a South African television station, which reportedly earned him £100,000. He was required to answer a string of questions that could not have been more harmless had his lawyers drawn them up, which they possibly did. The programmes were so schmaltzy that viewing figures actually fell, but the public were generally supportive. 'It's been one of the hardest of times ... but also one of the greatest of times because of all the support we've had,' Cronje's brother, Frans, said.[23]

He sold another interview to Australian television for about £80,000 in which he claimed his conduct equated with that of Warne and Waugh. 'They basically confessed to taking money from bookmakers and supplying information and it's exactly what I did in a lot of my dealings,' he argued.[24] There were also reports that he planned to write a book.

He did go through genuinely difficult times. The King hearings were particularly traumatic, for obvious reasons. For a start, getting his story straight must have been a trial. Bob Woolmer, who remained remarkably sympathetic, spoke to him on the phone at this time and described him as 'a broken man, full of remorse'.[25] Dave Richardson said, 'Those close to him saw what it did to him, he's a bit of a wreck'.[26] One newspaper erroneously reported his suicide.[27] A few weeks later Cronje said he was finding it hard 'to forgive myself for what I did ... There were days when I was really weak, days when I didn't want to get out of bed, days when I didn't want to face the world.'[28]

He received a bad blow when King said in his interim report that Cronje had more to tell, had contradicted himself and been evasive; and another when the South African board banned him for life from all its cricketing activities, including coaching, commentating and even attending grounds. 'That's the end of Hansie,' said Percy Sonn, who probably came to regret an intemperate remark about Cronje not even being allowed to play cricket on the beach, because it suggested due process was not being observed.[29] Cronje was given seven days to appeal, but his legal team did nothing – though this did not stop them subsequently disputing the ban on the grounds that no appeal was granted. The board seemed intent on continuing to let Cronje take the flak while it sought to clean up the affair in advance of staging the 2003 World Cup. The policy bore fruit. Under Shaun Pollock's leadership, the South Africa team, shorn only of its former captain, re-established itself as the second-best side behind Australia. 'I was very fearful when it all broke that the whole team would break apart,' Bacher said. 'But South Africans are resilient people. They have been through many hardships.'[30]

Backed by his religion and his friends, Cronje pulled himself round. He got his golf handicap down, studied for a second business degree and worked for an internet company. He became more trenchant about his sullied past. When he met Woolmer several months later, he pulled him to one side and, with bottom lip quivering, insisted, 'Coach, I want you to know that I never fixed a game of cricket involving South Africa or any other team.'[31]

What would have heartened Cronje most was that the political will to root out corruption rapidly evaporated, a situation his lawyers exploited by finding legal arguments to delay the King Commission reconvening. The mood had changed: the desire to uncover ugly truths had been supplanted by anxieties over the expense the hearings entailed and the damage they might do to the image of South Africa and its cricket. The sports minister was in favour of winding them up and Bacher concurred: 'We believe the commission has done a good job. We have our doubts whether there's any more to come out … It's time to wrap it up.'[32]

The hearings were eventually abandoned after Cronje's lawyers raised doubts over the validity of the commission itself, arguing that a serving judge could not head a special investigating unit, a point that was never resolved but was sufficient to prompt a closure. Had the hearings continued, a number of former international players were subpoenaed to appear and Cronje's legal team would have come under pressure to provide financial documents they had so far failed to deliver. So much for Cronje's early claim that his innocence could be established by checking his bank account.

Cronje and his legal team fought a tenacious rearguard, refusing to concede ground in any area. They prepared to sue the South African board in the courts over its ban, and when Judge King predictably declined to grant Cronje immunity from criminal prosecution and passed the verdict over to the director of public prosecutions, they were in a position to negotiate a deal: no appeal in the courts against the ban in exchange for no criminal prosecution. But they still hoped to win Cronje the right to attend or commentate on games. Indeed, said Cronje, with no apparent shame or remorse, he still hoped to coach South Africa. 'One day I would certainly like to have that opportunity ... I certainly tried my entire career to make South Africa the number-one cricket-playing country in the world. That's what I lived for, trained for, breathed for.'[33]

In theory, Cronje still faced possible criminal prosecution in India. The Delhi police still had aspirations to try several people, including himself and Sanjiv Chawla. But without an extradition treaty between South Africa and India, there was no chance of him being handed over to the Indian authorities, especially as they had been unable to provide South Africa with copies of the Cronje tapes.

Cronje had one last practical contribution to make to cricket. He was asked to star in an instructional video warning young players of what might happen if they got involved with bookmakers.

Some might have been forgiven for thinking that the lesson was just how much it was possible to get away with.

CHRONOLOGY

1979–80: Earliest allegations of match-fixing surround Pakistan's tour of India

1983: India win World Cup in England, transforming cricket on the subcontinent

1990: Bookmaker Mukesh Gupta becomes involved with India players Ajay Sharma and Manoj Prabhakar

1992: South Africa readmitted to international cricket

1994: India docked points after losing one-day match to West Indies. Pakistan and Sri Lanka conduct internal inquiries. Hansie Cronje and Salim Malik appointed captains respectively of South Africa and Pakistan

1995: Azharuddin first meets Mukesh Gupta. Cronje first approached by bookmaker. Australian newspapers allege Salim Malik tried to bribe Shane Warne, Mark Waugh and Tim May. Inquiry clears Malik

1996–97: Cronje and Azharuddin take bribes from Mukesh Gupta during reciprocal tours between South Africa and India. South Africa team turns down $250,000 to throw one-dayer

1997: Manoj Prabhakar alleges in *Outlook* magazine that unnamed teammate tried to bribe him

1998: Emerges Warne and Mark Waugh were secretly fined in 1995 for taking money from bookmaker. O'Regan inquiry launched. Pakistan launches inquiry under Judge Qayyum

1999: Favourites South Africa lose World Cup in England. Pakistan lose to Bangladesh, prompting inquiry. Chris Lewis approached to fix England–New Zealand Test at Old Trafford

Jan 2000: Cronje paid to ensure South Africa–England Test at Centurion does not end in draw

Feb–Mar 2000: South Africa tour India. Cronje approaches six teammates about possible match-fixing; Herschelle Gibbs and Henry Williams agree but fail to effect deal. Delhi police operation alights on telephone calls between Cronje and 'bookie'

Apr 2000:	Cronje and other South Africans charged by Delhi police, who release phone transcripts. Cronje confesses to taking money from bookmakers and is withdrawn from South Africa team. King Commission launched
May 2000:	Qayyum report leads to life bans for Salim Malik and Ata-ur-Rehman. Six others are fined, including Wasim Akram, who is barred from captaincy. India launches investigation under Central Bureau of Investigation. Prabhakar names Kapil Dev as person who tried to bribe him; Kapil denies the allegation but later steps down as India's coach. ICC sets up anti-corruption unit
Jun 2000:	Cronje admits dealings with Mukesh Gupta to King Commission
Oct 2000:	Cronje banned for life by South African board from all its activities; he later appeals
Nov 2000:	CBI publishes report in which Mukesh Gupta implicates several non-Indians. India bans Azharuddin and Ajay Sharma for life, Prabhakar and Ajay Jadeja for five years; Kapil Dev cleared
Feb 2001:	King Commission wound up
May 2001:	Lord Condon's anti-corruption unit publishes interim report
Jul–Aug 2001:	Alec Stewart and others cleared of Mukesh Gupta's allegations

NOTES

CHAPTER ONE

1 For Steyn's account of his encounter with Cronje, testimony to King Commission, 8 June 2000; interview with telhelka.com, 23 June 2000

2 For Cronje crumpling on sofa, Tony Greig, 11 April 2000

3 'To get lost…', King Commission, first interim report, 11 August 2000

4 'I don't want to get into a situation…', Cronje's cross-examination at King Commission

5 'It used to annoy me…', Donald, *White Lightning* (2000), p.15

6 'happy-go-lucky', Donald, *White Lightning* (2000), p.128

7 'Apparently the girl ran out…', Donald, *White Lightning* (2000), pp.127–8

8 John Blair doubting Cronje's credentials, cited by Ray White, president of UCBSA, 3 June 2000; confirmed by Blair to author, telephone conversation, 29 May 2001

9 'UCBSA is certain…', press statement, 7 April 2000

10 Bacher on the government running with the ball, conversation with author, 8 April 2000

11 Indian government taking a battering, Dr Ashwin Desai, member of UCBSA's Transformation Monitoring Committee, interview with Karen McGregor, 13 April 2000

12 'Strength of evidence', Dr Ashwin Desai, interview with Karen McGregor, 13 April 2000

13 Police quote, Ajay Ray Sharma, agency reports, 11 April 2000

14 Pahad conveys his concern to Cronje, Ronnie Mamoepe, Pahad's spokesman, interview with Karen McGregor, 13 April 2000

15 'I'm certain…', Dr Ashwin Desai, interview with Karen McGregor, 13 April 2000

16 On Cronje's conversation with McCauley, his spokesman Ron Steele, 11 April 2000

17 On phone call between Bacher and Cronje at game-park, Bacher's testimony to King Commission, 12 June 2000

18 Bacher on Cronje knowing he was sacked, conversation with author, 4 May 2000

19 On Pahad suggestion Cronje holds press conference, Ronnie Mamoepe, interview with Karen McGregor, 13 April 2000

CHAPTER TWO

1 'I honestly struggled…', Cronje interview with *Sixty Minutes* programme, Channel Nine, 16 July 2000

2 Wilkinson on 'kind of a snort laugh', King Commission, first interim report, 11 August 2000

3 Cronje, *News of the World* interview, 23 July 2000

4 'any sum of money…', Cronje press conference, Durban, 9 April 2000

5 Cronje alters statement, Steyn's testimony to the King Commission, 8 June 2000

6 Ngconde Balfour, Cape Town press conference, 11 April 2000

7 Bacher interview with author, Cape Town, 14 April 2000

8 'Hansie knows you want to kill him…', *Sunday Times*, 16 April 2000

9 'brought about by my own foolishness…', *Cape Times*, 14 April 2000

10 Cronje's hand-written statement, read out to King Commission, 8 June 2000

11 'The poor man needed desperately to sin…', Max du Preez, *Business Day*, 13 April 2000

12 'Even when we have made it in the sophisticated world…', Max du Preez, *Business Day*, 13 April 2000

13 'When money talks, even the angels listen,' Volsteedt, Deon Gouws, p.73

14 'Hansie is our hero, we shall not be moved!' Deon Gouws, p.73

15 'The refusal to countenance…', *Business Day*, 12 April 2000

16 Letter on boys and girls, *Citizen* newspaper, 13 April 2000

17 Cronje on his 'unfortunate love of money', evidence to King Commission, 21 June 2000

18 'You could see Hansie was just fascinated by this boat…', Matthews, Deon Gouws, p.87

19 'I am not an alcoholic…', Cronje's evidence to King Commission, 22 June 2000

20 Details of Cronje's estimated earnings were given in the South African *Sunday Times*, 16 April 2000, and also referred to during the King Commission hearings, 21 June 2000

21 It has been alleged that the Deloitte & Touche report for the King Commission was leaked by the United Cricket Board to undermine Cronje's efforts to rehabilitate himself; it was seen by the *Sunday Telegraph*, which published a report on 22 July 2001, claiming Cronje owned eight properties and nineteen bank accounts, but this was over the course of several years, not concurrently

22 'He played the stock market...', Bob Woolmer, *Wisden Cricket Monthly*, June 2000, p.19

23 Cronje's prospective business deals, Deon Gouws, p.117

24 'I am not trying to boast...', Cronje's evidence to King Commission, 21 June 2000

25 'He was adored...', letter to the *Star*, 13 April 2000

26 *Cape Times*, 12 April 2000

27 'his downfall is a moral fable...', *Business Day*, 12 April 2000

CHAPTER THREE

1   'It takes a lifetime...' Conversation with author, 6 August 2001

2   Calcutta toss: Abbasi to Qayyum; Narottam Puri, *Fallen Heroes*, p.53; Chetan Chauhan, quoted on agencies, 13 April 2000. On Asif and 1990–91 story, see also *Sunday Times*, 19 February 1995

3   'Viswanath has denied...' Conversation with author, 6 August 2001

4   'None of the players were directly involved,' Amarnath, *Fallen Heroes*, p.84

5   CBI report into match-fixing

6   'Corrupt practices took place...', Condon report into match-fixing, 30 April 2001, paragraphs 87–89

7   Asif 'wondered' about matches at Sharjah, *Sunday Times*, 27 May 2001

8   'They change their locations...', Mumbai police officer, quoted 17 April 2000

9   CBI report

10 'The gangsters got into fixing...', anonymous source to author, 23 June 2000

11 Asif on 1987 allegations, *Sunday Times*, 19 February 1995

12 'the entire team has to be in the know', Azharuddin, *Outlook*, 22 January 2001

13 Salim Malik, quoted in the *News of the World*, 21 May 2000

14 CBI report

15 For background on Ibrahim and Rajan, see *India Today*, 2 October 2000; *Outlook*, 20 November 2000

16 Test player admits approach from Abu Salem, CBI report, summary of Azharuddin's testimony

17 'We are punters, not fixers,' Chohtta Shakeel to Stephen Grey, May 2000

18 Managers, captains ... are involved,' Subodh Mehta, quoted in *India Today*, 29 May 2000

19 Salim Malik, *News of the World*, 21 May 2000

20 'The players do not do it just for money...', Fareshteh Gati to author, 16 November 2000

21 Qasim Omar stories, see *News of the World*, 5 November 2000 and the *Observer*, 21 January 2001; *The People*, 10 March 1996. *Wisden Cricket Monthly*, March 2001, p.9

22 'One day, he was walking...', Mukesh Gupta's testimony to CBI report

23 'since he thought Ajay Sharma...', Mukesh Gupta's testimony to CBI report

24 'arguably the biggest cricketer-bookie...', police source, *India Today*, 1 May 2000

25 'based on that information...', Mukesh Gupta's testimony to CBI report

26 'According to MK, Manoj...', Mukesh Gupta's testimony to CBI report

27 'They say I was involved...', *The Times*, 3 November 2000

28 Jones offered £30,000, *The Times*,14 February 1995, O'Regan report

29 'MK was always determined to make it big...', *Outlook*, 4 July 2000

30 'The secret of his success...', *Outlook*, 4 July 2000

31 'MK was very secretive...', Anand Saxena testimony to CBI

32 'Whatever he told us...', RN Sawani, director of CBI, quoted on *Panorama*, 20 May 2001

33 The CBI never cross-examined Prabhakar about Gupta's claims regarding his fixing of matches in Australia in 1992 or against England in 1993

34 Gupta tells CBI he made £800,000 through 'insider information', *Outlook*, 20 November 2000

35 'It was only in 1994–95...', CBI source, quoted 23 June 2000

36 'not especially reliable...', *Daily Telegraph*, 23 February 1995

37 For details of Colombo Test of 1992 and 1994 inquiry, see *Sunday Times*, 30 April 2000

38 Qayyum report, Part I, Background to Inquiry

39 Conversation with author, 18 March 2001

CHAPTER FOUR

1 Mongia on Kanpur, testimony to Madhavan
2 For Prabhakar's allegations against the Indian management, *Outlook*, 11 June 1997
3 Halbish on 'cricket's greatest crisis...', *Wisden* 1996, p.17
4 Mushtaq–Border story, *The Times*, 14 February 1995; *Guardian*, 13 February 1995
5 Intikhab on ugly rumours, *The Times*, 15 February 1995
6 Salim Malik's denials, and Sohail quote, *The Times*, 16 February 1995
7 Sohail quotes, *The Australian*, 17 February 1996
8 Sarfraz Nawaz on 1994 investigation, *Wisden* 1996, p.18
9 'It is very unfortunate...', Intikhab, *The Times*, 25 February 1995
10 Aaqib Javed, saw Cadbury 'freely mixing with the players...', testimony to Qayyum
11 'going into the rooms...', Basit Ali testimony to Qayyum
12 Javed Miandad on Idress Cadbury saying Wasim and Waqar 'on his brother's books', testimony to Qayyum. Wasim Akram's counsel argued before Qayyum that Miandad's statement was merely hearsay
13 Pakistan team 'very close to a bookie named Hanif Cadbury...', Mukesh Gupta's testimony to CBI, November 2000
14 For Richards–Abbasi correspondence, see the *Sunday Times*, 14 May 2000
15 John Reid, *The Times*, 16 February 1995
16 For summary of Ebrahim inquiry, see *Wisden* 1996, pp.17–18
17 Minutes of PCB meeting, *Outlook*, 30 July 1997
18 Sohail, *Outlook*, 9 April 1997
19 Latif fax to David Richards, see *Sunday Times*, 14 May 2000
20 Bahal–Magazine conversation, *Not Quite Cricket*, p.34
21 For Prabhakar–Bahal stories, *Outlook*, 11 June 1997
22 'Unfortunately, in situations where monkey deals...', *Outlook*, 11 June 1997
23 'It became obvious...', Sakyasen Mitra, *Fallen Heroes*, p.104
24 'Things really snowballed...', *Fallen Heroes*, p.29
25 'brusque and dismissive...', *Fallen Heroes*, p.19
26 'I have been a loner...', *Fallen Heroes*, p.33
27 'Prabhakar's face reflected...', Pradeep Magazine, *Not Quite Cricket*, p.61

28 Vinod Mehta, conversation with author, 17 April 2000

29 'If I name the player...', Prabkahar quoted in Pradeep Magazine, *Not Quite Cricket*, p.63

30 'He wanted to disclose everything...', Madhavan report

31 After the Chandrachud report cleared everyone, the Indian board filed defamation proceedings against Prabhakar and the magazine, but no hearing ever took place

32 'The board is making me...', Prabhakar, *Fallen Heroes*, p.159

33 'still had a few more years...', *Fallen Heroes*, p.31

34 'Perhaps the good is overshadowed...', *India Today*, 22 May 2000

CHAPTER FIVE

1 'John...', O'Regan report

2 'Little by little...', Conn to author, 2 May 2001

3 'I don't know what...', Conn to author, 2 May 2001

4 'protect the reputation of Australian cricket...', Speed, press conference, 8 December 1998

5 'We felt the way ICC was constituted...', Richards, 8 December 1998

6 'If he did not have a legal obligation...', Qayyum report

7 'He had players...', O'Regan report

8 'In my opinion...', O'Regan report

9 'There was no chance...', *Wasim: The Autobiography* (1998), p.127

10 Pakistan Cricket Board 'had arrived at the conclusion...', Qayyum report

11 'The allegation that the Pakistan team...', Qayyum report

12 Qayyum pressured during Bhutto's trial, 'Bugging tapes reveal "fixing" of Bhutto trial' by Nick Fielding, *Sunday Times*, 4 February 2001

13 'There was no legislation on match-fixing...', Qayyum report, Part II

14 'A number of people...', Qayyum report

15 'The government message...', Fareshteh Gati, Pakistan journalist, conversation with author, 16 November 2000

16 'I am convinced...', Qayyum to Reuters, 17 April 2000

17 When Malik was secretly caught on tape by the *News of the World*, it was alleged he said the Singer World Series was the target of a double-fix, with Pakistan and Australia both trying to lose. An investigation by Greg Malick,

Australia's anti-corruption officer, found no evidence of Australian involvement.

18 'When Mushtaq Ahmed appeared before this commission…', Qayyum report
19 Ata-ur-Rehman forced to move house, Fareshteh Gati to author, 16 November 2000
20 Kidnapping, Condon report, paragraph 15
21 Wasim 'not above board' and following quotes, Qayyum report
22 'Waqar Younis had not even heard…', Qayyum report

CHAPTER SIX

1 'It was clear from the beginning…', Deon Gouws, p.81
2 'Hansie ended up a total introvert…', Deon Gouws, p.82
3 'Hansie came to me with a huge smile…', Deon Gouws, p.82
4 'This thing is rife…', Wessels, *Star*, 8 April 2000
5 'He would often just make a fleeting remark…', Deon Gouws, p.117
6 Cronje 'never sort of stood down to anyone', Katis testimony to King Commission,13 June 2000
7 'He hates criticism,' Deon Gouws, p.115
8 Cronje–de Klerk incident, Deon Gouws, p.180
9 'Maybe I should have stuck it out…', Deon Gouws p.82
10 'I was approached by an Indian or Pakistani man…', Cronje's statement to King Commission, 15 June 2000
11 'It is such a big temptation…', Cronje interview on *Sixty Minutes*, Channel Nine, 16 July 2000
12 'Hansie called me to his room…', Symcox to King Commission, 22 June 2000
13 Rashid Latif on Mandela Trophy final, Qayyum report
14 Cronje on meetings with Sunil, King Commission interim report, 11 August 2000
15 'He called me to a room in the hotel…', this and following comments by Cronje, statement to King Commission, 15 June 2000
16 Smuggled $30,000 out of India – Cronje's cross-examination, King Commission, 22 June 2000
17 'I asked him if he was joking…', Crookes to King Commission, 8 June 2000
18 'The team was unhappy about the match…', Symcox testimony to King

Commission, 7 June 2000. Although Symcox said it was the first time he had heard of such an offer, he was in fact made a personal offer about 'getting involved in some betting' on the same tour. The offer came in a hotel lobby in Mumbai from one of the Indian players, whom Symcox has declined to name. Symcox declined to get involved but never officially reported the approach

19 'In any other circumstances...', Richardson's testimony to King Commission, 13 June 2000

20 'If we took the money...', Woolmer in *Daily Telegraph*, 10 May 2000

21 'openly bragging of the money they have made...', Cullinan to author, 12 April 2000

22 'We had heard that other teams had been approached...', Richardson to author, 16 April 2000

23 'The game was a farce...', Bob Woolmer in *Daily Telegraph*, 10 May 2000

24 Cronje was 'very annoyed with myself', King Commission first interim report, 11 August 2000

25 Derek Crookes confirmed the players' vow of secrecy – which extended to their wives and girlfriends – to the King Commission on 8 June 2000

26 'I did engage in a fleeting conversation...', Bacher to the *Citizen*, 24 June 2000

CHAPTER SEVEN

1 'He set about tackling...', R Mohan, *Wisden Almanack* 1991, p.66

2 'One day I met Azhar...', Ayaz Memon, *The Nation*, 19 November 2000

3 'I like to spend money...', Pradeep Magazine, *Not Quite Cricket*, p.71

4 'What's wrong in having Armani suits...', *Outlook* interview, 22 January 2001

5 Azhar's estimated wealth at around £25 million, Vishv Bandhu Gupta, *Fallen Heroes*, p.69

6 Azhar properties, CBI report. Azhar claimed to the CBI that the bungalow in Hyderabad actually belonged to an aunt

7 For details of their dealings, see the testimonies to the CBI of Azharuddin, Mukesh Gupta, Ajay Sharma and Dr Ali Irani

8 Irani no doubt about Jadeja's involvement with Azhar, see Madhavan report

9 Azharuddin speaks to Anees Ibrahim on phone, *Outlook*, 22 December 1997

10 'South Africa have been involved from the beginning,' Maria, *Fallen Heroes*, p.59

11 Police evidence against several Indian players during Titan Cup, *Fallen Heroes*, pp.119–120. Rakesh Maria was unhappy about being secretly taped and claimed he was misquoted

12 'Counter-fixing...', *Outlook*, 11 June 1997

13 Irani said Steel 'gave me money for Azhar on a number of occasions...', Irani's testimony to Madhavan

14 'He scored two runs in the match...', Indian official quoted in *Outlook*, 26 June 2000

15 Sunil Dev tour report, *Outlook*, 11 June 1997

16 'MK thought...', Gupta's testimony to CBI

17 Irani on Azhar doing matches with Anees Ibrahim, testimony to CBI; also *Outlook*, 20 November 2000

18 Irani altered the evidence he gave to the CBI when questioned by the Indian cricket board's match-fixing investigator, K Madhavan, saying that India did not play to their potential in Bridgetown, but Madhavan said he was 'not inclined to accept the revised version'. For the St Vincent match, see *Outlook*, 11 June 1997

19 'explosive documents' and Tiger Memon photographs break down Azharuddin, *Outlook*, 13 November 2000

20 'We have established his connections...', Income Tax officer interviewed by tehelka.com, 2 August 2000

21 CBI report, summary of evidence against Azhar

22 'He was the captain...', Madhavan report

23 'He suspected...', Tendulkar testimony to CBI

24 Gupta in Galle pavillion, anonymous source to author, March 2001

CHAPTER EIGHT

1 Woolmer 'breathless', *Woolmer on Cricket* by Bob Woolmer, p.3

2 'quite disgraceful', *Woolmer on Cricket*, p.133

3 'Apparently my name was mud...', *Woolmer on Cricket*, p.136

4 'There were times...', *Woolmer on Cricket*, p.75

5 'Hansie's face is like a book...', *Woolmer on Cricket*, p.170

6 Woolmer on 'Recently colleagues...', *Daily Telegraph*, 10 May 2000

7 Cronje on equal opportunity, interview with Mike Haysman on M-Net

television, quoted in Deon Gouws, p.169

8 Cronje denies Leeds Test fixed, *News of the World*, 23 July 2000

9 Bacher's evidence to King Commission, 12 June 2000. Bacher's claims were based on what he had been told by Majid Khan

10 Javed Akhtar's denial, 19 April 2000

11 Noakes, *Cape Times*, 12 April 2000

12 'There was absolutely no defensible reason...', Noakes in *Woolmer on Cricket*, pp.xvi–xvii

13 Indian actress Anju Mahendroo, quoted in *Fallen Heroes*, pp.444–445

14 For Ajay Gupta's dealings with Azhar, see CBI report and Madhavan report

15 Anonymous conversation with author, 26 April 2000

16 Test captain laughing at Pakistan performance v Bangladesh, quoted in *Wisden Cricket Monthly*, p.30, November 2000

17 Comparative earnings of Pakistan and Australian players, see Qayyum report

18 'received a low single figure percentage...', Condon report, paragraph 79

19 Sarfraz Nawaz, phone conversation with author, 10 May 2000

20 Sarfraz Nawaz, phone conversation with author, 7 November 2000

21 'I think people are forcing it to happen...', Gordon Greenidge, quoted in *Wisden Cricket Monthly*, p.30, November 2000

22 Richard Pybus, phone conversation with author, 12 October 2000

23 'I went to the...', Gaekwad, quoted 12 June 2000

24 Bookies may have applied pressure, *Sunday Telegraph*, 23 April 2000

25 Dawood aide, Chohtta Shakeel interview with Stephen Grey, May 2000. For more on bookies going off bets on England–Pakistan match, *Daily News* (Pakistan), 14 April 1999

26 Cadbury's body mutilated, Rashid Latif to Ghulan Hosnain, 21 April 2000

27 Report of Cadbury's death in Pakistan *Daily News*, 21 May 1999

28 'The immediate word,' quote, Ghulan Hasnain, to author, 20 April 2000

29 Cadbury robbed on way home from casino, *Guardian*, 24 May 2001; Mumbai bookie Subodh Mehta quoted in *India Today*, 29 May 2000

30 'He had received a phonecall...', Miandad testimony to Qayyum inquiry

31 'because [the] Holy Quran was not available...', Wasim Akram testimony to Qayyum inquiry

32 An analysis of telephone records linked Ratan Mehta to Sanjiv Chawla; see

India Today, 10 July 2000. A witness told the author that he saw Mehta in the company of Kishen Kumar in London during the World Cup, telephone conversation, 23 June 2000

33 'Small-time actresses,' Abhishek Verma, an acquaintance of Mehta's, to author, 23 June 2000

34 For details of Mehta's movements in London, see *India Today*, 26 June 2000

35 'I saw him taking calls…', Abhishek Verma to author, 23 June 2000

36 'After my case…', Mona Mehta, quoted in *India Today*, 10 July 2000

37 'I may have met him in a hotel lobby,' Wasim Akram, phone conversation with author, 11 November 2000

38 Ratan Mehta, on relationship with players, testimony to CBI

39 'like a father' referred to in Madhavan report; Kapil Dev on Jadeja's dubious friends, testimony to CBI report

40 'Asked about his association…', Jadeja testimony to CBI

41 Sanjiv Kohli and Pawan Puri, evidence to CBI inquiry. Puri's testimony about Ahmedabad was supported by another bookmaker, Deepak Rajouri, who said that it was known in Delhi's bookmaking circle that Ratan Mehta had advance information the game would be drawn

42 Tendulkar on the Ahmedabad follow-on, testimony to CBI report

43 Telephone contact between Jadeja and bookie Uttam Chand, CBI Report

44 Sunil Dev, India's manager, predicts one-day series will sit at 2–2, *India Today*, 29 May 2000

45 *Sunday Telegraph*, 23 April 2000

46 Malik on Bangladesh game, *News of the World*, 21 May 2000

CHAPTER NINE

1 Lewis as 'Outcast', *India Today*, 22 May 2000

2 For Jadeja contract, Pradeep Magazine, *Not Quite Cricket*, p.157

3 Khetrapal on his film career, interview with Damandeep Singh, 21 April 2000

4 'All along the drive to Delhi…', Pradeep Magazine, *Not Quite Cricket*, p.157

5 'Two days before…', this and following explanation of events by Khetrapal given in an interview with Damandeep Singh, 21 April 2000

6 Khetrapal's movements in England gleaned from police charge sheet. See *India Today*, 22 May 2000. When he checked into the Holiday Inn at Hanger,

Khetrapal gave his passport number as A5283263, whereas on his visa application form submitted to the British High Commission in Delhi it appeared as A5385917

7 Khetrapal telephones Chawla, Scotland Yard source to author, 24 January 2001; see also *India Today*, 22 May 2000. Khetrapal and Chawla denied knowing each other to police. It was understood that Sodha may also have known Chawla – he featured in the Cronje tapes recorded by Delhi police, trying to place bets with 'Sanjay'

8 'Somebody that I've known from time to time...', Lewis's interview with *Extra Cover* programme, Sky Sports television, 22 April 2000

9 'Jatesh', see *India Today*. Lewis could not recall anyone called Sodha, conversation with Dipesh Gadher, 14 June 2000

10 'What is in it for me?' and other quotes, Khetrapal to Damandeep Singh

11 'They wanted me...', Lewis, speaking on *Panorama*, 20 May 2001

12 'I was obviously shocked...', *Extra Cover* interview

13 'nearly fell off his chair...', *News of the World*, 16 April 2000

14 'When they initially asked me to fix...', *Extra Cover* interview

15 'They are all famous players...', *News of the World*, 16 April 2000

16 'He didn't say what it was for...' and 'At the time I actually just listened', *Extra Cover* interview

17 'The ECB have consistently told players...', *Extra Cover* interview

18 'As regards to how true...', *Extra Cover* interview

19 'I was told a week later by the board...', *Extra Cover* interview

20 Lord MacLaurin's statement, 27 April 2000

21 'If my name had come out...', *News of the World*, 16 April 2000

22 'I spoke to one of three players...', conversation with author, 22 November 2000

23 'left extremely bitter memories...', letter from Dalmiya to Khetrapal, 22 October 1999

24 Inland Revenue investigations into players, see *Sunday Times*, 27 May 2001

CHAPTER TEN

1 Kumar on friendships with Kalra and Chawla, here and subsequently, Kumar press conference, 12 April 2000

2 'We struck an instant rapport', Kalra on 8 April 2000

3 'The ambience of the shop...', agency report, 12 April 2000

4 'I don't think he has that sort of money...', Khurana in *Sunday Times*, 9 April 2000. Chawla held two directorships, with Commercial Clothing Company and Waterlow Nominees

5 'Sanjiv is a deep water fish...', Kalra, agency source, 7 April 2000

6 'More interested in gambling on cricket...', Hamid Cassim, testimony to King Commission, 26 June 2000

7 'He was near broke...', Ishwar Singh, quoted by Damandeep Singh, 14 April 2000

8 Calcutta police raid, *Fallen Heroes*, p.284; 'arguably the biggest cricket betting operator...', agency reports, 7 April 2000

9 'held several meetings...', *Statesman* newspaper, 4 May 2000

10 Kalra said $400,000–$500,000 was the figure raised to fix the India–South Africa one-day series in February 2000. He was contacted in prison by *India Today* on 8 April 2000. On 'massive' amount sent to London bank, police sources, 13 April 2000

11 'I did not put my money in betting', and 'too busy to indulge in such things', Kumar press conference, 12 April 2000

12 'threatened me to name some people falsely...', Kumar quoted on release on bail, 14 June 2000

13 'I have met them...', Kumar press conference, 12 April 2000

14 Chawla knew Azharuddin, *Fallen Heroes*, p.67

15 'Retired players...', *Outlook*, 5 June 2000

16 For summary of Prabhakar's activities in retirement, see *India Today*, 22 May 2000

17 Among other evidence, telephone records suggested there was contact; see *India Today*, 22 May 2000

18 'He was a disaster waiting to happen...', *Sunday Telegraph*, 11 June 2000

19 Chawla contacts Cassim, Cassim testimony to King Commission, 26 June 2000

20 'We became very good friends,' Cassim testimony to King Commission

21 Azharuddin 'The entire team...', *The Mercury*, Durban, 13 April 2000

22 'I would attend games...', Cassim to King Commission, 26 June 2000

23 'They all call me Maamu...', tehelka interview, 14 August 2000

24 Cronje on 'regular hanger-on', statement to King Commission, 15 June 2000

25 'If you call me...', Cassim, tehelka interview, 14 August 2000

26 'He kept calling me...', Cassim, tehelka interview, 14 August 2000

27 'In the time...', Cassim testimony to King Commission, 26 June 2000

28 'I'm definitely not...', Cassim, tehelka interview, 14 August 2000

29 Clive Lloyd sees Chawla in Bacher's VIP box, *The Times*, April 2000

30 'That's bullshit,' anonymous source to author, June 2000

CHAPTER ELEVEN

1 Aronstam on ex-player, interview with CricInfo, 11 November 2000

2 Cronje on conversations with Aronstam, statement to King Commission, 15 June 2000 and cross-examination, 22 June 2000

3 Cronje denies other players were willing to be involved, King Commission, 22 June 2000

4 'I couldn't believe it...', Aronstam, testimony to King Commission, 23 June 2000

5 Cronje on breakfast debate, press conference, 18 January 2000

6 Kallis opposed to Centurion finish, testimony to King Commission, 13 June 2000

7 text message to Aronstam, Aronstam on *Panorama*, 21 May 2001

8 Stewart and Hussain on offer, conversations with author, 19 January 2000

9 Strydom, testimony to King Commission, 9 June 2000

10 text message to Aronstam, Aronstam on *Panorama*, 21 May 2001

11 Cullinan on Cronje's declaration, phone conversation with author, 12 April 2000

12 'We are very proud of our country...', Bacher to author, 18 January 2000

13 Hussain and Atherton on Centurion, *Sunday Telegraph*, 18 June 2000

14 Aronstam maintains only pitch reports, 21 June 2000

15 Cronje admits extra payment from Aronstam, cross-examination before King Commission, 21 June 2000

16 Aronstam on drop in ocean, testimony to King Commission, 23 June 2000

17 Cronje meeting with Reena Desai, Cassim interview with tehelka, 14 August 2000; testimony to King Commission, 26 June 2000

18 'made himself some good money...', Cronje's statement to King Commission, 15 June 2000

19 'Since that day...', Cronje's written confession, 11 April 2000

20 Telephone records outlined to the King Commission on 26 June 2000 showed that Cassim called Cronje 180 times during a period of a few weeks. He also made 33 calls to Daryll Cullinan, 30 to Paul Adams, 28 to Lance Klusener, 18 to Ghulam Raja, the South African team manager, 14 to Herschelle Gibbs, 11 to Jonty Rhodes, 6 to Fanie de Villiers and 3 to Shaun Pollock. Cronje called him 11 times. Cassim's explanation for his calls to Cronje, tehelka interview, 14 August 2000

21 Chawla's solicitors deny he met Cronje, *Outlook*, 29 January 2001

22 Cronje's account of Durban meeting, statement to King Commission, 15 June 2000

23 'Keep this and we'll talk later,' Cassim to King Commission, 26 June 2000

24 Bacher admits to surmising, conversation with author, 14 April 2000

25 'I told him that maybe...', Cronje's written confession, 11 April 2000

26 'I realise now...', Cronje's statement to King Commission, 15 June 2000

CHAPTER TWELVE

1 Kishen Kumar pays Chawla's hotel bill, and Kumar's denials, Kumar press conference, 12 April 2000; agency reports and *The Hindu*, 13 April 2000

2 Cassim on calls from Chawla in India, evidence to King Commission, 26 June 2000. Phone records showed Chawla called Cassim 29 times during a period covering the one-day series in South Africa and India; Cassim was unable to explain to the King Commission the nature of many of them

3 Cronje and Chawla both phone Cassim from same hotel, agency reports, 10 April 2000

4 Role of Yasmeen, police sources, 25 April, 5 May

5 Chawla's call from hotels, agency reports, 15 April 2000

6 Cronje receiving harassing phone calls, statement to King Commission, 15 June 2000

7 'to encourage the team...', Cronje to King Commission, 15 June 2000

8 'I never knew anything...', unnamed South African player, quoted in South Africa's *Mail* and *Guardian*, 14 April 2000

9   Strydom on Mumbai approach, testimony to King Commission, 9 June 2000

10 Cronje's comments on Strydom, statement to King Commission, 15 June 2000

11 Bangalore offer: Klusener and Boucher, to King Commission, 12 June 2000;
    Kallis, 13 June 2000

12 'thinking that if we could…', Cronje to King Commission, 15 June 2000

13 Cronje was less forthcoming in his statement to the King Commission than in
    his original letter of confession; in the letter he said Cassim phoned him on
    the morning of the Kochi game and that Cronje had phoned him back to say
    he had spoken to other players and the deal was on

14 'I suggested that I would speak…', Cronje to King Commission, 15 June 2000

15 'I was happy to go along…', Gibbs to King Commission, 8 June 2000

16 'When I got back to the hotel…', Cronje to King Commission, 15 June 2000

17 Kalra tells police Sanjay lost money, agency reports, 10 April 2000

18 'Hamid kept phoning me…', Cronje to King Commission, 15 June 2000

19 Chawla leaves for London, Asian Age, quoting CBI sources, 8 July 2000;
    shortly before he left India, Chawla may also have visited Dubai, according to
    police sources quoted on 15 April 2000

20 Paul said Chawla–Cronje met in Delhi hotel on 14 March 2000, quoted
    7 April 2000

21 Phone belonged to Chawla, Delhi police, 8 April 2000

22 In his statement to the King Commission, Cronje said of the mobile given
    him by 'Sanjay': '[He] gave me a local sim-card so that he could call me for
    information and which would also be helpful for internet connectivity and e-
    mails. This was not compatible with my cellphone and could not be used. I
    later received a cellphone, sent up to my room, with which it was compatible.'

23 Cronje quote on free phone, Independent newspapers of South Africa,
    12 April 2000

CHAPTER THIRTEEN

1   For background to extortion threats, see *The Hindu*, 13 April 2000

2   Kumar seeks police help, Pradeep Magazine, p.xxiv

3   'We began monitoring…', Police source, 15 April 2000

4   'Available information…', Pradeep Srivastava, Delhi police statement, 7 April
    2000

5   There were conflicting reports about the number of tape-recordings: Delhi police themselves said twelve tapes at their first press conference; the following week, another police source said there were five cassettes of recordings of 90 minutes each

6   'horrible sinking feeling', interview in *News of the World*, 23 July 2000

7   'stringing him along', Cronje to King Commission, 22 June 2000

8   'Klusener called up police...', *Gulf News*, 12 April 2000

9   'Prior to the third...', Cronje statement to King Commission, 15 June 2000

10 Transcript released by Delhi police, 7 April 2000

11 'I know nothing of this entire issue...', Klusener, 12 April 2000. Two days after the Gulf News story appeared, one of our journalists at the *Sunday Times* was told by a South African board official that he had heard a South Africa player had blown the whistle on Cronje, but it was not Klusener (Dr Ashwin Desai to Karen McGregor, 13 April 2000)

12 'At no stage in this process...', Bhasin in South African *Sunday Times*, 16 April 2000

13 'They were talking...', Strydom, testimony to King Commission, 9 June 2000

14 Summary of conversations on eve of Baroda one-dayer, see *India Today*, 26 June 2000

15 Subba Row, conversation with author, April 2000

16 'During the second...', Cronje to King Commission, 15 June 2000

17 Sanjay complains to girlfriend about Cronje's erratic forecasting, *Guardian*, 14 April 2000

18 'Azharuddin transcript', published in *Midday*, Mumbai evening newspaper, 17 June 2000

19 Kalra asked to phone Chopra, testimony in CBI report

20 Transcript leaked to NDTV, Indian television station, 12 April 2000

21 Crookes to King Commission, 8 June 2000

22 'I started well...', Crookes, 13 April 2000

23 'A discussion with Sanjay...', Cronje to King Commission, 15 June 2000

24 'I gave in...', Cronje to King Commission, 15 June 2000

25 Transcript released by Delhi police, 7 April 2000

26 'I said yes...', Gibbs to King Commission, 8 June 2000

27 'I also agreed...', Williams to King Commission, 9 June 2000

28 'I batted like a steam train...', Gibbs to King Commission, 8 June 2000

29 Indian names 'blurred' on tapes, agency reports, 9 April 2000; come up only 'in passing', 13 April 2000

30 Transcript naming Azharuddin, published in *Midday*, Mumbai evening newspaper, 17 June 2000

31 Azharuddin in contact with bookie (Ajay Gupta) during South Africa's tour, CBI report

32 Azhar and Sharma phone contact, *India Today*, 1 May 2000

33 Jadeja in contact with Uttam Chand, Chennai bookmaker, see respective testimonies in CBI report

34 'He indicated that Sanjay...', Cronje to King Commission, 15 June 2000

CHAPTER FOURTEEN

1 King quotes St John, King Commission, 15 June 2000

2 Rory Steyn on 'Herschelle, don't worry...', Steyn testimony to King Commission, 8 June 2000

3 Gibbs told not to tell the truth, Gibbs testimony, King Commission, 8 June 2000

4 Strydom 'the furore was about one-day internationals', Deon Gouws, p.30

5 Cronje admits probably would not have admitted approaches himself, cross-examination before King Commission, 21 June 2000

6 Cronje, why only referred to India, evidence to King Commission, 21 June 2000

7 'I'll be back...', Cronje's written confession, 11 April 2000

8 McCauley on Cronje not being asked everything, Deon Gouws, p.115

9 Dr Ian Lewis's testimony to King Commission, 21 June 2000

10 Cronje realised wrong to take money, evidence to King Commission, 21 June 2000

11 '$8,200 and a joke...', Ray McCauley, the *Star* newspaper, 7 June 2000

12 'playing along', Cronje's statement read by Ngconde Balfour, 11 April 2000; 'stringing along', Bacher to author, 14 April 2000

13 'Ninety-five per cent of the time...', Cronje to King Commission, 22 June 2000

14 Speculation that Cronje physically threatened in India, *Sunday Telegraph*, 11 June 2000

15 'not readily reconciliable…', King's interim report

16 'May I suggest…', King Commission, 23 June 2000

17 'This was something that should, after all, not happen to any idol,' Deon Gouws, p.47

18 'It is hard not to equate…', *Sunday Times*, 11 June 2000

19 Boje on Cronje saying he had 'just thrown a few names around', to King Commission, 9 June 2000

20 Gibbs on protecting Cronje, evidence to King Commission, 8 June 2000

21 'If you don't come clean…', Boucher, quoted in *Sunday Times*, 11 June 2000

22 'Agreeing to the deal…', Gibbs, 1 January 2001

CHAPTER FIFTEEN

1 If the people…', Kamal Morarka, Indian board vice-president, on Star Television, 15 April 2000

2 Government tells Prabhakar to keep quiet, *Fallen Heroes*, p.91

3 'cockiness of crooks who had covered their trails well,' Bahal, *Fallen Heroes*, p.18

4 'I think if we hadn't…', Bahal, *Fallen Heroes*, p.20

5 'I wanted to prove that I did not lie,' Prabhakar, *Fallen Heroes*, pp.30–31

6 'No one was willing…', Prabkahar, *Fallen Heroes*, p.34. Shastri advised Prabhakar to put his complaint in writing but he never did so

7 'Everybody knows,' Wadekar, *Fallen Heroes*, p.176

8 'Wadekar and Azhar destroyed my life,' Prabhakar, *Fallen Heroes*, p.142

9 'According to the bookie…', Rakesh Maria, Mumbai police commissioner, *Fallen Heroes*, pp.118–119

10 'I have only said what Prabhakar told me,' Bindra, CNN interview, 4 May 2000

11 'wild and baseless allegations', Kapil Dev, quoted 4 May 2000

12 'I would commit suicide…', Kapil Dev, BBC World interview, 7 May 2000; broadcast 10 May 2000

13 'What is Jadeja, is all Kapil…', Jaywant Lele, former secretary of Indian cricket board, *Fallen Heroes*, p.61

14 'We have gathered substantial…', Dhananjaya Kumar, deputy finance minister, speaking to Indian parliament, 8 August 2000

15 'As far as I know...', Azharuddin, quoted, 18 June 2000

16 'We thought it would be best...', Chandu Borde, 2 September 2000

17 'enjoy his holiday', see *Sunday Times*, 23 July 2000

19 'The cricketing fraternity...', CBI report

19 'Look at this man's conscience...', Bedi, *Fallen Heroes*, p.90

20 'This is the beginning of our crusade...', Jai Bhagwan Goyal, quoted, 11 November 2000

21 'These hard decisions...', AC Muttiah, quoted, 5 December 2000

22 'The BCCI should be commended...', Richards, quoted, 5 December 2000

23 'let some holy cows off the hook', Sarfraz Nawaz, quoted by Associated Press of Pakistan, 11 November 2000

24 Dr Ashwin Desai, member of UCBSA's transformation monitoring committee, to Karen McGregor, 13 April 2000

25 'The media refused to believe me...', Kapil Dev, quoted, November 2000

26 'His stability...', Lord Condon, conversation with author, 18 June 2001

27 'We found no reason...', RN Sawani, CBI director, quoted in *Sydney Morning Herald*, 3 February 2001

28 'increasingly frustrated', ACU press statement, issued 15 June 2001

29 'let us know that he is willing...', Lord Condon, press conference, Lord's, 18 June 2001

30 'He either travels...', Condon, conversation with author, 18 June 2001

31 'They will no doubt...', ACU press release, 2 July 2001

32 'Gupta's evidence...', Lord Condon, press conference, Lord's, 18 June 2001

33 'If at any stage...', Condon, conversation with author, 18 June 2001

34 'There exists...', Lord MacLaurin, 11 July 2001

CHAPTER SIXTEEN

1 'We endured a fractious and unpleasant meeting...', AC Smith, chief executive of the Test and County Cricket Board, quoted in *Wisden Cricketers' Almanack* 1994, p.1292

2 Kenya's meeting with Lancaster Holdings, Sharad Ghai, Kenyan cricket official, telephone conversation with author, 19 May 2000

3 On Bukhatir's Sharjah profits, *Daily Telegraph*, 23 June 2001

4 For allegations by Sri Lankan board president Upali Dharmadasa against

WorldTel, see *Daily Telegraph*, 1 November 1997

5 Details of the rights row over the contract for the ICC Knockout were outlined in a letter from Mark Mascarenhas, head of WorldTel, to Malcolm Gray,
president of ICC, on 13 June 2001, a copy of which the author has seen

6 Indian players allegedly received money in Sharjah, *Outlook*, 22 December
1997; players betting on matches in which they played, Inderjit Singh Bindra,
former board president, speaking in Star television interview, 15 April 2000

7 'not possible', Jaywant Lele, quoted, 3 September 2000

8 'What was the BCCI doing all these years?' CBI report

9 'A compelling case...', Condon report, paragraphs 100–104

10 'should develop an internal audit function...', Condon report, paragraph 134

11 'I am a cricketer...', Asif Iqbal, *Daily Telegraph*, 7 April 2001

12 To avoid UK corporation tax, the ICC, whose administrative headquarters
were in London, had created an offshore company, ICC Development
International, in the British Virgin Islands in 1993 and was under no obligation to make public its accounts

13 Declaration forms, Condon report, paragraphs 56–57

14 'more transparent and accountable', Condon report, paragraph 132

15 Mark Taylor, quoted in *Sunday Times*, 27 May 2001

16 'Only a minority of professional cricketers...', Tim May, chief executive of
Fica, the players' global union, *Sunday Times*, 27 May 2001

17 'It was embarrassingly easy...', Condon, press conference, 18 June, 2001

18 'known corruptors', ACU statement, 2 June 2001. Condon said newspaper
reports that the plot was to influence the England–Pakistan Tests in 2001 were
wrong. He believed Tests and one-dayers were still being fixed; conversation
with author, 18 June 2001

19 'We should be focusing on the future...', this and following statements from
Gray and Condon, press conference in London, 18 June 2001

20 'I have let down...', Cronje statement, 26 June 2000

21 'My son has acknowledged...', Ewie Cronje, quoted, 25 June 2000

22 'two or three times', Bacher, press conference, 22 June 2001

23 'It's been one of the...', Frans Cronje, *Sunday Telegraph*, 15 February 2001

24 'They basically confessed...', Cronje interview on *Sixty Minutes*, Channel Nine
television, 16 July 2000

25 'a broken man, full of remorse', Woolmer, *Daily Telegraph*, 21 June 2000

26 'Those close to him...', Dave Richardson, *Sunday Telegraph*, 15 February 2001

27 Suicide report, *Cape Times*, 28 June 2000

28 'to forgive myself for what I did...', Cronje interviews on *Sixty Minutes*, Channel Nine television, 16 and 17 July 2000

29 'That's the end of Hansie,' Percy Sonn, quoted, 10 October 2000

30 'I was very fearful...', Bacher, press confernece, 22 June 2001

31 'Coach, I want you...', Woolmer, *Daily Telegraph*, 5 June 2001

32 'We believe the commission...', Bacher, quoted in *Sunday Telegraph*, 15 February 2001

33 Cronje, interview on BBC Radio 4, 24 July 2001

SOURCES

OFFICIAL REPORTS

All the following reports can be accessed on the internet. The Condon interim
report is available at www.icc.cricket.org/anti-corruption unit and provides
links to the O'Regan, Qayyum, CBI and King reports. The Madhavan report is
available at www.tehelka.com/sports

'ACB Player Conduct Inquiry Report', by Rob O'Regan, February 1999
'Justice Qayyum's Report', released by Pakistan Cricket Board, 24 May 2000
'Commission of Inquiry into Cricket Match-Fixing and Related Matters', by Judge
Edwin King, first interim report, 11 August 2000; second interim report,
12 December 2000
'The CBI Report on Cricket Match Fixing and Related Malpractices',
1 November 2000
'The Madhavan Report', K Madhavan on behalf of the Board of Control for
Cricket in India, 24 November 2000
'Report on Corruption in International Cricket', by Sir Paul (subsequently Lord)
Condon, director of the ICC's anti-corruption unit, published on the internet,
23 May 2001

BOOKS

Donald, Allan, *White Lightning*, Collins Willow (2000)
Gouws, Deon, ... *And Nothing But the Truth?*, Zebra Press (2000)
Magazine, Pradeep, *Not Quite Cricket: The Explosive Story of How Bookmakers
Influence the Game Today*, Penguin India (2000)
tehelka.com, *Fallen Heroes: The Story that Shook the Nation*, Buffalo Books (2000)
Woolmer, Bob, *Woolmer on Cricket*, Virgin (2000)

PERIODICALS AND NEWSPAPERS

*Sunday Times, The Times, Daily Telegraph, Sunday Telegraph, Guardian, Mirror, Mail
on Sunday, News of the World, Observer, The People, Wisden Cricket Monthly, Wisden
Almanack* (England); *India Today, Outlook, The Hindu, The Statesman, Midday*
(India); *Cape Times, Business Day, The Citizen, The Star, The Mercury, Sunday Times*
(South Africa); *Sydney Morning Herald, The Australian* (Australia); *The Nation, Daily
News* (Pakistan); *Gulf News* (UAE).

ACKNOWLEDGEMENTS

I would like to thank my sports editor at the *Sunday Times*, Alex Butler, for vigorously supporting our coverage of the match-fixing scandal; Graham Coster, at Aurum Press, for his enthusiasm for putting the story into book form, and for his care and attention throughout; and to Graeme Wright, for reading the manuscript.

I am also indebted to, among others, the following:

SUNDAY TIMES: Maurice Chittenden, James Clark, Nick Fielding, Dipesh Gadher, Stephen Grey, Peter Roebuck, Jonathan Ungoed-Thomas.

ENGLAND: Scyld Berry, Lord Condon, Stephen Fay, Steve Gwilliam, Martin Hawkins, Peter Hayter, Chris Lewis, Lord MacLaurin, Ehsan Mani, Robert Matusiewicz, David Norrie, Owen Slot, Qamar Ahmed, Ian Smith, Ivo Tennant, the ICC Anti-Corruption Unit.

AUSTRALIA: Malcolm Conn.

INDIA: Aniruddha Bahal, Harshe Bogle, Sayantan Chakravarty, Sumit Dasgupta, Murali Krishnan, Vijay Lokapally, Vinod Mehta, R Mohan, Damandeep Singh, Abishek Verma.

KENYA: Harad Ghai.

NEW ZEALAND: Don Cameron.

PAKISTAN: Arif Abbasi, Asif Iqbal, Fareshteh Gati, Ghulan Hasnain, Majid Khan, Rashid Latif, Sarfraz Nawaz, Richard Pybus.

SOUTH AFRICA: Luke Alfred, Ali Bacher, Shamila Batohi, John Blair, Colin Bryden, Daryll Cullinan, Karen McGregor, Ronnie Mamoepe, Neil Manthorp, David Richardson, Peter Robinson, Ron Steele, the King Commission team.

SRI LANKA: Charlie Austin, Ranjan Madugalle, Ana Punchahawa, Sidath Wettimuny, Lal Wickrematunga.

INDEX